D1209727

RETRIEVING THE AMERICAN PAST

A CUSTOMIZED U.S. HISTORY READER

COMPILED BY

University of Houston
Sections 04405, 04408 and 04406

PEARSON CUSTOM PUBLISHING

Director of Database Publishing: Michael Payne
Acquisitions Editor: Ellen M. Kuhl
Editor: Colby R. Lawrence
Marketing: Hester Tinti-Kane, Nathan L. Wilbur
Operations Manager: Eric M. Kenney

Printed in the United States of America

10 9 8 7 6 5 4 3 2 1

0-536-62618-9
BA 5567

PEARSON CUSTOM PUBLISHING
75 Arlington Street, Suite #300/Boston, MA 02116
Pearson Education Group

CONTRIBUTORS

Senior Editors
Michael Les Benedict
Mark Grimsley
Susan M. Hartmann
Margaret E. Newell
Carla Gardina Pestana
Leila J. Rupp
David L. Stebenne
Warren R. Van Tine

Current Managing Editor
John Day Tully

Assistant Managing Editor
Brian C. Etheridge

Copy Editor
Ann Heiss

Contributing Editors

Tyler Anbinder
Kenneth J. Andrien
Jean Harvey Baker
Michael Les Benedict
Mansel Blackford
Paul C. Bowers
Rowland Brucken
John D. Buenker
John C. Burnham
Joan E. Cashin
William R. Childs
Albert J. Churella
Steven Conn
Saul Cornell
Jeanette Davis
Merton L. Dillon
Daniel Feller
Charles Coleman Finlay
Mark Grimsley
Bernard N. Grindel
Peter L. Hahn
Susan M. Hartmann
Mary Ann Heiss
Earl J. Hess
Michael J. Hogan

Bruce Karhoff
Terence Kehoe
K. Austin Kerr
James McCaffrey
Allan R. Millett
Pamela J. Mills
Daniel Nelson
Margaret E. Newell
Josef Ostyn
Carla Gardina Pestana
Patrick D. Reagan
Randolph A. Roth
John A. M. Rothney
Leila J. Rupp
Richard D. Shiels
David Sicilia
C. Edward Skeen
Amy L. S. Staples
David L. Stebenne
David Steigerwald
Marshall F. Stevenson, Jr.
Warren R. Van Tine
Christopher Waldrep
J. Samuel Walker

Contents

The Indians'
New World:
Native Americans after
the European Invasion,
1585–1783

Margaret E. Newell

INTRODUCTION

As historian James Merrell points out, in the wake of the European invasion, America's native inhabitants faced a radically altered way of life—a "new world" almost as foreign to them as America was to the European colonizers. First, European diseases wrought a terrible mortality among the Indians, resulting in the destruction of entire tribes and traditions. Second, European settlers and traders, and their African slaves, introduced new goods, technologies, and agricultural methods to America, all of which affected the Indians' way of life. The new arrivals also competed with the native inhabitants for resources and military control. Native Americans in turn influenced the course of European settlement. The following readings explore relations between Europeans and Indians during the first two centuries of contact in North America, focusing on the Indians' responses.

The Indian experience was as diverse as the tribes that inhabited North America. Although the eastern coastal peoples succumbed quickly to disease and military conquest, Native Americans in the interior remained a force to be reckoned with well into the nineteenth century. Survivors migrated to escape sickness, creating diversely populated villages and new tribal alliances. Powerful groups like the six-tribe Iroquois Confederation, the Choctaws of Louisiana, and the Creeks and Cherokees of the southeast outnumbered white settlers and retained much of their land and independence for over a century.

During the colonial period, Indians and Europeans interacted in numerous ways short of war, most commonly in the related activities of trade and diplomacy. Indeed, in their early years, the small scattered European settlements depended upon the Indians

2

for survival. Thus both groups had numerous opportunities to observe each other's culture and manners. The Indians adopted some aspects of European culture, but they also forced Europeans to adjust to the native inhabitants' presence and expectations. Some of the technology that the Dutch, French, and English introduced—guns, knives, kettles, hoes—made the Indians' agriculture, hunting, and cooking more efficient, and many tribes eagerly sought access to trade with Europeans. Indians also used English and French agents as mediators to resolve conflicts with neighboring tribes, or solicited their help in conquering their enemies. In return, the Europeans received food, furs, deerskins, information, and military aid. As the French and English battled to extend their respective empires in America, the Indians played an important role in what historian Gary Nash calls the "three-cornered fight for a continent." They took advantage of European rivalries, playing the French against the English and the colonies against each other, seeking the most advantageous trading terms and refusing to be pawns in European wars.

Relations between Indians and whites entered a new phase in 1763 after England's victory in the Seven Years' War (the French and Indian War). The elimination of the French reduced the Indians' ability to pit one enemy against another. The dramatic growth of the English colonies' population led authorities to pressure the Indians for ever-larger land cessions; with Indians and whites living side-by-side, the potential for conflict increased. In addition, the adoption of European technology had unanticipated consequences. For example, guns made war in the post-contact era a much more deadly affair for Indians, and hunters armed with muskets nearly wiped out some of the species they depended upon. Other goods, such as liquor, found wide acceptance, with devastating consequences for Indian societies. Many Native Americans grew dependent upon European cloth, guns, and ammunition, even as their ability to pay for such goods diminished. Some tribes survived by ceding their land. The Revolution left the Indians in an even more vulnerable position; after 1783, the Indians had only one partner to negotiate with—the Americans, whose land hunger outstripped that of both the English and French.

CULTURAL EXCHANGES AND CULTURAL CLASHES

The following documents offer insight into the Indians' economic, military, and cultural relations with Europeans. These sources present several methodological problems, however; because the Indians had no indigenous written language, all the speeches, letters, petitions, and legal documents included here were written or transcribed by whites. Rather than the Indians' direct words and thoughts, the written record consists of second- and third-hand accounts of what the Indians said and did, often written long after the fact. Such sources are useful, but we must read them critically and be aware of the writers' biases, interests, and errors. Those who sympathized with the Indians sometimes glorified native oratory, while hostile government officials portrayed Indians more negatively.

First Encounters

In this selection taken from his history of the "Lost Colony" of Roanoke, Captain John Smith—promoter, soldier of fortune, and key figure in the colonization of Virginia—recounts the Algonquin Indians' response to the outbreak of disease following the English landing in North Carolina in 1585. From John Smith, "The Generall Historie of Virginia, the Somer Iles, and New England . . ." in The Complete Works of Captain John

Reprinted from *The Complete Works of Captain John Smith* (1580–1631), Vol. 2, edited by Philip L. Barbour. Copyright © by University of North Carolina Press.

5

Smith (1580–1631), ed. *Philip L. Barbour, (Chapel Hill, 1986),* 2:80–81.

One other strange Accident . . . will I mention before I end, which mooved the whole Country that either knew or heard of us, to have us in wonderfull admiration.

There was no Towne where they had practised any villany against us . . . but within a few dayes after our departure, they began to dye; in some Townes twenty, in some forty, in some sixty, and in one an hundred and twenty, which was very many in respect of their numbers. And this hapned in no place (we could learn) but where we had bin. . . . And this disease was so strange, they neither knew what it was, nor how to cure it; nor had they knowne the like time out of minde. . . . [T]hey were perswaded it was the worke of God through our meanes: and that we by him might kill and slay whom we would, without weapons, and not come neare them. . . .

This marveilous Accident in all the Country wrought so strange opinions of us, that they could not tell whether to thinke us gods or men. And the rather that all the space of their sicknesse, there was no man of ours knowne to die, or much sicke. They noted also we had no women, nor cared for any of theirs: some therefore thought we were not borne of women, and therefore not mortall. . . . Some would Prophesie there were more of our generation yet to come, to kill theirs and take their places.

Interdependence and Exchange in Colonial Louisiana

When the French began to settle the Lower Mississippi region in the late seventeenth century, they quickly sought to ally themselves with the twenty thousand member Choctaw Nation. France's settlements at New Orleans and Biloxi, which never contained more than five thousand white and four thousand black inhabitants, relied on the Choctaws for food, deerskins, and military aid against the English. This anonymous French account from the early 1700s details how the Indians sought trade contacts with the Europeans, but set the terms of exchange, demanded "presents" in the form of yearly tribute, and forced the French to use Indian ceremonies. Excerpted from John R. Swanton, "An Early Account of the Choctaw Indians," in Memoirs of the American Anthropological Association *(Lancaster, Pennsylvania, 1918), 5:54–55.*

The Chaquetas [Choctaws] are a hundred leagues north of Mobile. There are about four thousand bearing arms. . . . This nation is warlike against similar people. . . . The French always having needed to depend upon them in war, it has made them so insolent that they despise the French and would receive the English among them. They are much accustomed to receiving presents from the French. . . . They think that it is a right, that the French pay them for the lands which they occupy. It is this which they try to make them understand in the speeches which they make to the commandants of the posts where they go, saying:

> Formerly our ancestors occupied the place where you now live and came there to hunt; they have ceded it to you as to people who wished to be their friends, in consideration for which you have promised them a certain quantity of goods, and length of time has not cancelled the continuance of the gift, and of the friendship, which, having reigned between our ancestors and the French, reigns still between you and us. You know that every time you have asked us to take vengeance on your enemies who have insulted you, we have had pity, since, being few in numbers, you were unable to go to war, and that we, regarding you as our brothers, have left our wives, children, houses, villages, harvests, and periods of hunting to attack your enemies and stain our arms with their blood; that we have often lost our people there. You know that many times on returning from war we have taken credit for the goods that you have promised us, gained at the price of our blood, because they had not yet arrived by vessel from France. You know that the English are always at our doors importuning us to make an alliance with them, and sell them our deerskins at fairer prices than you offer. We have hopes then that in consideration of all these things you will look with pity on us and will share with us as your brothers in order that we may return to our village loaded with the presents you shall have given us.

7

The Narragansetts Challenge Massachusetts Bay's Authority

In the 1640s, the English colony of Massachusetts Bay moved aggressively to incorporate new lands and to extend its jurisdiction over nearby Indians. The Narragansetts of Rhode Island, who earlier had fought alongside English colonists in a common war against the Pequot tribe, began to fear their former allies. When their leader, Miantonomo, was captured and executed by Mohegin Indians at Massachusetts's instigation, the Narragansetts fought back in a way that demonstrated a sophisticated grasp of English imperial politics. They submitted directly to English royal authority in 1644, which gave them equal status with the Bay Colony, and announced their intention to seek mediation in London, not Boston, in the future. The following document is taken from "The Act and Deed of the Voluntary and Free Submission of the Chiefe Sachem . . .of the Nanhigansets . . . ," in Records of the Colony of Rhode Island . . . , *ed. John Russell Bartlett, (Providence, Rhode Island, 1856), 1:134–37.*

KNOW ALL MEN, Colonies, Peoples, and Nations, unto whom the fame hereof shall come; that wee, the chiefe Sachems, Princes or Governours of the Nanhigansets (in that part of America, now called New-England), together with the joynt and unanimous consent of all our people and subjects, inhabitants thereof, do upon serious consideration, . . . submit, subject, and give over ourselves, peoples, lands, rights, inheritances, and possessions whatsoever, in ourselves and our heires successively for ever, unto the protection, care and government of that worthy and royal Prince, Charles, King of Great Britaine and Ireland, his heires and successors forever, to be ruled and governed according to the ancient and honorable lawes and customes, established in that so renowned realme and kingdome of Old England; . . . *upon condition of His Majesties' royal protection,* and wrighting us of what wrong is, or may be done unto us, according to his honorable lawes and customes, exercised amongst his subjects, in their preservation and safety, and in the defeating and overthrow of his, and their enemies; not that we find ourselves necessitated hereunto, . . . with any of the natives in these parts, knowing ourselves sufficient defence and able to judge in any matter or cause in that

8

respect; but have just cause of jealousy and suspicion of some of His Majesty's pretended subjects. Therefore our desire is, to have our matters and causes heard and tried according to his just and equall lawes, in that way an order His Highness shall please to appoint: *Nor can we yield over ourselves unto any, that are subjects themselves in any case;* having ourselves been the chief Sachems, or Princes successively, of the country, time out of mind. . . .

Here followeth a copy of a letter sent to the Massachusetts, by the Sachems of the Narrangansetts, (shortly after their subjection to the State and Government of Old England) they being sent unto by the Massachusetts, to make their appearance at their General Court, then approacing [approaching].

We understand your desire is, that we should come downe into the Massachusetts, at the time of your Courte, now approaching. Our occasions at this same time are very great; and the more because of the loss . . . of our late deceased brother [Miantonomo]. . . . Our brother was willing to stir much abroad to converse with men, and we see a sad event at the last thereupon. Take it not ill, therefore, though we resolve to keep at home, . . . and so, at this time, do not repair unto you, according to your request. . . . [We] have subjected ourselves, our lands and possessions, with all the rights and inheritances of us and our people, either by conquest, voluntary subjection or otherwise, unto that famous and honorable government of that Royal King, Charles, and that State of Old England, . . . hereby being subjects now (and that with joint and voluntary consent), unto the same King and State yourselves are. So that if any small things of difference should fall out betwixt us, only the sending of a messenger may bring it to right again; but if any great matter should fall (which we hope and desire will not . . .), then neither yourselves, nor we are to be judges; and both of us are to have recourse, and repair unto that honorable and just Government.

Covering the Dead

The native inhabitants of America waged wars against each other long before Europeans arrived. Sometimes they fought over resources and power, but sometimes the motive was revenge for earlier killings. The

9

Creeks, Hurons, Iroquois, and Ohio Valley tribes called this "covering the dead"; those responsible had to compensate relatives of the victims with trade goods, or with their own lives. In this selection, Sir William Johnson, the chief British Indian agent in the northern colonies from 1754 until the revolution, offered to compensate the Seneca for casualties suffered in a clash with the British. Johnson was desperately trying to gain the Iroquois' support for war against the French. (The phrase "a belt" referred to the gifts of wampum belts that Johnson presented to them during his speech.) Taken from Documents Relative to the Colonial History of the State of New-York . . . , *ed. E. B. O'Callaghan, M.D., (Albany, 1856), 7:54–55.*

[At a meeting of the Six Nations and their allies, 18 February 1756]

Bretheren of the Caijougas and Tedirighroonas,

By constant experience we discover that the life of Man, is as the Flower of the Field, in this transitory scene therefore Resignation becomes us under the loss of our nearest and dearest friends, comfort yourselves therefore under the losses you have sustained as becomes reasonable creatures With this Belt I cover all your dead, that they may no more offend your sight

A Belt [hands over belt].

Bretheren of the Onondagas, Oneidas, Tuskaroras, Skaniadaradighroonas, Aughquageys, and the Mohawks of both Castles.

I perform the same ceremony to you

After this ceremony six French Prisoners some of those who were taken at the late Battle near Lake George were delivered with great ceremony to the Indians in order to replace the following Indians who were killed in that Battle. . . . [T]hey received the Prisoners with the greatest mark of Gratitude and Satisfaction, every nation giving the Shout of approbation, and then carried off the Prisoners to their respective familys

Thus ended the Ceremony necessary on those occasions agreeable to their Customs

10

[The Answer of the Six Nations and their Allies, 19 February 1756]

Brother Warraghiyagey [Johnson]

We the Sachims and Warriours of the Seneca Nation return you our sincere [and hearty] thanks for your great affection in drying our Tears, and driving Sorrow from our Hearts, and we in return perform the same ceremony to you, with the like Hearty Affection.

A String of Wampum [presents wampum]

Brother Warraghiyagey

We are sensible of your goodness expressed to us in removing the cause of our Grief, and tenderly taking the Axe out of our Heads

A Belt

Brother Warraghiyagey

We are thankful to you for cleansing the Blood out of our sight agreeable to the antient Custom of our Forefathers

A Belt

White Indians

As historian Daniel Richter notes, aside from covering the dead with goods, the Iroquois waged "mourning wars" in which they sought captives to replace relatives who had died. High mortality from war and disease in the late 1600s and early 1700s increased this practice. Sometimes the Iroquois tortured these Indian and white captives to death before ceremonially "adopting" them, but often they incorporated captured women and children into the tribe. Mary Jemison, an Irish immigrant living in Pennsylvania, was only fifteen in 1758 when a combined force of French troops and Shawnee Indians kidnapped her family. After scalping her parents and siblings, the Shawnee handed her over to a

Seneca tribe living in Ohio; she lived with the Indians for the rest of her life. Jemison's account of her experiences appeared in James E. Seaver, A Narrative of the Life of Mrs. Mary Jemison . . . *(Canandaigua, New York, 1824), 34–39.*

I was now left alone in the fort, deprived of my former companions, and of every thing that was near or dear to me but life. But it was not long before I was in some measure relieved by the appearance of two pleasant looking squaws of the Seneca tribe, who came and examined me attentively for a short time, and then went out. After a few minutes absence they returned with my former masters, who gave me to them to dispose of as they pleased.

The Indians by whom I was taken were a party of Shawanees, if I remember right, that lived, when at home, a long distance down the Ohio. . . . At night we arrived at a small Seneca Indian town. . . . Having made fast to the shore, the Squaws left me in the canoe while they went to their wigwam or house in the town, and returned with a suit of Indian clothing, all new, and very clean and nice. My clothes, though whole and good when I was taken, were now torn in pieces, so that I was almost naked. They first undressed me and threw my rags into the river; then washed me clean and dressed me in the new suit they had just brought, in complete Indian style; and then led me home and seated me in the center of their wigwam.

I had been in that situation but a few minutes, before all the Squaws in the town came in to see me. I was soon surrounded by them, and they immediately set up a most dismal howling, crying bitterly, and wringing their hands in all the agonies of grief for a deceased relative.

Their tears flowed freely, and they exhibited all the signs of real mourning. At the commencement of this scene, one of their number began, in a voice somewhat between speaking and singing, to recite some words to the following purport, and continued the recitation till the ceremony was ended . . . :

"Oh our brother! Alas! He is dead—he has gone; he will never return! Friendless he died on the field of the slain, where his bones are yet lying unburied! Oh, who will not mourn his sad fate? . . . Oh where is his spirit? His spirit went naked, and hungry it wanders, and thirsty and wounded it groans to return! . . . Though he fell on the

12

field of the slain, with glory he fell, and his spirit went up to the land of his fathers in war! Then why do we mourn? With transports of joy they received him, and fed him, and clothed him, and welcomed him there! Oh friends, he is happy; then dry up your tears! His spirit has seen our distress, and sent us a helper whom with pleasure we greet. Dickewamis [Mary Jemison's Indian name] has come: then let us receive her with joy! She is handsome and pleasant! Oh! she is our sister, and gladly we welcome her here. In the place of our brother she stands in our tribe. With care we will guard her from trouble; and may she be happy till her spirit shall leave us."

In the course of that ceremony, from mourning they became serene—joy sparkled in their countenances, and they seemed to rejoice over me as over a long lost child. I was made welcome amongst them as a sister to the two Squaws. . . .

I afterwards learned that the ceremony I at that time passed through, was that of adoption. The two squaws had lost a brother in Washington's war, sometime in the year before, and in consequence of his death went up to Fort Pitt, on the day on which I arrived there, in order to receive a prisoner or an enemy's scalp, to supply their loss.

It is a custom of the Indians, when one of their number is slain or taken prisoner in battle, to give to the nearest relative to the dead or absent, a prisoner, if they have chanced to take one, and if not, to give him the scalp of an enemy. On the return of the Indians from conquest, which is always announced by peculiar shoutings, demonstrations of joy, and the exhibition of some trophy of victory, the mourners come forward and make their claims. If they receive a prisoner, it is at their option either to satiate their vengeance by taking his life in the most cruel manner they can conceive of; or, to receive and adopt him into the family, in the place of him whom they have lost. All the prisoners that are taken in battle and carried to the encampment or town by the Indians, are given to the bereaved families, till their number is made good. And unless the mourners have but just received the news of their bereavement, and are under the operation of paroxysm of grief, anger and revenge; or, unless the prisoner is very old, sickly, or homely, they generally save him, and treat him kindly. But if their mental wound is fresh, their loss so great that they deem it irreparable, or if their prisoner or prisoners do not meet their approbation, no torture, let it be ever so cruel, seems sufficient to make

13

them satisfaction. . . .

It was my happy lot to be accepted for adoption; and at the time of the ceremony I was received by the two squaws, to supply the place of their brother in the family; and I was ever considered and treated by them as a real sister, the same as though I had been born of their mother.

Sources of Conflict

The Iroquois consistently frustrated both English and French attempts to win the unqualified support of the Indian confederation in their battles for control of North America. Both sides redoubled their efforts to woo the Iroquois after the outbreak of the Seven Years' War in 1754. Peter Wraxhall, the British secretary for Indian affairs, explained the difficulty of winning over the Iroquois in a 1756 report to the newly appointed Superintendent, Sir William Johnson. Wraxhall noted that the real obstacle to alliance was the Indians' fear that victory by either side would upset the balance of power and threaten the Iroquois' control of their lands. Excerpted from Documents Relative to the Colonial History of the State of New-York . . . , *ed. E. B. O'Callaghan, M.D., (Albany, 1856), 7:14, 17–18.*

To Major Generall William Johnson His Majestys sole superintendant of the affairs of the Northern Indians &c

Sir

In consequence of your Request and upon the plan I received from you, I herewith offer you Some Thoughts on the British Indian Interest &c.

. . . [One] cause by which our Interest & Influence amongst the Indians hath been greatly injured, their esteem for and confidence in us fatally weakened, hath been from the exorbitances and Impositions of our . . . Traders [from Albany]: This not only with the six Nations but with the Western or far Indians . . .

The ill consequences to our true Interest of this reproachful and impolitic conduct, are too obvious to require my expatiating on—

... [O]ne of the most fatal Causes of the decrease of our Indian Interest & influence, and which hath not only weakened their good opinion and affection towards us, but has made numbers of them our enemies, sown a gloomy discontent and suspicion of our Intentions amongst the whole confederacy hath been very near loosing us their Alliance, and will in all probability wholly do it, if proper measures are not fallen on to give them satisfaction & security. This Cause is relating to their Lands

An unaccountable thirst for large Tracts of Land without the design of cultivation, hath prevailed over the inhabitants of this and the neighbouring Provinces with a singular rage Patents have been lavishly granted (to give it no worse term) upon the pretence of fair Indian purchases, some of which the Indians have alleged were never made but forged—Others bought of Indians who were no Proprietors some by making two or three Indians Drunk and giving them a trivial consideration—They say also the Surveyors have frequently run Patents vastly beyond even the pretended conditions or limits of sale

There has certainly been a great deal of unrighteous conduct in these matters Many years ago the Indians requested of our Governors, & indeed have ernestly repeated it to almost every Governor, that no Patents might be granted, but for Land sold at their General and public meetings—this hath been as often promised ...

The vast Grant of Land to the Ohio company is ... one of the most material articles of discontent & Jealousy to the confederate Nations and their allies, aggravated by many other Patents granted by the Governors of Virginia and Maryland

There is reason to beleive the last Pensilvania Purchase, tho' agreed to at a publick meeting, is a matter of no small Grievance to many of the six Nations, and so disgusting to the Delaware & Shawanese Indians, as hath probably occasioned those Indians now ravageing our back Settlements

That memorable and important act by which the Indians put their Patrimonial and conquered Lands under the Protection of the King of Great Britain their Father against the incroachments or Invasions of the French is not understood by them as a cession or Surrender as it seems to have been ignorantly or willfully supposed by some, they intended and look upon it as reserving the Property and Possession of the Soil to themselves and their Heirs.

15

This Property the Six Nations are by no means willing to part with and are equally averse and jealous that any Forts or Settlements should be made thereon either by us or the French

These are their hunting Grounds, by the profits of which they are to maintain themselves and their Families, they are therefore against any settlements there because the consequence would be the driving away Game & destroying their Livelyhood and Riches. . . .

Our Six Nations and their Allies at least the Polititians amongst them look upon the present disputes betw'n the English and French in this part of the world notwithstanding our plausible pretences of rescuing their Lands, and some such pretences the French plead on their side, as a point of selfish Ambition in us both and are apprehensive that which ever Nation gains their Point will become their Masters not their deliverers—They dread the success of either and their ablest Politicians would very probably rather wish us to continue destroying each other than that either should be absolute conquerors, could the various nations of Indians form a cenfederacy equal to the Attempt there is reason to suppose they would unite and drive us and the French to a greater distance from their Hunting Grounds. . . . But the Indians suspect we have different views; that to restore their Lands to their natural state and deliver 'em over to them as Proprietors of the soil are not the ends we aim at.

Petition of the Chickasaw Headmen

Europeans also excelled at the tactics of divide and conquer, and nowhere were these tactics more successful than in the Carolinas, where, Gary Nash contends, "a white population of only about 1,500 males . . . succeeded in employing the larger tribes to enslave and shatter nearly a dozen coastal tribes." The English traders' superior goods won the allegiance of the powerful Chickasaws, but the relationship proved costly for the Indians. Disease, warfare, and the trade in Indian slaves decimated allies and enemies of the English alike, while overhunting and the loss of lands eroded their economic base. Others found themselves ever

Reprinted courtesy of South Carolina Department of Archives and History.

deeper in debt to the trading posts. In the spring of 1754, the Chickasaws explained their plight to Governor Glen and asked for aid. Excerpted from Colonial Records of South Carolina, Documents Relating to Indian Affairs, May 21, 1750–August 7, 1754, *ed. William L. McDowell, Jr. (Columbia, South Carolina, 1958), 512–13.*

To His Excellency James Glen, Esq., Governor of South Carolina, and the Honourable Council from the Head Men and Warriours of the Chickesaw Nation.

We have heard your friendly Talk . . . which together with your kind Presents confirms in us the Oppinion we have long had of your Desire that we should live and injoy our Lands against all the Attempts of our Enemies. Though your Lands and ours is far distant from each other, and that of our Enemies, the French, but a little Way from us, yet we look on you not only as our best Friends, but as our Fathers haveing always found a Readyness in you to assist us whenever we made Application to you, and although we are Red People, we can and ever will make a true Distinction between the English and ever other Nation, and shall love and esteem them all our Days.

It's true some Years ago we did not mind how many our Enemies were, but that is not our case at Present, our Number being reduced to a Handful of Men, and thereby we are rendered uncapable of keeping our Ground without a Continuance of your friendly Assistance, we not being able to hunt nor are we free from the Hands of our Enemies even in our Towns, so that it is impossible for us to kill Dear to buy Cloathing for ourselves, our Wives, and Children, or even to purchase Amunition. This the English Traders that comes amongst us is too sencable off from the small Quantity of Skins they have carried out of this Nation these two last Years to what they used to do formerly. It's needless to trouble you with an Account of what People we have lost in a few Months. . . . Nothing but our present Necessity could oblige us at this Time to ask you for a further Suply of Guns and Ammunition, without which we must either stand and be shott, or defend the Enemies' Bullets with our Hatchets as we have nothing else at Present. Our Traders is tired out with trusting us with Ammunition and Guns, nor can we be angry with them as it has not been in our Power to pay them for it, and many other Things we had from them, so that we may now say our Lives is in your Power to save or to let the Enemy have their Desire off us. It has always been your Desire as well as our own that we should keep this Ground from the French which we have hitherto done, but now this is our very case; we must either run from it and save our Lives or die upon it, and either Ways give it up to them unless assisted by you. In former Times when we either went or sent to you we had Presents of all kinds of Cloths, Duffels, Red Coats, and a great many good Things, but now we do not desire any other then Guns and Amunition to preserve our Lives with. We still love our Lands and Liberties nor shall we chuse ever to give it up but with the Loss of our Lives.

A great many of our People has left us; a Thing we are sorry at, but young People will rather go from us to live in Peace than stay here where they are in Danger every Day. . . . If you think good to take Pity on us and send us some Ammunition and at the same Time four of your Guns that make a great Noise and will kill our Enemys at a great Distance we will either keep our Land or die along side of them Guns, and if we should be all killed the Guns would still remain on our Ground to shew the French how much the English loved us. All your old good Talks is still fresh with us, and so shall this your last Talk nor shall we ever throw them away.

Dreams of Rebellion

In 1763, the Seneca Indians abandoned neutrality and attacked English forts and settlements from Virginia to the Great Lakes. Their leader, Pontiac, was inspired by a prophet named Neolin, who claimed that the "Master of Life" had appeared to him in a dream and called on the Indians to unite in order to drive the whites out of America. Neolin's religion included elements of Christianity but emphasized the rejection of European goods and liquor and a return to the Indians' former independent life of hunting and agriculture. Pontiac's Rebellion failed, but Neolin's Dream was the first of many such "nativist" Indian movements that resurfaced in the nineteenth century. Excerpted from Anthony F. C. Wallace with the assistance of Sheila C. Steen, The Death and Rebirth of the Seneca *(New York, 1970), 117–18.*

I am the Master of Life, whom thou wishest to see, and to whom thou wishest to speak. Listen to that which I will tell thee for thyself and for all the Indians. I am the Maker of Heaven and earth, the trees, lakes, rivers, men, and all that thou seest or hast seen on the earth or in the heavens; and because I love you, you must do my will; you must also avoid that which I hate; I hate you to drink as you do, until you lose your reason; I wish you not to fight one another; you take two wives, or run after other people's wives; you do wrong; I hate such conduct; you should have but one wife, and keep her until death. When you go to war, . . . you sing the medicine song, thinking you speak to me; you deceive yourselves; it is to the Manito that you speak; he is a wicked spirit who induces you to evil, and, for want of knowing me, you listen to him.

The land on which you are, I have made for you, not for others: wherefore do you suffer the whites to dwell upon your lands? Can you not do without them? I know that those whom you call the children of your great Father supply your wants. But, were you not wicked as you are, you would not need them. Before those whom you call your brothers had arrived, did not your bow and arrow maintain you? You needed neither gun, powder, nor any other object. The flesh of animals was your food, their skins your raiment. But when I saw you inclined to evil, I removed the animals into the depths of the forests, that you might depend on your brothers for your necessaries, for your clothing. Again become good and do my will, and I will send animals for your sustenance. I do now, however, forbid suffering among you your Father's children; I love them, they know me, they pray to me; I supply their own wants, and give them that which they bring to you. Not so with those who are come to trouble your possessions. Drive them away; wage war against them. I love them not. They know me not. They are my enemies, they are your brothers' enemies. Send them back to the lands I have made for them. Let them remain there.

Here is a written prayer which I give thee; learn it by heart, and teach it to all the Indians and children. It must be repeated morning and evening. Do all that I have told thee, and announce it

Reprinted from *The Death and Rebirth of the Seneca*, by Anthony F. C. Wallace, with the assistance of Sheila C. Steen, 1970, pp. 117–118. Published by Alfred A. Knopf, New York, © 1969 by Anthony Wallace.

to all the Indians as coming from the Master of Life. Let them drink but one draught [of liquor], or two at most, in one day. Let them have but one wife, and discontinue running after other people's wives and daughters. Let them not fight one another. Let them not sing the medicine song, for in singing the medicine song they speak to the evil spirit. Drive from your lands those dogs in red clothing; they are only an injury to you. When you want anything, apply to me, as your brothers [i.e., the Christian whites] do, and I will give to both. Do not sell to your brothers that which I have placed on the earth as food. In short, become good, and you shall want nothing.

Questions

1. *How did the Indians react to the newcomers? What cultural differences divided Indians and Europeans in the century following contact? Who had the upper hand in relations between the two?*

2. *What strategies did the Indians use to preserve their power? Which were the most successful, and why? What did the Europeans and Indians have to offer one another?*

3. *What caused the balance of power between Native Americans and Euro-Americans to shift in favor of the latter?*

FURTHER READING

William Cronon's Changes in the Land: Indians, Colonists, and the Ecology of New England *(New York, 1983), discusses the New England Indians' interactions with their environment and describes the impact of European settlement on both the landscape and the native inhabitants. In* The Middle Ground: Indians, Empires, and Republics in the Great Lakes Region, 1650–1815 *(New York, 1991), historian Richard White stresses the cultural adjustments that both Europeans and Indians made through two centuries of contact in the upper midwest. Daniel Usner introduces a third element—the importance of black slaves—in his account of French, English, Spanish, and Indian relations in the lower Mississippi Valley,* Indians, Settlers, & Slaves in a Frontier Exchange Economy: The Lower Mississippi Valley Before 1783 *(Chapel Hill, 1992). James Merrell's* The Indians' New World: Catawbas and Their Neighbors from European Contact through the Era of Removal *(Chapel Hill, 1989) focuses on a single tribe—the Catawbas of the Carolina Piedmont—and traces their changing fortunes through the 1830s.*

What Did it Mean to Be a Puritan?

Carla Gardina Pestana

INTRODUCTION

Puritans suffer from a bad reputation. Since the early twentieth century when American social critic H. L. Mencken ridiculed the first English settlers in New England, the word "puritan" conjures up images of sexual prudery, censoriousness, and hypocrisy. Although American school children are told that the Puritans came to America to establish religious freedom, as adults we learn that they in fact repressed dissent. Not only that, they limited political participation to (adult male) church members, even though admission to the church was by no means automatic. Many college students learning anew about early New England history wonder: Why would anyone be a Puritan?

The English men and women who migrated to New England between 1630 and 1642 to settle the Massachusetts Bay Colony would probably not be surprised that they have an unflattering image. By the time they left England they were accustomed to being ridiculed. In part they departed because they were committed to a religious movement that was increasingly coming under attack. In their view, the Church of England (established by Henry VIII in 1534) ought to participate more fully in the Protestant Reformation that had converted many on the European continent. Their criticisms of religious practices and social mores had ceased to be tolerated in the years leading up to their exodus, and Archbishop William Laud was intent on suppressing their movement. Financial hardships and religious woes combined to persuade over thirteen thousand people to leave the island of their birth to travel to northern North America in the dozen years after 1629.

They carried on—in spite of the travails they experienced—because they believed that God required it of them. To understand the Puritans, we must think about that conviction and the meaning that it gave to their lives. Many women and men braved first the displeasure of the English authorities and then the dangers of colonization because of their belief that they were fulfilling God's will. Early New England residents embraced the faith that we call "Puritan" out of the sense of personal commitment to reformed Protestantism. Theologically, they generally followed the teachings of John Calvin, a leading Protestant reformer of the previous century. The Puritans' church organization has been described as "non-separating congregationalism." Congregationalists rejected the ecclesiastical hierarchy of the Church of England (with its bishops, like their old nemesis Archbishop Laud, and its system of courts); they believed that the individual congregation should be autonomous, with the power to call a minister and to admit and discipline members. They earned the appellation "non-separating" because—unlike the separatists ("Pilgrims") who settled Plymouth—they refused to renounce their affiliation with the Anglican church, claiming that they wished to work for its reformation from within. Although we may find it difficult to comprehend their beliefs and the depth of their convictions, we must understand the Puritans as people dedicated to a cause. This cause guided them to New England in the first place and led them to create a unique society once they arrived. Their commitment to their cause was their reason for being Puritans.

RELIGION IN EARLY NEW ENGLAND: FROM PERSONAL PIETY TO SOCIAL FORCE

The selections that follow have been drawn from a massive literature on early New England. They attempt to convey something of the appeal that this religious faith held for the men and women who embraced it. Like all religions, Puritanism provided meaning and offered comfort, as some of these readings suggest. In addition, Puritanism shaped basic social attitudes and, hence, colonial New England society. As you read, you may conclude that a number of the accusations against the Puritans had some grounding in reality—for instance, they did police one another's behavior; but notice, too, how they thought about what they were doing. Do you consider them hypocritical and repressed after reading these selections?

Lay Puritans Form a Police Force

No scholar has done more to make the Puritans comprehensible to the modern reader than Edmund S. Morgan. In his biography of early Massachusetts governor John Winthrop (1588–1649), Morgan discusses sin and temptation as social problems for Puritans like Winthrop. This selection gives a sense of how the community viewed its obligation to monitor the activities of its members. Think about the charge of hypocrisy as you read Morgan's sympathetic account. Excerpted from Edmund S. Morgan, The Puritan Dilemma: The Story of John Winthrop, *(New York, 1958), 69, 71.*

27

John Winthrop (1588–1649) served as governor of Massachusetts for most of its first twenty years. His portrait reveals the relatively simple clothing favored by well-to-do Puritans of his era. (Courtesy of The American Antiquarian Society.)

TO PLEASE God the Puritans demanded of themselves a standard of behavior not far different from that required by most modern codes of morality. They did not think it necessary to be either prudes or prohibitionists. They did not dress in drab clothes or live in drab houses or speak in drab words. The people who appear in the pages of Winthrop's journal, the good men and women who showered him with venison and partridges and fat hogs to celebrate Margaret's arrival [i.e., Margaret Tyndal Winthrop, John's third wife], the boys and girls who skipped rope on the decks of the *Arbella*, the men who built ships and caught fish and planted corn were all human enough.

Nevertheless, the Puritans did make strong demands on human nature, for they were engaged in a mission that required great exertion. They had undertaken to establish a society where the will of God would be observed in every detail, a kingdom of God on earth. While still aboard the *Arbella*, Winthrop had explained to his fellow emigrants their solemn commitment to this task. Every nation, they all knew, existed by virtue of a covenant with God in which it promised to obey His commands. They had left England because England was failing in its promise. In high

Reprinted from *The Puritan Dilemma: The Story of John Winthrop* by Edmund S. Morgan, edited by Oscar Handlin. Published by HarperCollins Publishers, 1958. Copyright © 1958 by Edmund S. Morgan.

hope that God was guiding them and would find their efforts acceptable, they had proposed to form a new society. Now God had demonstrated His approval. He had made way for them by a "special overruling providence." By staying His wrath so long and allowing them to depart in peace, by delivering them safe across the water, He had sealed a covenant with them and given them a special responsibility to carry out the good intentions that had brought them into the wilderness. . . .

Winthrop was determined that Massachusetts should not deal falsely with God. Before arriving in New England, he and the other leaders of the exodus had thought long and hard about the articles of God's special commission, and they were confident that they knew what was required of them. They knew, in the most elementary terms, that they must punish every sin committed in Massachusetts. And punish they did, with the eager cooperation of the whole community, who knew that sin unpunished might expose them all to the wrath of God. Families became little cells of righteousness where the mother and father disciplined not only their children but also their servants and any boarders they might take in. In order that no one should escape this wholesome control, it was forbidden for anyone to live alone: unmarried men and maids were required to place themselves in some family if their own had been left behind. Parents were obliged to take care that all their children and apprentices learned to read, so that everyone would be able to see for himself in the Bible what opportunities for salvation God offered to man and what sins He forbade. The churches were thronged every Sunday with willing and unwilling worshipers—everyone was required to attend—and church members guarded each other's morals by censuring or excommunicating those who strayed from the straight path.

With virtually the whole population for a police force Winthrop found it no problem to punish sin.

Religion as a Source of Safety and Comfort

Samuel Sewall (1652–1730), a leading member of the Boston, Massachusetts community, was an educated, respectable, and pious man. His diary provides a rich source of information about his activities and attitudes. In

the excerpt that follows, historian David D. Hall describes the comfort that Sewall took from various religious practices. As you will see, some of the things that Sewall did—such as driving a pin into the frame of his new house—might be classified by us as superstition. But these activities, along with those that grew more directly out of his religious faith, all drew upon supernatural forces to give Sewall a feeling of safety. Taken from David D. Hall, Worlds of Wonder, Days of Judgment: Popular Religious Belief in Early New England (*Cambridge, Massachusetts, 1990), 217–19.*

Samuel Sewall (1652–1730), a leading New Englander of the second generation, was a judge at the Salem witch trials. He also wrote an important condemnation of slavery. His attire, like Winthrop's, remains simple, but note the subtle changes. (Painting by John Smibert. Courtesy of the Museum of Fine Arts, Boston.)

CRAVING SAFETY for himself, Sewall sought it earnestly for others as well. As he went about this task, he could not separate the welfare of his wife and children from the welfare of New England. Family, church, town, and country, all shared a collective destiny. He linked them together at a private fast: "Pray'd for Sister Dorothy, my family, New England, that God would fit me for his good pleasure in doing and suffering." At another fast, he begged for blessings upon his children and their kin, the governor and the General Court, Third Church and missionaries to the Indians, Connecticut and New York, "all the European Plantations in

Reprinted from *Worlds of Wonder, Days of Judgment* by David D. Hall. Copyright © 1989 by David D. Hall. Reprinted by permission of Alfred A. Knopf, Inc.

America," the Queen and "Europe." The close at hand and the distant were both deserving of his care. Yet the family always had priority. There were steps he took to safeguard his children that they alone enjoyed. A new addition to his house was under way. Before construction began, Sewall consulted with a minister as to whether the times were propitious. While the floor was being laid he drove a pin into the frame, an act he repeated for the houses of close friends and kin, and for ships and meetinghouses. Soon after he and his family moved into their new rooms, they held a private fast asking God to bless the place where they now lived. Some years later, Sewall set up stone carvings on gateposts in front of the house, two "cherubims heads" that symbolized the presence of protecting forces.

The children born to him and Hannah were carried to the meetinghouse their first week of life to be baptized. In later life Sewall looked back fondly on those moments when he held a newborn child in his arms "upon the Sabbath Day in the Solemn Assembly of God's saints." Giving names to newborn children was no casual task, since the right choice could add protection. "I named Joseph, in hopes of the accomplishment of the Prophecy, Ezek. 37th and such like: and not out of respect to any Relation, or any other person, except the first Joseph." "I named my little daughter Sarah . . . I was struling whether to call her Sarah or Mehetabel; but when I saw Sarah's standing in the Scripture . . . I resolv'd on that side. Also Mother Sewall had a sister Sarah. . . ." For his children he also sought the benefit of "Blessing" from old men; on one occasion he transported the whole family to the bedside of a man whose word (or touch?) he deemed of special worth, and on another he presented "all my stock" to the Reverend Nehemiah Walter of Roxbury and "desired his Blessing of them; which he did."

Back within their home, father, mother, and children gathered daily for a service of devotion. The routine they practiced was that prescribed by the clergy, who envisaged every household as a "little commonwealth" exemplifying moral order. Year in and year out the Sewalls sang psalms and read Scripture at these family meetings. The prayers they offered were explicit in their reference to family problems like a son's quest for a suitable apprenticeship. Scripture-reading proceeded by a schedule that took them "in Course" from Genesis to Revelation, a sequence

31

they resumed once the cycle was completed. Everyone within the family took his turn at reading, Joseph starting at age ten, one sister at age eight.

The psalms they sang together had particular significance. Sewall listed them by number in the diary. Here he also listed psalms he sang in Third Church, in the "closet" of his bedchamber, and in private meetings he shared with a group of laymen. This attention to the psalms was in keeping with their place in popular tradition—not the popular tradition of maypoles and Christmas, but the new vernacular tradition that emerged in post-Reformation England. For Sewall, the music that his friends and family made together was a means of imitating life as saints in heaven. "I give you this Psalm-Book," he told a relative, "in order to your perpetuating this Song; and I would have you pray that it may be an Introduction to our Singing with the Choir above." Noting the death of a Harvard classmate, he recalled that they had "sung many a Tune in Consort; hope shall sing Hallelujah together in Heaven." Together with his family he anticipated heaven as they sang the stanzas of their favorite psalms.

Puritanism's Appeal to Women

Amanda Porterfield is interested in explaining why women found Puritanism appealing. In the passage that follows, she makes an argument about how religion functioned as a source of authority for women. Although the power that pious Puritan women exercised may strike us as indirect and severely limited, a case can be made that even this degree of power represented an increase for early modern women. Porterfield contributes here to an on-going debate about the impact of the Protestant Reformation on the position of women in society. Excerpted from "Women's Attraction to Puritanism," Church History *60 (June 1991): 196–200.*

In 1566 when the Puritan ministers John Gough and John Philpot were suspended from their pulpits and banished from

"Women's Attraction to Puritanism," by Amanda Porterfield, as it appeared in *Church History*, Vol. 60, No. 2, June 1991. Copyright © 1991 by The American Society of Church History.

London for their refusal to wear the white outer robe, or surplice, marking their special holiness as priests of the church, a crowd of more than two hundred women gathered at London Bridge to cheer them on as they left the city. As Gough and Philpot crossed the bridge, the women pressed bags of food and bottles of drink on them, all the while "animating them most earnestly to stand fast in the same their doctrine." That same year, when John Bartlett was also ordered to step down from his pulpit in London for refusing to wear the surplice, sixty women assembled at the home of his bishop to protest the suspension. Such demonstrations of women's support for Puritan ministers were not isolated events. As the historian of Elizabethan Puritanism Patrick Collinson asserted, "it was the women of London who occupied the front line in defence of their preachers, and with a sense of emotional engagement hardly exceeded by the suffragettes of three and a half centuries later."

Women's support for Puritan theology, and for Puritan preachers, was no less formidable in seventeenth-century New England. By 1660 women comprised the majority of communicants in every New England church whose membership records have been preserved. Women comprised 84 percent of new communicants in the New Haven church in the 1660s, over 70 percent of new communicants in the Charlestown, Boston Third, and New London churches in the 1670s, 70 percent or more of new communicants in the Salem, Beverley, Boston First, and Hartford Second churches in the 1680s, and 76 percent and 75 percent of new communicants in the Salem and Boston Third churches during the 1690s. In 1692 Cotton Mather estimated that women made up between two-thirds and three-fourths of the membership of a church close to his home, perhaps Boston's Second Church, where he was minister, and implied that a preponderance of women church members was characteristic of all New England churches. In fact, female admissions to communion in each decade from 1660 to 1700 never dipped below 54 percent in any church in Massachusetts or Connecticut.

The seating arrangements in New England meeting houses represented the prominence of women saints in New England society as well as the relatively intimate relationship that obtained between them and their ministers. For example, during church services in seventeenth-century Dorchester, women sat on the right side of the meetinghouse, directly in front of the minister, while men sat on the left, behind the deacons. When the Dorchester congregation expanded, a new double seat "at ye righthand of ye Pulpit" was installed for women and later, a "2d Seat to ye Double Seat," also for women, was added alongside, effectively nestling the pulpit in the laps of women.

In light of such evidence of women's prominence as supporters of Puritan theology and Puritan ministers, the question of what attracted women to Puritanism arises. Which aspects of Puritan theology and Puritan culture led women to emerge as champions of Puritan ministers during Elizabeth's reign and as custodians of church membership in New England after 1660? Such questions arise with special sharpness because of the emphasis placed in recent scholarship on the patriarchal character of Puritan theology and Puritan culture. Lyle Koehler, Ben Barker-Benfield, Rosemary Skinner Keller, and Margaret Olfson Thickstun have all pointed to the laws and conventions of Puritanism that supported male dominance and discriminated against women. For example, Koehler asserts that "the need to define all women as weak and dependent was . . . deeply embedded in the character of American Puritanism." As Koehler sees it, "Puritans attempted to keep women subordinate and dependent by limiting their educational opportunities, separating the sexes whenever possible, providing no possibility of female economic security outside marriage, censuring 'old maids,' depriving women of the vote in church and commonwealth, forcing wives to relinquish control over their realty, and placing married women under the effectual supervision of their husbands." If Puritan theology and Puritan ministers represented and abetted this system of male dominance, why did women embrace Puritanism so passionately? Why did New England women outnumber men as the church members who sustained and exemplified Puritan culture?

Women were drawn to them partly because of the seductiveness of Puritan theology and Puritan ministers. Especially when delivered by an inspiring preacher, images of Christ as a ravishing Bridegroom and God as an omnipotent Father answered women's desires for powerful love objects. Thus Puritan sermons on the nature of conversion and the devotional characteristics of faith in God offered women imaginary experiences of erotic satisfaction and emotional security.

This seductive power of Puritan theology is illustrated in the conversion story of Joanna Tothill Drake (1585?–1625). In 1618 when her husband hired the forceful young preacher Thomas Hooker (1586–1647) to serve as her personal minister as well as rector of St. George's church in Esher, Surrey, Joanna Drake was distraught and angry about the sinful state of her soul. Before Hooker's arrival, she had been suicidal and violent toward others; she had swallowed pins and struck the eminent Puritan John Dod, in the midst of his prayers for her, with part of her bedstead. Under Dod's ministrations, her physical violence had subsided, but she was still terrified of hell and insistent on the hopeless state of her soul. Moreover, she had grown skillfully disputatious as a result of her arguments with the dozen ministers her husband had enlisted to cure her. With Hooker, however, Mrs. Drake was "mervellously delighted." Her spirits improved steadily under his attentions. Her arguments and debilitating sense of sinfulness disappeared and, on her deathbed, she enjoyed a prolonged and ecstatic experience of God's grace.

Hooker cured Joanna Drake by encouraging her to think about Christ as a magnificent bridegroom and about God as a strong Father. In a treatise based on his cure of Drake, Hooker identified the Christian's acceptance of Christ's suit as the means of her reunion with God; Christ's husbandly love was her "title to the promise" of union with God the Father. Moreover, Hooker exposed Drake's protestations of unworthiness as resentful claims to a better lot and urged her to relinquish her sullen displeasure with her life and rejoice in the grace she already had. Thus in the treatise that grew out of Drake's cure, Hooker likened the Christian who insisted on her unworthiness to "a sullen child that will not eat his milk because he hath it not in the golden dish." With a disarming mixture of encouragement, admonition, and titillation, Hooker encouraged Christians to "hear the best part" of themselves and not "turn the backside of our hearts to the promise." Just as a bride does not have to win her spouse's love but only accept it, so "there is nothing required on our side," wrote Hooker, "but only to receive him as a husband."

This presentation of Christ's suit must have had a very familiar ring to Joanna Drake: her own father had married her against her will to a man who seems to have wanted her love, or at least cared enough about satisfying her to enlist a dozen ministers to alleviate her unhappiness. Hooker led Joanna Drake to accept her husband's love, and her father's authority, by representing their relationships to her in the symbolic language of Puritan theology.

By picturing Christ's husbandly love and God's fatherly authority as pleasurable solutions to her soul's distress, and thereby providing her with religious symbols of sexual satisfaction and emotional security, Hooker led Joanna Drake to feel content with her life and to accept the love and authority of her husband and father. Hooker helped Drake control her anger by identifying it and making her feel guilty about it; his argument that anger was behind her preoccupation with sinfulness led her to confront that anger, and to feel that it was unworthy of a Christian. The remarkable effectiveness of inducing self-control by means of guilt resulted from the attractiveness of the images associated with that strategy; Drake was willing to take responsibility for her anger because her willingness was associated with images of God and Christ that elicited imaginary experiences of erotic satisfaction and emotional pleasure. In effect, the process of embracing Christ advocated by Hooker entailed accepting symbols of emotional gratification for the price of emotional restraint.

Puritan theology and Puritan preachers attracted women not only because they offered women symbols of emotional gratification, but also because Puritan theology and Puritan culture enabled women to exercise an indirect, often public and deliberate authority. These two sources of women's attraction to Puritanism were not unrelated; women's ability to exercise influence over their preachers was part of the same interpersonal, cultural system as their emotional vulnerability to symbols of espousal to Christ, and to erotically charged relationships with the preachers who represented themselves as Christ's ambassadors. Joanna Drake exerted considerable influence in Thomas Hooker's life through her responsiveness to his guidance. His reputation grew out of her acceptance and support; she indirectly shaped Hooker's career as the subject of his first published work, *The Poor Doubting Christian Drawn Unto Christ,* which established his reputation as a pastoral theologian. As was the case with many Puritan preachers, Hooker's success derived in part from his ability to please women.

Puritan Attitudes Toward Sex

One of the charges most frequently leveled against the Puritans is that of sexual prudery, so much so that the popular connotation of the term "Puritan" suggests repressed sexuality. This view comes largely from such early twentieth-century critics of Puritanism as H. L. Mencken, who attacked the mores of late nineteenth century American society by derisively labelling them "Puritan." In one of his earliest publications on early New England history, Edmund S. Morgan defended the Puritans against the charge of prudery. Morgan's definition of what constitutes a "healthy attitude" toward sex may seem somewhat dated now, however. Abridged from Edmund S. Morgan, "The Puritans and Sex," New England Quarterly 15 (December 1942):591–94.

[The nineteenth-century historian] Henry Adams once observed that Americans have "ostentatiously ignored" sex. He could think of only two American writers who touched upon the subject with any degree of boldness—Walt Whitman and Bret Harte. Since the time when Adams made his penetrating observation, American writers have been making up for lost time in a way that would make Bret Harte, if not Whitman, blush. And yet there is still more truth than falsehood in Adams's statement. Americans, by comparison with Europeans or Asiatics, are squeamish when confronted with the facts of life. My purpose is not to account for this squeamishness, but simply to point out that the Puritans, those bogeymen of the modern intellectual, are not responsible for it.

At the outset, consider the Puritans' attitude toward marriage and the role of sex in marriage. The popular assumption might be that the Puritans frowned on marriage and tried to hush up the physical aspect of it as much as possible, but listen to what they themselves had to say. Samuel Willard, minister of the Old South Church in the latter part of the seventeenth century and author of the most complete textbook of Puritan divinity, more than once expressed his horror at "that Popish conceit of the Excellency of Virginity." Another minister, John Cotton, wrote that

"The Puritans and Sex," by Edmund S. Morgan, as it appeared in *The New England Quarterly*, Vol. 15. Copyright © 1942 by *The New England Quarterly*. Reprinted by permission of Northeastern University.

Women are Creatures without which there is no comfortable Living for man: it is true of them what is wont to be said of Governments, *That bad ones are better than none:* They are a sort of Blasphemers then who dispise and decry them, and call them *a necessary Evil,* for they are *a necessary Good.*

These sentiments did not arise from an interpretation of marriage as a spiritual partnership, in which sexual intercourse was a minor or incidental matter. Cotton gave his opinion of "Platonic love" when he recalled the case of

one who immediately upon marriage, without ever approaching the *Nuptial Bed,* indented with the *Bride,* that by mutual consent they might both live such a life, and according did sequestring themselves according to the custom of those times, from the rest of mankind, and afterwards from one another too, in their retired Cells, giving themselves up to a Contemplative life; and this is recorded as an instance of no little or ordinary Vertue; but I must be pardoned in it, if I can account it no other than an effort of blind zeal, for they are the dictates of a blind mind they follow therein, and not of that Holy Spirit, which saith *It is not good that man should be alone.*

Here is as healthy an attitude as one could hope to find anywhere. Cotton certainly cannot be accused of ignoring human nature. Nor was he an isolated example among the Puritans. Another minister stated plainly that "the Use of the Marriage Bed" is "founded in mans Nature," and that consequently any withdrawal from sexual intercourse upon the part of husband or wife "Denies all reliefe in Wedlock vnto Human necessity: and sends it for supply vnto Beastiality when God gives not the gift of Continency." In other words, sexual intercourse was a human necessity and marriage the only proper supply for it. These were the views of the New England clergy, the acknowledged leaders of the community, the most Puritanical of the Puritans. As proof that their congregations concurred with them, one may cite the case in which the members of the First Church of Boston expelled James Mattock because, among other offenses, "he denied Coniugall fellowship vnto his wife for the space of 2 years together vpon pretense of taking Revenge upon himself for his abusing of her before marryage." So strongly did the Puritans insist upon the sexual character of marriage that one New Englander considered himself slandered when it was reported, "that he Brock his deceased wife's hart with Greife, that he wold be absent from her 3 weeks together when he was at home, and wold never come nere her, and such Like."

There was just one limitation which the Puritans placed upon sexual relations in marriage: sex must not interfere with religion. Man's chief end was to glorify God, and all earthly delights must promote that end, not hinder it. Love for a wife was carried too far when it led a man to neglect his God:

> ...sometimes a man hath a good affection to Religion, but the love of his wife carries him away, a man may bee so transported to his wife, that hee dare not bee forward in Religion, lest hee displease his wife, and so the wife, lest shee displease her husband, and this is an inordinate love, when it exceeds measure.

Sexual pleasures, in this respect, were treated like other kinds of pleasure. On a day of fast, when all comforts were supposed to be foregone in behalf of religious contemplation, not only were tasty food and drink to be abandoned but sexual intercourse, too. On other occasions, when food, drink, and recreation were allowable, sexual intercourse was allowable too, though of course only between persons who were married to each other. The Puritans were not ascetics; they never wished to prevent the enjoyment of earthly delights. They merely demanded that the pleasures of the flesh be subordinated to the greater glory of God: husband and wife must not become "so transported with affection, that they look at no higher end than marriage it self." "Let such as have wives," said the ministers, "look at them not for their own ends, but to be fitted for Gods service, and bring them nearer to God."

Toward sexual intercourse outside marriage the Puritans were as frankly hostile as they were favorable to it in marriage. They passed laws to punish adultery with death, and fornication with whipping. Yet they had no misconceptions as to the capacity of human beings to obey such laws. Although the laws were commands of God, it was only natural—since the fall of Adam—for human beings to break them. Breaches must be punished lest the community suffer the wrath of God, but no offense, sexual or otherwise, could be occasion for surprise or for hushed tones of voice.

Puritanism as a Source of Social Stability

In an important essay on the social stability that characterized early New England society, Timothy H. Breen and Stephen Foster suggest that Puritanism played an important role in creating that stability. If most New Englanders approved of the society that Breen and Foster describe, they would have appreciated their faith all the more for the kind of community that it helped them to erect. Abridged from "The Puritans' Greatest Achievement: A Study of Social Cohesion in Seventeenth-Century Massachusetts," Journal of American History 60 (June 1973): 10–13.

Left to themselves, however, the Massachusetts colonists found Congregationalism a source of stability. Flexible enough to accommodate moderate differences of opinion, the orthodox faith still served as a useful test for detecting and expelling extremists, thereby precluding any prolonged clash over religious fundamentals. Irreconcilables quickly discovered the charms of Rhode Island and left the Bay Colony in relative peace. Nathaniel Ward, the colony's most exuberant propagandist, explained this phenomenon in his *Simple Cobler of Aggawam:* "True Religion is *Ignis probationis* [a testing fire] which doth *congregare homogenea & segregare heterogenia* [bring together the alike and drive away the different]."

Ward was correct to emphasize the homogenizing effect of "true religion," any true religion, providing it could be widely and exclusively inculcated as in Massachusetts. The Bay Colony fortunately possessed an official priestly caste supported at public expense and periodically replenished by the graduates of Harvard College. Unhampered by anything but the most futile and sporadic opposition, the authorized interpreters of the exclusive faith provided the citizens of the Bay Colony with meaning for their present, a mission for their future, and, what was more, and perhaps most of all, a synthetic but compelling past. . . .

"The Puritans' Greatest Achievements: A Study of Social Cohesion in Seventeenth-Century Massachusetts," by Timothy H. Breen and Stephen Foster, as it appeared in *The Journal of American History* (formerly *The Mississippi Valley Historical Review*), Vol. 60, No. 1, June 1973. Copyright © 1973 by the Organization of American Historians.

Puritanism gave to Massachusetts the same kind of provincial identity that was supplied by local tradition in the counties of seventeenth-century England. Indeed, in its physical situation no less than in its mental set the Bay Colony would have made a typical county community. The colony was small in extent, its population was about the right size and relatively compact in distribution, it possessed a coherent intellectual and gentry class, and it was ready to offer fierce resistance to central power emanating from London. . . .

1653 cartoon depicts "Father Christmas" (center) being turned away by a Puritan while another man welcomes him. The image was intended to lampoon Puritan hostility to Christmas which they regarded as a pagan holiday. Which of the two men flanking Father Christmas is wealthier? Why did the artist choose to distinguish the two in that way? (Courtesy of The Library of Congress.)

By contributing a common ideology to the Bay Colony, Puritanism did much to create in America the kind of community capable of maintaining order within its borders. If anything, the artificiality of Massachusetts "countyness" assisted its function. Conflicting loyalties to patrons, family, or guilds, which could tear apart even the most traditional European community, were all comparatively weak or absent in New England. In this sense the social utility of Puritanism lay in its position as the monopoly faith rather than in its particular tenets. Hinduism might have served equally well if Harvard could have turned out genuine Brahmins trained in the learned exposition of the *Bhagavad-gita* and the printing press, pulpit, and schools been adapted to the inculcation of the Word in Sanskrit. But the specific preachings of the Puritan Word also had a contribution to make.

From the very first the leaders of New England spoke of love as the foundation of their society. While still aboard the *Arbella*, John Winthrop set the tone for life in the Bay Colony, urging the settlers to be "knitt together in this worke as one man" and warning that their failure to do so would make them "a story and a by-word through the world." Winthrop and the other Puritans who moved to Massachusetts assumed that the Lord had made a covenant with them as He had once done for the people of England. This initial "national Covenant" was followed by a proliferation of other covenants on every level of life in New England. The Massachusetts Puritans organized churches, towns, indeed, the entire commonwealth upon the contractual model. The essential ingredient in this contract was free will: the individual voluntarily promised to obey civil and scriptural law, for the seventeenth-century Puritans believed that meaningful obedience could only grow out of voluntary consent, never out of coercion. With this principle in mind, Thomas Hooker insisted that the man who desired to enter a social convenant had to "*willingly* binde and ingage himself to each member of that society . . . or else a member actually he is not." The strong sense of communal responsibility that developed out of this voluntary commitment influenced the character of conflict within the Bay Colony. It was incumbent upon all men to work out their disputes as peacefully as possible, thinking always of their greater obligation to the commonwealth as a whole and ultimately to God himself. Thus, when the future townsmen of Dedham drew up their covenant, they pledged to practice "everlasting love," and should that bond ever be strained by local differences "then, such party or parties shall presently refer all such differences unto some one, two or three others of our said society to be fully accorded and determined without any further delay."

The logic of the covenant determined that the towns and churches of New England would be homogeneous units. Puritan villagers excluded anyone from their midst whom they believed endangered their way of life, and unwanted strangers were frequently "warned out" when they failed to meet the community's standards. In Winthrop's time the concern for social purity was so great that colonial authorities sometimes asked newcomers to present evidence of good character before allowing them to settle.

Such conscious self-selection strengthened social cohesion within Massachusetts by forcing potential troublemakers to find homes in other parts of America. Historians have often criticized the leaders of the Bay Colony for their intolerance of other men's opinions, but when one considers Catholics fighting Protestants in colonial Maryland or the Dutch quarreling with the English in New York, one begins to understand why the Puritan fathers acted as they did.

Questions

1. *Both Hall and Porterfield discuss the appeal of Puritanism for the individual believer, but the issues they emphasize differ. Compare and contrast the two discussions, then think about ways in which their points of view might be integrated.*

2. *Edmund S. Morgan directly addresses the older criticisms of Puritanism with regard to the questions of "community watchfulness" and sexuality. What does he assert in an effort to force us to reconsider our view of the Puritans? How persuasive do you find his arguments?*

3. *Why would any of the people described in these selections have wanted to be a Puritan? What was appealing about the society that they created? What do you find unappealing?*

PURITAN FAITH:
THE PERSONAL AND THE POLITICAL

Since the popular negative image of Puritanism is a fairly recent develop-ment, the Puritans themselves did not respond systematically to the various charges that have been levelled against them. Thus, the written records they left—a sampling of which is reprinted below—do not neces-sarily address our issues. For the Puritans, the compelling question— Am I saved or damned?—was unanswerable in this life. Unable to know their fates, each wondered how can I handle not knowing my fate, and how does God require me to live my life? As they struggled with these issues, they produced a wide variety of documents that can suggest to us why they made the choice to join the Puritan movement and what that decision meant for the society that they created in New England.

God's Judgment as a Lesson

Increase Mather (1639–1723), an influential Boston minister, wrote a best-selling book that recounted examples of "God's Providence"—that is, God's direct intercession in people's lives. Mather collected stories from all over New England to illustrate that God did take an active role in daily life. In the preface to his book, he related the following incident from an earlier English manuscript that made his point quite well; Mather criticizes then-prevailing religious practices (such as church discipline) even as he approvingly relates the tale of poor Mr. Juxon. From the unpaginated preface to An Essay for the Recording of Illustrious Providences . . . *(Boston, 1684).*

This M. *SS.* [manuscript] doth also mention some most *Remarkable Judgments* of God upon Sinners, as worthy to be Recorded for Posterity to take notice of. It is there said, that when Mr. *Richard Juxon* was a Fellow of *Kings Colledge* in *Cambridge*, he led a most vicious life: and whereas such of the Students as were serious in matters of Religion, did endeavour by solemn Fasting and Prayer to prepare themselves for the Communion which was then (this was about the year 1636) on *Easter-Day*. This *Juxon* spent all the time of preparation in Drunken wild Meetings, and was up late and Drunk on . . . Saturday night. Nevertheless, on the Lords day, he came with others to the Communion, and sat next to the Relator [storyteller], who knowing his Disorder the night before, was much troubled: but had no remedy; Church-Discipline not being then so practiced as ought to have been. The Communion being ended, such of the Scholars as had the fear of God in their hearts, repaired to their Closets [or small rooms]. But this *Juxon* went immediately to a Drunken-meeting, and there to a Cock-fight, where he fell to his accustomed madness, and pouring out a volley of Oaths and Curses; while these were between his Lips, God smote him dead in the twinkle of an eye. And though *Juxon* were but young, and of a comely person, his Carcase was immediately so corrupted as that the stench of it was insufferable, insomuch that no house would receive it; and his Friends were forced to hire some base Fellows to watch the Carcase till night; and then with Pitch and such like Gums covered him in a Coffin, and so made a shift to endure his Interment. There stood by a Scholar, whose name was *George Hall*, and who acted his part with *Juxon* in his prophaneness: but he was so astonished with this amazing Providence of God, as that he fell down upon his knees, begging pardoning mercy from Heaven, and vowing a Reformation; which vow the Lord enabled him to keep, so as that afterwards he became an able and famous Minister of the Gospel.

Preface to "An Essay for the Recording of Illustrious Providences," by Increase Mather, published by Samuel Green for Joseph Browning, Boston, 1684.

46

John Dane Grapples with His Sinfulness

Every Puritan thought about his (or her) spiritual state, confronting the sinful inclinations inherent in human nature and praying for God's help in overcoming temptation. Shortly before his death in 1683, John Dane (born in 1612) composed an autobiography intended to edify his children and grandchildren, from which the following excerpt is extracted. His narrative gives some insight into the attitudes of lay people. Taken from "A Declaration of Remarkabell Prouedenses in the Corse of My Lyfe," in New England Historical Genealogical Register, *(Boston 1854) 8:149–51) [In the following selection, the Latin "u" is often substituted for the English "v".]*

Consarning my self; when I was but a lettell boy, being edicated under godly parents, my Conshans [conscience] was ueary apt to tell me of euells that I should not doe. Being now about aight yers ould, I was giuen mutch to play and to run out without my fathers Consent and againe his comand. One a time, I haueing gone out most parte of the day, when my father saw me cum home, he toke me and basted [beat] me. I then cept [kept] home, and folowed my busenes two or thre dase. My father and mother Comended me, and tould me that god would bles me if I obeyed my parents, and what the contrary would ishew [issue] in. I then thout in my harte, o that my fatther would beat me more when I did amis. I fard [feared], if he did not, I should not be good. . . .

I did think myself in a good condishon. I was conuinsed that I should pray and durst doe no other, and Red and here sarmons and durst doe no other; yet I was giuen to pastime and to dansing, and that I thout lawfull. Now uppone a time, when I was groune 18 yers of age or thare abouts, I went to a dansing scoll to larne to dans. My father hering of it, when I cam home tould me, if I went agayne, he would bast me. I tould him, if he did he should neuer bast me againe. With that, my father toke a stick and basted me. I toke it patiently, and said nothing for a day or [two], but on morning betimes I Res and toke 2 shurts on my back and the best sute I had, and a bybell in my pocet, and set the dores open and went to my fathers chamber dore and said, god by father, god by mother. Why, whether are you going? To seke my fortin, I

47

answared. Then said my mother, *goe whare you will, god he will find you out.* This word, the point of it, stuck in my breast, and afterwards god struck it home to its head.

Allthough I thout my fatther was two Strict, I thout Soloman said, be not holy ouer mutch, and daued [David] was a man after gods oun harte, and he was a danser [dancer]: but yet I went my Journey, and was from him half a yere before he hard whare I was. I first settled in barcumsted, and thare Rought on a shobord that had bene improud that waie. On a nyte [night], when most folke was a bead, a mayd cam into the shopbord and sat with me, and we Jested togetther; but at the last she cared it so, and put huself in sutch a poster, as that I made as If I had sum speshall ocashon abrod and went out; for I fared, If I had not, I should haue cumitted foley with hur. But I ofen thout that it was the prayers of my parents that preuaild with god to kepe me. I then gaue my self mutch to dansing and staying out and heatting myself and lying in haymowes, the pepell being a bed whare I abod that I lost my culler and neuer Recuferd it a gaine. . . .

I now being at harford, M'[ister] Goodin preacht thare, and he preacht consarning prayer. But on saboth day, not being in that trim that i would haue bene in [i.e., not being able to dress as he would like], . . . I would not goe to metting but walkt in the filds close by a meadow sid. Thare was, whetther fly, wasp or hornet, I cannot tell, but it struck my finger, and watter and blod cam out of it and paind me mutch. I went up to a hous and shoud it, but thay knew not what a sting I had at my harte. Now I thout of my mothers words, that god would find me out. I hastend home to the Chamber I lay in, at my masters house; and when i cam thare I toke my bybell and lokt ouer sum instructions my father had Ret, and I weapt sorly. The payne and swelling increast & sweld up to my shoulder. I prayd ernistly to god that he would pardon my sinn and heall my arme. I went to a surgin and askt him what it was. He said it was *the take.* I askt him what he meant. He said it was taken by the prouedens [providence] of god. This knoct home on my hart what my mother said, *god will find you out.* Now I made great promises that if god would here me this time I would Reforme.

An Artist Contemplates the Struggle to Overcome Sin

The Puritan poet Anne Bradstreet (1612?–1672) approaches the struggle over sin that engaged John Dane and indeed all Puritans from a more philosophical perspective in the poem reprinted below. In "The Flesh and The Spirit" the natural (or sinful) side of the Christian believer debates with the spiritual side. Note that the spirit derides worldly pleasures, contrasting these with spiritual pleasures to come. Reprinted from The Complete Works of Anne Bradstreet, *ed. Joseph R. McElrath, Jr., and Allan P. Robb (Boston, 1981), 175–77.*

The Flesh and the Spirit.

In secret place where once I stood
Close by the Banks of *Lacrim* flood
I heard two sisters reason on
Things that are past, and things to come;
One flesh was call'd, who had her eye
On worldly wealth and vanity;
The other Spirit, who did rear
Her thoughts unto a higher sphere:
Sister, quoth Flesh, what liv'st thou on
Nothing but Meditation?
Doth Contemplation feed thee so
Regardlesly to let earth goe?
Can Speculation satisfy
Notion without Reality?
Dost dream of things beyond the Moon
And dost thou hope to dwell there soon?
Hast treasures there laid up in store
That all in th' world thou count'st but poor?
Art fancy sick, or turn'd a Sot
To catch at shadowes which are not?
Come, come, Ile shew unto thy sence,

"The Flesh and the Spirit," by Anne Bradstreet, reprinted from *The Complete Works of Anne Bradstreet*, Joseph R. McElrath, Jr. and Allan P. Robb, editors. Published by Twayne Publishers, 1981. Copyright © 1981 by G.K. Hall & Co.

Industry hath its recompence.
What canst desire, but thou maist see
True substance in variety?
Dost honour like? acquire the same,
As some to their immortal fame:
And trophyes to thy name erect
Which wearing time shall ne're deject.
For riches dost thou long full sore?
Behold enough of precious store.
Earth hath more silver, pearls and gold,
Then eyes can see, or hands can hold.
Affect's thou pleasure? take thy fill,
Earth hath enough of what you will.
Then let not goe, what thou maist find,
For things unknown, only in mind.
Spir. Be still thou unregenerate part,
Disturb no more my setled heart,
For I have vow'd (and so will doe)
Thee as a foe, still to pursue.
And combate with thee will and must,
Untill I see thee laid in th' dust.
Sisters we are, yea twins we be,
Yet deadly feud 'twixt thee and me;
For from one father are we not,
Thou by old Adam wast begot,
But my arise is from above,
Whence my dear father I do love.
Thou speak'st me fair, but hat'st me sore,
Thy flatt'ring shews Ile trust no more.
How oft thy slave, hast thou me made,
When I believ'd, what thou hast said,
And never had more cause of woe
Then when I did what thou bad'st doe.
Ile stop mine ears at these thy charms,
And count them for my deadly harms.
Thy sinfull pleasures I doe hate,
Thy riches are to me no bait,
Thine honours doe, nor will I love;
For my ambition lyes above.
My greatest honour it shall be
When I am victor over thee,

And triumph shall, with laurel head,
When thou my Captive shalt be led,
How I do live, thou need'st not scoff,
For I have meat thou know'st not off;
The hidden Manna I doe eat,
The word of life it is my meat.
My thoughts do yield me more content
Then can thy hours in pleasure spent.
Nor are they shadows which I catch,
Nor fancies vain at which I snatch,
But reach at things that are so high,
Beyond thy dull Capacity;
Eternal substance I do see,
With which inriched I would be:
Mine Eye doth pierce the heavens, and see
What is Invisible to thee.
My garments are not silk nor gold,
Nor such like trash which Earth doth hold,
But Royal Robes I shall have on,
More glorious then the glistring Sun;
My Crown not Diamonds, Pearls, and gold,
But such as Angels heads infold.
The City where I hope to dwell,
There's none on Earth can parallel;
The stately Walls both high and strong,
Are made of pretious *Jasper* stone;
The Gates of Pearl, both rich and clear,
And Angels are for Porters there;
The Streets thereof transparent gold,
Such as no Eye did e're behold,
A Chrystal River there doth run,
Which doth proceed from the Lambs Throne:
Of Life, there are the waters sure,
Which shall remain for ever pure,
Nor Sun, nor Moon, they have no need,
For glory doth from God proceed:
No Candle there, nor yet Torch light,
For there shall be no darksome night.
From sickness and infirmity,
For evermore they shall be free,
Nor withering age shall e're come there,

But beauty shall be bright and clear;
This City pure is not for thee,
For things unclean there shall not be:
If I of Heaven may have my fill,
Take thou the world, and all that will.

Drawing Upon Faith in the Face of Affliction

Although Puritans—like religious peoples in many other faith traditions—feared divine judgment, they also found solace in their religious faith. When dealing with the death of a loved one, Puritans often sought comfort in their religious beliefs. Anne Bradstreet wrote the following poem while struggling to come to terms with the death of her granddaughter. From The Complete Works of Anne Bradstreet, *ed. Joseph R. McElrath, Jr., and Allan P. Robb (Boston, 1981), 187.*

In memory of my dear grand-child . . .
Who deceased June 20. 1669. *being three years and*
seven Moneths old.
With troubled heart & trembling hand I write,
The Heavens have chang'd to sorrow my delight.
How oft with disappointment have I met,
When I on fading things my hopes have set?
Experience might 'fore this have made me wise,
To value things according to their price:
Was ever stable joy yet found below?
Or perfect bliss without mixture of woe.
I knew she was but as a withering flour,
That's here to day, perhaps gone in an hour;
Like as a bubble, or the brittle glass,
Or like a shadow turning as it was.
More fool then I to look on that was lent,

"In memory of my dear grand-child . . . who deceased June 20, 1669, being three years and seven months old," by Anne Bradstreet, reprinted from *The Complete Works of Anne Bradstreet,* Joseph R. McElrath, Jr. and Allan P. Robb, editors. Published by Twayne Publishers, 1981. Copyright © 1981 by G.K. Hall & Co.

As if mine own, when thus impermanent.
Farewel dear child, thou ne're shall come to me,
But yet a while, and I shall go to thee;
Mean time my throbbing heart's chear'd up with this
Thou with thy Saviour art in endless bliss.

"To Walke Together":
The Role of the Puritan Congregation

The preceding selections from Mather, Dane, and Bradstreet dealt with religion on a personal level, but Puritans believed that their spirituality ought to have a public component as well. One way in which they expressed their commitment publicly was by joining a church. In seventeenth-century Massachusetts and Connecticut, only those who seemed to their peers to be saved—that is, to have undergone a legitimate conversion experience—could become church members. Once accepted into a congregation, new members entered into a church covenant. In many churches, such as the one founded in Salem, Massachusetts in 1629, a written covenant was publicly endorsed by all members. The text of the Salem covenant explains why the Puritans thought it necessary to organize churches. Taken from The Records of the First Church in Salem Massachusetts, 1629–1736, *ed. Richard D. Pierce (Salem, Massachusetts, 1974), 3–5.*

Wee whose names are here under written, members of the present Church of Christ in Salem, haveing found by sad experience how dangerous it is to sitt loose to the Covenant wee make with our God: and how apt wee are to wander into by pathes, even to the looseing of our first aimes in entring into Church fellowship: Doe therefore, solemnly in the presence of the Eternall God both for our owne comforts and those which shall or maye be joyned unto us renewe that Church covenant we find this Church bound unto at theire first begining. vizt: That we Covenant with the Lord and one with an other, and doe bynd our selves in the

"To Walk Together," excerpted from *The Records of the First Church in Salem Massachusetts 1629–1736*, Richard D. Pierce, editor, published by Essex Institute, 1974. Copyright © 1974 Essex Institute, Salem, Massachusetts.

presence of God, to walke together in all his waies, according as he is pleased to reveale him selfe unto us in his Blessed word of truth. And doe more explicitely in the name and feare of God, profess and protest to walke as followeth through the power and grace of our Lord Jesus.

1. first wee avowe the Lord to be our God, and our selves his people in the truth and simplicitie of our Spirits

2. Wee give our selves to the Lord Jesus Christ, and the word of his grace, fore the teaching, ruleing and sanctifyeing of us in matters of worship, and conversation resolveing to cleave to him alone for life and glorie; and oppose all contrarie wayes, cannons and constitutions of men in his worship.

3. Wee promise to walk with our brethren and sisters in the Congregation with all watchfullness, and tendernis avoyding all jelousies, suspitions, backbyteings, conjurings, provoakings, secrete riseings of spirit against them, but in all offences to follow the rule of the Lord Jesus, and to beare and forbeare, give and forgive as he hath taught us.

4. In publick or private, we will willingly doe nothing to the ofence of the Church but will be willing to take advise for ourselves and ours as ocasion shall be presented.

5. Wee will not in the Congregation be forward eyther to show our owne gifts or parts in speaking or scrupuling [2] or there discover the fayling of our brethren or sisters butt attend an orderly cale there unto; knowing how much the Lord may be dishonoured, and his Gospell in the profession of it, sleighted by our distempers, and weaknesses in publyck.

6. Wee bynd ourselves to studdy the advancment of the Gospell in all truth and peace, both in regard of those that are within, or without, noe waye sleighting our sister Churches, but useing theire Counsell as need shalbe; nor laying a stumbling block, before any, noe not the Indians, whose good we desire to promote, and soe to converse, as wee may avoyd the verrye appearance of evill,

7. Wee hereby promise to carrye ourselves in all lawfull obedience, to those that are over us in Church or Common weale, knowing how well pleasing it wilbe to the Lord, that they should have incouragement in theire places, by our not greiveing theyre spirites through our iregulareties.

8. Wee resolve to prove our selves to the Lord in our particular calings, shunning ydlenes as the bane of any state, nor will wee

deale hardly, or opressingly with Any, wherein wee are the Lords stewards: alsoe

9. promyseing to our best abilitie to teach our children and servants, the knowledge of God and his will, that they may serve him alsoe and all this, not by any strength of our owne, but by the Lord Christ, whose bloud we desire may sprinckle this our Covenant made in his name.

A Puritan Justifies Intolerance

The New England Puritans were criticized for more than leaving England at a time of intense struggle; they were also attacked as religious bigots. In the following selection, Puritan legal scholar Nathaniel Ward (1570–1653) attempts to justify intolerance. Although he and his coreligionists were criticized for these attitudes in their own day, we must bear in mind that principled opposition to religious diversity was fairly common among their contemporaries. This passage is taken from The Simple Cobler of Aggawam in America, *5th ed. (Boston, 1713), 5–6. Aggawam was an early name for the town of Ipswich, Massachusetts.*

My heart hath natura'ly detested four things: The standing of the Apocrypha in the Bible; Forainers dwelling in my Country, to crowd out Native Subjects into the corners of the Earth; Alchymized Coines; Tolerations of divers Religions, or of one Religion in segregant shapes: He that willingly assents to the last, if he examines his heart by day-light, his Conscience will tell him, he is either an Atheist, or an Heretick, or an Hypocrite, or at best a captive to some Lust: Poly-piety is the greatest impiety in the World. True Religion is *Ignis probation is* which doth *congregare homogenea & segregare heterogenea [True Religion is a Testing Fire which doth Bring Together the alike and drive away the different or heterodox].*

Excerpted from *The Simple Cobler of Aggawam in America,* Fifth Edition, by Nathaniel Ward a.k.a. Theodore de la Guard, printed by J.D. & R.I. Reprinted for Daniel Henchman at his shop in King Street, Boston, Massachusetts, 1713.

55

Not to tolerate things meerly indifferent to weak Consciences, argues a Conscience too strong: pressed uniformity in these, causes much disunity: To tolerate more than indifferents, is not to deal indifferently with God: He that doth it, takes his Scepter out of his hand, and bids him stand by. Who hath to do to institute Religion but God. The power of all Religion and Ordinances, lies in their Purity: their Purity in their Simplicity: then are mixtures pernicious. I lived in a City, where a Papist Preached in one Church, a Lutheran in another, a Calvinist in a third; a Lutheran one part of the day, a Calvinist the other, in the same Pulpit: the Religion of that Place was but motly and meagre, their affections Leopard-like.

If the whole Creature should conspire to do the Creator a mischief, or offer him an insolency, it would be in nothing more, than in erecting untruths against his Truth, or by sophisticating his Truths with humane medleyes: the removing of some one iota in Scripture, may draw out all the life, and traverse all the Truth of the whole Bible: but to authorize an untruth, by a Toleration of State, is to build a Sconce against the walls of Heaven, to batter God out of his Chair: To tell a practical lye, is a great Sin, but yet transient; but to set up a Theorical untruth, is to warrant every lye that lyes from its root to the top of every branch it hath, which are not a few.

Edward Johnson Exhorts All People to Follow Christ

In this final excerpt, lay author Edward Johnson interrupts his history of early New England to call all nations to Christ. Because he sees New England as the fulfillment of God's plan for humanity, this call seems to him not an interruption, but an integral part of the history he is relating. The language he uses in this passage is inspired by the Bible. Taken from Edward Johnson, A History of New-England *[better known as* Wonder-working Providence*] (London, 1654), 32–33.*

An Exhortation to all People, Nations and Languages, to indeavour the advancing of the Kingdome of Christ in the purity of his Ordinances, seeing he hath done such admirable Acts for these poore shrubs.

AND now all you whose affections are taken with wonderfull matters (Attend) and you that thinke Christ hath forgotten his poore despised people (Behold) and all you that hopefully long for Christs appearing to confound *Antichrist* (Consider) and rejoyce all yee his Churches the World throughout, for the Lambe is preparing his Bride, and oh! yee the antient Beloved of Christ, whom he of old led by the hand from *Egypt* to *Canaan*, through that great and terrible Wildernesse, looke here, behold him whom you have peirced, preparing to peirce your hearts with his *Wonder-working Providence*, and to provoke you by this little handfull of his people to looke on him, and mourne. Yet let no man think these few weake Wormes would restraine the wonderfull Workes of Christ, as onely to themselves, but the quite contrary, these but the Porch of his glorious building in hand, and if hee have shewed such admirable acts of his providence toward these, what will he doe when the whole Nation of *English* shall set upon like Reformation according to the direct Rule of his Word? Assured confidence there is also for all Nations, from the undoubted promise of Christ himselfe.

The Winter is past, the Raine is changed and gone, come out of the holes of the secret places, feare not because your number is but small, gather into Churches, and let Christ be your King, yee *Presbytery*, Lord it not over them or any Churches, but feed every one, that one flock over which Christ hath made you overseers, and yee people of Christ give your *Presbytery* double honours, that they with you may keepe the watch of the Lord over his Churches. Yee *Dutch* come out of your hods-podge, the great mingle mangle of Religion among you hath caused the Churches of Christ to increase so little with you, standing at a stay like Corne among Weeds, Oh, yee *French*! feare not the great swarmes of *Locusts*, nor the croking *Frogs* in your Land, Christ is reaching out the hand to you, look what hee hath done for these *English*, and sure hee is no Respecter of Persons, &c. yee *Germanes* that have had such a bloudy bickering, Christ is now comming to your aide, then cast off your loose, and carelesse kinde of Reformation, gather into Churches, and keepe them pure, that Christ may delight to dwell among you: oh *Italy*! The Seat and Center of the Beast, Christ will

---

Excerpted from *A History of New England*, better known as *Wonder-working Providence*, printed for Nath. Brooke at the *Angel* in Corn Hill, 1654.

now pick out a People from among you for himselfe, see here what wonders hee workes in little time. Oh! yee *Spaniards* and *Portugalls*, Christ will shew you the abominations of that beastly Whore, who hath made your Nations drunke with the Wine of her Fornication. Dread not that cruell murtherous Inquisition, for Christ is now making Inquisition for them, and behold, here how hee hath rewarded them, who dealt cruelly with these his people.

Finally, oh all yee Nations of the World, behold great is the worke the glorious King of Heaven and Earth hath in hand; beware of neglecting the call of Christ: and you the Seed of *Israel* both lesse and more, the ratling of your dead bones together is at hand, Sinewes, Flesh and Life.

Questions

1. *Some of the passages above suggested that these religious beliefs caused people to feel fearful, other passages suggested that these religious beliefs that they served as a source of comfort. Which aspect of the experience seems comprehensible to you? Can the fear and comfort be integrated somehow? How did the Puritans integrate them?*
2. *What obligations did the Puritans' faith place upon them, in terms of their personal behavior, their churches, and their society?*
3. *What impact do you think Puritanism as a social or religious force had on the history of New England?*
4. *Why would a seventeenth-century English man or woman have found the Puritan message and movement appealing? Why would some people have been outraged by the very existence of such a movement?*

FURTHER READING

Edmund Morgan's biography of John Winthrop, The Puritan Dilemma: The Story of John Winthrop *(Boston, 1958), offers a good starting place on the early history of Puritanism in Massachusetts.* Worlds of Wonder, Days of Judgment: Popular Religious Belief in Early New England *(New York, 1989) by David D. Hall treats popular religion in New England. A fairly basic general account of the experiences of the first migrants to Puritan New England can be found in Virginia DeJohn Anderson,* New England's Generation: The Great Migration and the Formation of Society and Culture in the Seventeenth Century *(New York, 1991). John Demos's* A Little Commonwealth: Family Life in Plymouth Colony *(New York, 1970), addresses the social history of an early New England settlement.*

The Causes of Bacon's Rebellion

Carla Gardina Pestana
and Charles Coleman Finlay

INTRODUCTION

By 1675, the royal colony of Virginia concentrated its agricultural efforts on growing tobacco for export. Tobacco cultivation demanded a large labor force, and the planters relied mainly on English, Irish, and Scottish indentured servants, some of them poor young men and women, others convicts sentenced to a period of labor in the New World. When their terms of servitude expired, they wanted land for themselves, which put them in competition with plantation owners (their former masters) who wanted to expand their holdings to replace land that had been depleted by the overcultivation of tobacco. New land was becoming scarce, because the colony was reaching the limits of its boundaries. Beyond those boundaries lived various groups of Native Americans who opposed continued English expansion onto their lands. The royally appointed governor, Sir William Berkeley, sought to avoid further conflicts with the Indians by reaching boundary agreements with them. These agreements primarily hurt the ex-indentured servants and the newly arrived planters, since these people would benefit most if additional lands were made available for settlement. Some of these people went to live on (or beyond) the borders of the colony, where their presence sparked the hostilities that Berkeley sought to avoid.

In 1675 and early 1676, a series of confrontations occurred along the Potomac River in the Chesapeake region, pitting Doeg and Susquehannock Indians against these English planters. Nathaniel Bacon, a well-born Englishman who had recently migrated to Virginia, sought official sanction for a general attack against the natives. After Governor Berkeley refused to authorize

Bacon's request, Bacon led a group of volunteers to massacre one of the friendly tribes. When Berkeley declared Bacon a rebel and moved to arrest him, the young man launched an attack on the governor, and the entire colony collapsed into civil war. The rebels burned Jamestown, the capital, to the ground, and a period of plunder ensued in which partisans on both sides looted the homes and property of their enemies.

For most of 1676 Virginia was engulfed by civil war. The uprising against Berkeley, led by Bacon and named after him, was the largest armed revolt against English authority in the American colonies until the Revolution a century later. It was only put down after King Charles II dispatched an expeditionary force to quell the rebellion. After they had helped Berkeley restore order to the colony, the king's commissioners replaced Berkeley and sent him back to England to justify himself to the king. After an extended career (1642–52, 1660–77) as governor in the first royal colony in America, Berkeley died in disgrace in England shortly after his return there.

Although Berkeley's handling of the crisis (along with some of the policies that led up to it) resulted in his fall from power, the rebels were judged yet more harshly at the time. Many of them lost their lives after the rebellion was put down. During the revolutionary era, however, it became popular to present Bacon as the heroic forerunner of later Virginian revolutionaries like George Washington and Patrick Henry. More recently, scholars have been less inclined to side wholeheartedly with Bacon. They now tend to study the rebellion for what it reveals about serious divisions within late-seventeenth-century Chesapeake society. Bacon's Rebellion was the only colonial revolt to involve Native Americans, Europeans, and Africans. As such, it offers a glimpse of the social and political development of early Virginia.

SCHOLARS DEBATE MOTIVATION

Ironically, Bacon's Rebellion "waited" almost one hundred years after it first erupted in 1676 to become an important historical event. During and after the American Revolution, people like Thomas Jefferson searched for examples of previous resistance to English authority in the American colonies and identified Nathaniel Bacon as a model for a later generation of Virginian rebels. Well into the twentieth century, this view that Bacon's Rebellion was an early example of Americans standing up against English tyranny continued to be widely accepted by historians. Over the last four decades, however, some scholars have questioned its accuracy and reconsidered the evidence to find alternative explanations. All three of the readings below focus on explaining what motivated the colonists to take up arms against their government.

Prelude to the American Revolution

Thomas Jefferson Wertenbaker defends the traditional interpretation of Bacon's Rebellion, explicitly comparing Nathaniel Bacon's revolt against a "tyrannical" Governor Berkeley with the American colonists' later revolution against King George. The excerpt below is abridged from Virginia Under the Stuarts, *which was reprinted as part of* The Shaping of Colonial Virginia *(New York, 1958), 115–16, 123, 127, 130–31, 133, 143–45.*

Never was a people doomed to more bitter disappointment [than the Virginians were after Charles II was restored to the throne of England in 1660]. The years which followed the Restoration were crowded with misfortunes greater than any that had

65

befallen the colony since the ghastly days of the Great Sickness [malaria epidemics]. Charles II, far from showing gratitude to his Old Dominion, overwhelmed it with injustice and oppression. The Virginians were crushed with tremendous duties on their tobacco and with ruinous restrictions upon their trade. The titles to their plantations were threatened by a grant of the entire colony to two unworthy favorites of the King. Governor Berkeley, embittered . . . and growing avaricious and crabbed with advancing years, soon forfeited that respect and love which his former good conduct had gained him. His second administration [1660–1677] was marred by partiality, oppression and inefficiency. The people were deprived of their right of suffrage by continued prorogation [dismissal] of the Assembly. Local government fell into the hands of small aristocratic cliques, while the poor were ground down with unequal and excessive taxes. Two wars with Holland added to the misfortunes of the colonists. Even the Heavens seemed to join with their enemies, for the country was visited by a terrific hurricane which swept over the plantations, destroying crops and wrecking houses. These accumulated misfortunes brought such deep suffering upon the colony that hundreds of families were reduced to poverty and many were forced into debt and ruin. No wonder that the commons, finally driven to desperation, should have risen in insurrection against the Governor and the King.

First among the causes of distress during this unhappy period must be placed the Navigation Acts. . . . [A series of laws intended to force the colonists to trade with England rather than other European countries.] Can there be any doubt that the Navigation Acts and the futility of all attempts to escape their baleful effects, were largely instrumental in bringing on Bacon's Rebellion? As prosperity and contentment are the greatest safeguards of the public peace, so poverty, nakedness and distress are breeders of sedition. Philip Ludwell spoke of Bacon's army as "a Rabble of the basest sort of People; whose Condicion was such as by a chaunge could not admitt of worse". Had England been less selfish in her treatment of Virginia, there would not have been so many indigent men in the colony eager to join in this wild uprising against the government. Berkeley himself admitted, in 1673, that at least one third of the freemen had been rendered so desperate by poverty and debt that in times of foreign war their loyalty to England could not be relied upon.

The wars of 1664 and 1672 with Holland added much to the distress in Virginia. The bold Dutch mariners, angered at the injury done them by the Navigation Acts, preyed upon the English merchantmen in every sea. Woe to the tobacco ship that encountered a hostile privateer, in its journey across the Atlantic! The English vessels were not safe even in the Virginia rivers, under the guns of their forts. Twice the daring Dutch came through the capes and into the James River itself, where they wrought great damage to the shipping. . . .

Great as was the distress caused by the depredations of the Dutch, the planters suffered even more during these wars by the stagnation of trade. The great risk incurred in crossing the ocean necessarily brought an increase both in freight rates and in the cost of manufactured goods. In 1667 the Governor and Council declared that the planters were "inforced to pay 12 pounds to £17 per ton freight" on their tobacco "which usually was but at seven pounds". Conditions were even worse during the second war. In 1673 Berkeley complained that the number of vessels that dared come to Virginia was so small, that they had "not brought goods and tools enough for one part of five of the people to go on with their necessary labor". "And those few goods that are brought," he added "have Soe few (and these hard Dealing) Sellers and Soe many Indigent and necessitous buyors that the Poore Planter gets not the fourth part . . . for his tobacco which he usually has had in other times."

In this period, so full of suffering and misfortune, the year 1667 was especially noteworthy for its long series of [natural] disasters. . . .

Perhaps the people of Virginia might have borne patiently all these misfortunes, had their Governor ruled them with wisdom and justice. Certain it is they would never have turned in wild anger to strike down his government, had that government not done much to make their condition intolerable. Sir William Berkeley was accused of destroying the representative character of the Assembly, of initiating a notorious spoils system, of intimidating Burgesses, of winking at embezzlement of public funds. And, although most of these charges were brought by the Governor's bitter enemies, some of them were undoubtedly true. . . .

It would not be just to give credence to all the accusations made against Berkeley. The King's commissioners who conducted

Charles II (1630–85), King of England during Bacon's Rebellion, recalled his long-time governor, William Berkeley in its aftermath. (Painting by Peter Lely. Courtesy of The Library of Congress.)

the investigation into his conduct, were his enemies; while many of the charges were brought by those who had taken part in the Rebellion. Thus the testimony against him is in most cases distinctly partisan. Moreover those that were closely associated with Sir William often expressed extravagant admiration for his ability and energy, and love for his character. "He hath," wrote the Council in 1673, "for neare 30 years governed this colony with that prudence and justice which hath gained him both love and reverence from all the Inhabitants here." . . .

But whatever is the verdict of posterity upon the conduct and motives of Sir William Berkeley, the causes of the Rebellion stand out with great clearness:—England's selfish commercial policy, . . . the Dutch wars, storms and pestilence, inefficient if not corrupt government, excessive taxes. The only wonder is that the insurrection did not occur earlier. In fact two mutinies did break out in 1674, when the excessively heavy taxes of that year were announced, but the rebels lacked leaders and were suppressed without great difficulty. As early as 1673 the defection of the planters was so great that it was feared many might attempt to deliver the colony into the hands of the Dutch. Berkeley wrote that a large part of the people were so desperately poor that they might reasonably be expected upon any small advantage of the enemy to "revolt to them in hopes of bettering their Condition by Shareing the Plunder of the Country with them". A certain John Knight reported "that the planters there doe generally desire a trade with the Dutch and all other nations and would not be singly bound to the trade of England, and speake openly there that they are in the nature of slaves, soe that the hearts of the greatest part of them are taken away from his Majesty". Thus the downtrodden planters, alienated from England, angered at the Governor, even distrusting their own Assembly, waited but an occasion and a leader to rise in open rebellion. A new Indian war offered the occasion, and they found their leader in young Nathaniel Bacon.

Conflict on the Frontier

Historian Wilcomb Washburn refutes the consensus Wertenbaker and many others shared on Bacon's Rebellion. He rejects comparisons with the Revolution and argues that the uprising must be understood in the context of Bacon's hatred for Native Americans and his desire for their frontier lands. Excerpted from Wilcomb E. Washburn, The Governor and The Rebel: A History of Bacon's Rebellion in Virginia *(Chapel Hill, 1957), 153, 159–60, 162–63, 166.*

What was the "cause" of Bacon's Rebellion? What motivated the 400 foot and 120 horse who marched with Bacon into Jamestown on June 23, 1676? Romantic historians like to see the rebellion as "a revolt of the lower classes of whites against the aristocratic families who governed Virginia," as "the cause of the poor against the rich, of the humble folk against the grandees.". . .

The more prosaic interests of the rebels have rarely been inquired into. It has been assumed that they were selfless patriots fighting a tyrannical government. We are told that Bacon was "a champion of the weak, a rebel against injustice, the forerunner of

---

"Causes of the Rebellion," reproduced from *The Governor and the Rebel: A History of Bacon's Rebellion in Virginia,* by Wilcomb E. Washburn. Published for The Institute of Early American History and Culture, Williamsburg, Virginia. Copyright © 1957 by The University of North Carolina Press. Used by permission of the publisher.

Washington, Jefferson and Samuel Adams." Others have compared Bacon to Patrick Henry, to Tiberius Gracchus, to Callimachus, and even to Leonidas at Thermopylae.

It is generally assumed, on the other hand, that the governor and his council were the "grandees" of the colony and that they possessed vast holdings of land while the rest of the colonists eked out a precarious existence on their small plantations. Like so many other assertions about Bacon's Rebellion, this one is not based on a study of the evidence. An investigation of the land holdings of the partisans on both sides reveals a surprising equality between them. The leaders on both sides had large holdings. The followers on both sides had more modest holdings. What is most significant is that the leaders of the rebellion against Governor Berkeley almost invariably owned great tracts of land on the frontier, frequently had a record of oppression and aggression against the neighboring Indians, and occasionally had been punished by Berkeley for their crimes against the natives.

Governor Berkeley strove throughout his career to restrain the aggressiveness of the frontier landowners. But his power was limited. For one thing he was not in control of the government from 1652 to 1660 when the most unregulated expansion took place. His ability to control expansion was further restricted when, in 1666, he lost the right to allow or disallow individual grants. The assembly successfully challenged his authority to limit the right to acquire land, and "henceforth it was recognised in practice that the Governor had no more power over land grants than that secured by his individual vote in the Council." ...

The connection between the colonists' itch for land and the Indian "troubles" is a close one. Since the Indian troubles set off the rebellion, it would seem fair to blame the rebellion in great part on those who caused the Indian troubles. But it seems an inescapable conclusion that the English, and particularly the rebellious frontiersmen themselves, were responsible for the Indian troubles. It was the frontiersmen's continuing violation of Governor Berkeley's efforts to settle the Indian-white relationship with fairness to both sides that precipitated the rebellion.

Colonel Moryson, one of the commissioners [who investigated the rebellion for the King], was well aware from his period in the Virginia government of the propensity of the frontiersmen to push the Indians off their land. He wrote in 1676 that there had not been a war with the Indians for the previous twenty-five years that had not been caused by the English coveting their land. When, therefore, Moryson and his fellow commissioners were presented the "grievance" of Henrico County that no satisfaction had been obtained against the Indians, they commented: "These Complainants never consider that the breach of the Peace and occasion of Bloodshed has still been on the side of the English, which was publickly Justified and affirmed in open Court in the face of a very great Assembly, and denied by none."

The one cause of Bacon's Rebellion that has been consistently overlooked, then, is the aggressiveness of the frontiersmen. The careful [Richard] Hildreth [a nineteenth-century historian] nearly stumbled onto this conception when he wrote, with unconscious humor, that "the Indian war, the immediate cause of all the late disturbances, seems to have subsided so soon as expeditions against the Indians were dropped." What has caused English and American historians to overlook the frontiersmen's aggressiveness? The reason lies partly in the white historian's unconscious immersion in his racial bias. According to the mythology of the white view of the world, the Indian is ever "primitive," "warlike," and "aggressive," while the "civilized" white man is constantly on guard against his attacks. But the aggressiveness of the frontiersmen has been overlooked for another reason, one based on our idea of our political beliefs. Most of the writers and historians who have dealt with Bacon's Rebellion have written from what they regarded as a "liberal" point of view, and it is part of the mythology of this view of history that the American frontiersman symbolizes America's freedom, democracy, and hatred of oppression. Actually the American frontiersman of the seventeenth century paid scant heed to such ideals. . . .

The causes of Bacon's rebellion are complex and profound. They cannot be explained in terms of Berkeley's "greed" and "oppression," Bacon's love of "liberty," the "savagery" of the Indians, or the "patriotism" of the frontiersmen; such explanatory descriptions are meaningless labels pasted on the actors by those who see all history as a morality play. Nor can the rebellion be explained in terms of the concealed identities and mysterious motives of a Gothic romance. Bacon does not change, with the hemispheres, from the spoiled son of a well-to-do English country squire to a dedicated democratic frontier hero. Nor does Governor

Berkeley, after being the "Darling of the People" for thirty-five years, suddenly reveal his true identity as their blackest oppressor. Both men remained true to the faults and virtues of their natures.

Nathaniel Bacon would be vastly amused to find himself the sainted hero of the guardians of the liberal traditions of western democratic government. No doubt he would receive the news with an expression of his profane amusement at the idiocy of men. "God damn my blood," he might exclaim; "how easily people are led!"

Exploitation of Labor

Edmund S. Morgan chooses to examine the motives of the masses of people who rebelled, rather than focusing on Berkeley and Bacon, the leaders on opposite sides of the rebellion. In the following selection, he places the uprising in a pattern of resistance by people whose labor was ruthlessly exploited throughout the first century of Virginia's history. Condensed from American Slavery, American Freedom: The Ordeal of Colonial Virginia *(New York, 1975), 253–61.*

When Berkeley heard that the Susquehannahs had been seen at the falls of the James, he called a special session of the assembly. It met on March 7 and adopted measures that added political grievances to the settlers' anxieties over the Indians. The legislators decided to build a fort at the head of each great river and to man the forts with a standing army of 500 soldiers drawn from the lower counties; the tributary Indians were to be enrolled against the enemy and rewarded with trading cloth, but private trade with the Indians was forbidden. To people in New Kent and the Southside, the act that was supposed to end the Indian menace looked like a prescription for profiteering. The frontier forts would contribute more to the wealth of the men who built them

Reprinted from *American Slavery, American Freedom: The Ordeal of Colonial Virginia,* by Edmund S. Morgan with the permission of W.W. Norton & Company, Inc. Copyright © 1975 by W.W. Norton & Company, Inc.

than to the security of the people they were supposed to protect. The new ones would doubtless be located on the unoccupied upriver lands of the "great men" who sat in the assembly and would thus help to raise the value of their speculative holdings. The soldiers, recruited in the lower counties, would be paid 1,500 pounds of tobacco apiece, more than a frontier farmer on poor land was likely to make in a year. There would have to be another huge levy to pay for the troops and the forts, and both would be useless against roving Indians who melted into the woods after every attack. It almost seemed that the assembly had wished to guarantee the ineffectiveness of the scheme, because they had included a provision that if the enemy was discovered, he was not to be attacked until the governor was notified and gave his approval, by which time, as every frontiersman knew, the Indians would have vanished. The provision may have arisen from Berkeley's anger at the reckless commanders who had murdered the Susquehannah chiefs at the fort when they came out to a supposed peace parley ("If they had killed my Grandfather and Grandmother, my father and Mother and all my friends, yet if

This image comes from a cartouche (an illustration that appeared on a map of Virginia) in the early eighteenth century. It shows a typical waterfront scene from a later era, when manual labor was performed almost exclusively by slaves. The casks contain tobacco. (Courtesy of M.P. Middleton.)

they had come to treat of Peace, they ought to have gone in Peace"), but it would scarcely reassure frontiersmen of the government's ability to handle the Indian danger. Among those not reassured was Nathaniel Bacon. . . .

One day in the following April [1676], Bacon and some of his neighbors, James Crews, Henry Isham, and William Byrd, got together for a sociable glass or two. Byrd had lost three servants killed by the Indians. Bacon had lost his overseer at the falls. They were all unimpressed by the measures the March assembly had taken and were "making the Sadnesse of the times their discourse, and the Fear they all lived in, because of the Susquahanocks, who had settled [i.e., encamped] a little above the Falls of James River." They were also uneasy about the tributary Indians who lived close by. It was said that these Indians were not planting corn, which suggested that they intended leaving their towns for the warpath. Bacon in particular believed the country must defend itself "against all Indians in generall for that they were all Enemies." "This," he told Berkeley later, "I have alwayes said and doe maintaine."

While Bacon and his friends were telling each other their troubles on the north side of the James, the less prosperous planters on the south side were doing the same. They were even more upset than Bacon about the assembly's measures and also about the assembly itself. The 150 pounds a day plus expenses that the burgesses allowed themselves was as much a grievance as the useless forts that would enrich the great men. And Giles Bland was apparently encouraging them to appeal to the king against the extortionary local magnates. Bland was ready to carry the message himself.

The immediate problem, however, was the Indians. The Southsiders were eager to march against them with their own arms and without pay, and had appealed to the governor to commission someone to lead them. When he declined to do so, they lost patience and began to gather on their own in an encampment at Jordan's Point, just below the mouth of the Appomattox. Hearing of the move, Bacon and his friends left their talk and crossed the river to see what was up. Bacon's feelings about Indians were evidently known. He was a friend of the governor, a member of the council; and his appearance in the crowd, doling out a supply of rum like a good politician, gave a semblance of governmental approval to the gathering. "A Bacon! a Bacon! a Bacon!" went the cry. The young man was evidently not displeased, and he agreed to lead them against the Indians, perhaps assuming that Berkeley would not deny a commission to *him*.

And, indeed, if Berkeley had been willing to follow the line of least resistance, he would have been well advised to grant the commission gracefully. In April of 1676, however, the Southsiders' proposed march on the Indians apparently looked more dangerous to the safety of the colony than the depredations of the Susquehannahs. For months Indian tribes up and down the continent had been restive. King Philip's War, a concerted attack on the New England settlers, had broken out at about the same time as the skirmishes on the Potomac, a fact that looked sinister in itself. It was rumored that the Susquehannahs were negotiating for assistance from tribes three hundred miles to the north. All in all, Berkeley was convinced that the Indians were "generally conspired against us in all the western parts of America." With a larger Indian war brewing, Berkeley thought it desirable to keep a firm but friendly grip on Virginia's tributary Indians, not only because they might be useful as spies against hostile tribes but also to prevent them from joining the enemy. Berkeley, knowing the frontiersman's contempt for all Indians and his greed for their lands, would not risk sending out an expeditionary force that might not differentiate between friend and foe any more carefully than the Westmoreland militia who had started the whole conflict with the Susquehannahs. Nor could Berkeley risk creating an armed force of his most disgruntled inhabitants, men who were even more likely to turn against him than those he had led against the Dutch. The assembly may have been swayed by this danger when voting to garrison the new forts with men from the downriver counties.

Although Bacon seriously differed with Berkeley about the way to deal with Indians, he fully appreciated the danger of rebellious freemen. Living in Henrico County, he was in a better position than Berkeley to sense their mood, and he was not likely to underestimate it. As a prosperous government official in an area surrounded by men angry with the government, he could anticipate a rough time if discontent turned to rebellion. By leading the discontented in their proposed expedition against the Indians, which he relished as much as they did, he would gain their good will and at the same time avert their anger from the governor and assembly. According to Bacon, his leadership at Jordan's Point had precisely that effect. "Since my being with the volunteers," he wrote to Berkeley, "the Exclaiming concerning forts and Leavys has beene suppressed and the discourse and earnestness of the people is against the Indians. . . ." Bacon was offering Berkeley a way to suppress a mutiny. The Indians would be the scapegoats. Discontent with upper-class leadership would be vented in racial hatred, in a pattern that statesmen and politicians of a later age would have found familiar.

Berkeley did not take the offer. Virginia needed the friendship of the local Indians, and he did not trust the freemen. Furthermore, he did not know whether to trust Bacon. . . . When Berkeley refused Bacon a commission, Bacon chose to proceed without one, but he issued a conciliatory "Humble Appeale of the Voluntiers to all well minded and Charitable People." The appeal recited the uselessness of the forts, the need for a "moving force," and the willingness of the volunteers to "become both actours and paymasters of this necessary defensive warr" without charge to the colony. It asked "the Enactours themselves of this late Act for forts," to judge in their consciences "whether our proffer be not wholly clear from any dregs of Rebellion, and mutiny, and be not rather to be esteemed an honourable purchase of our Countries quiett and benefitt with our owne hazard and charge." It closed with a denunciation of all Indians and their combination against His Majesty's good subjects, who were the only rightful inhabitants and possessors of Virginia. . . .

Whatever Bacon's intentions may have been in assuming leadership of the self-starting crusade against the Indians, he was guilty of a greater insubordination than Berkeley could tolerate. On May 10, in a public proclamation, Berkeley denounced him and removed him from the council. [Despite the Governor's orders not to, Bacon proceeded to march against the Indians and massacred the friendly Oaccaneechees.] . . .

The nature of those offenses was treason, and the proper punishment death. In order to make that plain, Berkeley issued a "Declaration and Remonstrance" in which he explained that the mightiest subject in the land, even a peer of the realm, would deserve death if he successfully protected the country against an enemy without authorization from the king. This was an unfortunate line of reasoning to a people who put preservation ahead of loyalty to a governor who was not, after all, quite a king. And among men who as a matter of course believed that all Indians were alike, Berkeley could not at this stage of the game start winning points by stating that he too was now against all Indians, especially when he added that earlier "I would have preservd those Indians that I knew were hourely at our mercy to have been our spies and intelligence to find out the more bloody Ennimies." He also misread the situation in stating that "Mr. Bacon has none aboute him but the lowest of the people." Those he had in plenty, but there were men of the better sort too who shared Bacon's racist hatred of Indians.

With Berkeley's Declaration not only Bacon but all his followers and supporters became, by definition, rebels. They undoubtedly retained their zeal for killing Indians, but they were now invited to save a share of their hostility for the governor and council, the biggest men in Virginia. In a colony where the level of discontent was already so high and the means of suppressing a rebellion were so scant, it required a degree of foolhardiness in the governing circles to adopt such a position. With the local Indians fleeing out of range, and the Susquehannahs too elusive to lay hands on, the dangerous young men of New Kent and the Southside might well consider attacking their rulers, especially if led by men who could themselves lay claim to high position. As Giles Bland had recognized some weeks earlier, a bona fide rebellion could easily develop out of the existing situation, precisely because the freemen were led "by persons of quality there, which was wanting to them in 1674 when they were suppressed by a Proclamation, and the advice of some discreet persons, that had then an Influence upon them; which is now much otherwise, for they are at this time Conducted by Mr. Nathaniel Bacon, lately Sworne one of the Councell, and many other Gentlemen of good Condition."

Questions

1. *In order to explain the cause of Bacon's Rebellion, these scholars examine the leaders of the rebellion, the people who rebelled, and the government against which they rebelled. Which method seems best?*
2. *Washburn criticizes certain aspects of Wertenbaker's explanation of Bacon's Rebellion. Are his criticisms persuasive? Why or why not? Does he ignore any aspects of Wertenbaker's argument?*
3. *Morgan explains the motivations of the poor freemen who rebelled even though he lacks access to any records or documents in their own words. How does he do so?*
4. *What do we gain by studying Bacon's Rebellion today? Do the lessons we draw from it depend on which causes we use to explain it?*

CONTEMPORARY VIEWS OF THE REBELLION

Only a few of the participants left records about their roles in the rebellion, and those were mostly the wealthy men who served as leaders of either faction. While we know that several different groups of Native Americans were involved, that women participated actively in both the Bacon and Berkeley camps, and that the last rebels out in the field were mostly European indentured servants and African or African-American slaves, we have few, if any, records from these people to explain their actions. The motives of all parties can only be interpreted through the limited existing records. (Throughout these documents, archaic abbreviations have been silently edited for greater clarity.)

Tensions on the Frontier

In the aftermath of the rebellion, commissioners sent from England by the king interviewed people and collected information about the rebellion to discover why it happened. The following selection describes the conflicts with local Native Americans that sparked a desire for revenge in Bacon and other frontier dwellers. Taken from the commissioners' report entitled "A True Narrative of the Rise, Progresse, and Cessation of the Late Rebellion in Virginia . . ." in Narratives of the Insurrections, 1675–1690, *ed. Charles M. Andrews (New York, 1952), 105–7.*

Few or none had bin the Damages sustained by the English from the Indians, other than occasionally had happen'd sometimes upon private quarells and provocations, untill in July, 1675,

79

certain Doegs and Susquahanok Indians on Maryland side, stealing some Hoggs from the English at Potomake on the Virginia shore (as the River divides the same), were pursued by the English in a Boate, beaten or kill'd and the hoggs retaken from them; whereupon the Indians repairing to their owne Towne, report it to their Superiors, and how that one [Thomas] Mathewes (whose hoggs they had taken) had before abused and cheated them, in not paying them for such Indian trucke [goods] as he had formerly bought of them, and that they took his hogs for Satisfaction [of the debt]. Upon this (to be Reveng'd on Mathews) a warr Captain with some Indians came over to Potomake and killed two of Mathewes his servants, and came also a second time and kill'd his sonne.

It happen'd hereupon that Major George Brent and Col. George Mason pursued some of the same Indians into Maryland, and marching directly up to the Indian Towne with a Party of 30 Virginians came to a certaine House and there killed an Indian King and 10 of his men upon the place; the rest of the Indians fled for their lives. . . .

The Indians persisting to Revenge themselves Inforted [fortified their position] in Maryland and now began to be bold and formidable to the English who Besieged them; their Boldness and daring behavior of late tymes and their promptnesse to Fire arms, being (indeed) wonderfull, over what they seem'd formerly indued with, which doubtlesse was of some advantage extraordinary to them considering their Small Body, [and the fact that] the Virginians and Marylanders that Besieged them being said to make neer a thousand men. The siege held 7 weekes, during which tyme the English lost 50 men, besides some Horses which the Indians tooke, and serv'd themselves to subsist on. But Provisions growing very scarce with them during this siege the Indians sent out 5 greate men to Treate of Peace, who were not Permitted to return to the Fort, but being kept Prisoners Some tyme were at last murdered by the English.

At length (whether through negligence or cowardize) the Indians made theire escape through the English, with all their wives, children and goods of value, wounding and killing some at their sally and going off. After which the English returning (as Report Saith), the Marylanders composed a Peace with the Salvages, and soe diverted the warr from themselves. . . .

But about the beginning of January, 1675–6, a Party of those abused Susquahanocks in Revenge of the Maryland businesse came suddainly down upon the weak Plantations at the head of Rappahanock and Potomaque and killed at one time 36 persons and then immediately (as their Custome is) ran off into the woods.

Berkeley Declares Bacon a Rebel

When Governor William Berkeley refused to authorize attacks against the Susquehannocks, Nathaniel Bacon, a wealthy planter, took matters into his own hands, leading a group of volunteers in a massacre of friendly Indians. In the selection below, Berkeley defends his own actions and declares Bacon a rebel. Originally printed in the Collections of the Massachusetts Historical Society, *4th Series, (Boston, 1871) 9:178– 81.*

Since that time that I returned into the Country [as Governor of Virginia: about 1660], I call the great God, Judge of all things in heaven and earth to wittness, that I doe not know of any thing relateive to this Country, wherein I have acted unjustly, corruptly, or negligently, in distributeing equall Justice to all men, & takeing all possible care to preserue [preserve] their proprietys, & defend them from their barbarous enimies. . . .

And now I will state the Question betwixt me as a Governor and Mr Bacon, and say that if any enimies should invade England, any Councellor Justice of peace, or other inferiour officer, might raise what forces they could to protect his Majesty's subiects [subjects], But I say againe, if after the Kings knowledge of this inuasion, any the greatest peere [or nobleman] of England, should raise forces against the kings p'hibition this would be now, & ever was in all ages & Nations accompted [accounted as] treason. Nay I will goe further, that though this peere was truly zealous for the preservation of his King, & subiects, and had better & greater abillitys than all the rest of his fellow subiects, to doe his King and Country seruice, yett if the King (though by false information) should suspect the contrary, itt were treason in this Noble peere to p'ceed after the King's prohibition, and for the truth of this I appeale to all the laws of England, and the Laws and constitutions of all other Nations in the world. . . .

Now my friends I have lived 34 yeares amongst you, as vncorrupt and dilligent as ever [a] Governor was, Bacon is a man of two yeares amongst you, his p'son and qualities vnknowne to most of you, & to all men else, by any vertuous action that ever I heard of, And that very action which he boasts of [the massacre of the Occaneechee Indians], was sickly & fooleishly, & as I am informed treacherously carried to the dishonnor of the English Nation, yett in itt, he lost more men then I did in three yeares Warr [against an Indian uprising several decades earlier], and by the grace of God will putt myselfe to the same daingers & troubles againe when I have brought Bacon to acknowledge the Laws are above him, and I doubt not but by God's assistance to have better success then Bacon hath had, the reason of my hopes are, that I will take Councell of wiser men then my selfe, but Mr Bacon hath none about him, but the lowest of the people.

Yett I must further enlarge, that I cannot without your helpe, doe any thinge in this but dye in defence of my King, his laws, & subiects, which I will cheerefully doe, though alone I doe itt, and considering my poore fortunes, I can not leave my poore Wife and friends a better legacy then by dyeing for my King & you: for his sacred Majesty will easeily distinguish betweene Mr Bacons actions & myne, and Kinges have long Armes, either to reward or punish. . . .

Lastly my most assured ffriends I would have preserued those Indians that I knew were howerly att our mercy, to have beene our spyes and intelligence, to finde out our bloody enimies, but as soone as I had the least intelligence that they alsoe were trecherous enimies, I gave out Comissions to distroy them all as the Comissions themselues will speake itt.

To conclude, I have don what was possible both to friend and enimy, have granted Mr Bacon three pardons, which he hath scornefully reiected, suppoaseing himselfe stronger to subuert [the laws] than I and you [are] to maineteyne the Laws, by which onely and Gods assisting grace and mercy, all men must hope for peace and safety. I will add noe more though much more is still remaineing to Justifie me & condemne Mr Bacon, but to desier that this declaration may be read in every County Court in the Country.

The Queen of Pamunkey
Negotiates for Her People

Once Bacon began attacking the frontier Indians, Virginia's leaders sought assistance from the Pamunkeys, the most powerful of the tributary, or "friendly," Indians. In the following passage, Thomas Mathew, an eyewitness, relates how and why the Queen of Pamunkey tried to keep her people from becoming involved. Taken from Thomas Mathew, "The Beginning, Progress, and Conclusion of Bacon's Rebellion . . .," re-printed in, Tracts and Other Papers, Relating Principally to the Origin, Settlement, and Progress of the Colonies in North America . . . , *ed. Peter Force, (Washington, D.C., 1836) 1:14–15.*

Our comittee being sat, the Queen of Pamunky (descended from Oppechankenough a former Emperor of Virginia) was introduced, who entred the chamber with a comportment gracefull to admiration, bringing on her right hand an Englishman interpreter, and on the left her son a stripling twenty years of age, she having round her head a plat of black and white wampum peague three inches broad in imitation of a crown, and was cloathed in a mantle of dress't deer skins with the hair outwards and the edge cut round 6 inches deep which made strings resembling twisted frenge from the shoulders to the feet; thus with grave courtlike gestures and a majestick air in her face, she walk'd up our long room to the lower end of the table, where after a few intreaties she sat down; th' interpreter and her son standing by her on either side as they had walked up, our chairman asked her what men she woud [would] lend us for guides in the wilderness and to assist us against our enemy Indians, she spake to th' interpreter to inform her what the chairman said, (tho' we believed she understood him) he told us she bid him ask her son to whom the English tongue was familiar, and who was reputed the son of an English colonel, yet neither woud he speak to or seem to understand the chairman but th' interpreter told us, he referred all to his mother, who being againe urged she after a little musing with an earnest passionate countenance as if tears were ready to gush out and a fervent sort of expression made a harangue about a quarter of an hour often, interlacing (with a high shrill voice and vehement

83

passion) these words "Tatapatamoi Chepiack, i.e. Tatapatamoi dead["] Coll. Hill being next me, shook his head, I ask'd him what was the matter, he told me all she said was too true to our shame, and that his father was generall in that battle, where diverse years before Tatapatamoi her husband had led a hundred of his Indians in help to th' English against our former enemy Indians, and was there slaine with most of his men; for which no compensation (at all) had been to that day rendered to her wherewith she now upbraided us.

Her discourse ending and our morose chairman not advancing one cold word towards asswaging the anger and grief her speech . . . nor taking any notice of all she had said, . . . he rudely push'd againe the same question "what Indians will you now contribute, &c.?["] of this disregard she signified her resentment by a disdainfull aspect, and turning her head half aside, sate mute till that same question being press'd, a third time, she not returning her face to the board, answered with a low slighting voice in her own language "six,["] but being further importun'd she sitting a little while sullen, without uttering a word between said "twelve,["] tho' she then had a hundred and fifty Indian men, in her town, and so rose up and gravely walked away, as [if] not pleased with her treatment.

Bacon Justifies Rebellion on Behalf of "the People"

Within months, the colony divided into factions that supported either Berkeley or Bacon, and both sides took up arms. On 30 July 1676, Bacon issued "The Declaration of the People," in which he defended his actions and attacked the policies of Berkeley's government. Reprinted from the Collections of the Massachusetts Historical Society, *4th Series, (Boston, 1871), 9:184–85.*

1st. For haveing . . . raised greate unjust taxes vpon the Comonality for the aduancement of private favorites & other sinister ends, but [without having] . . . in any measure aduanced this hopefull Colony either by fortifications Townes or Trade.

2d. For haveing abused & rendred contemptable the Magistrates of Justice, by aduanceing to places of Judicature, scandalous and Ignorant favorites.

3. For haveing wronged his Majestys prerogative & interest, by assumeing Monopolony of the Beaver trade, & for haveing in that unjust gaine betrayed & sold his Majestys Country & the lives of his loyall subiects to the barbarous heathen.

4. For haveing, protected, favoured, & Imboldned the Indians against his Majestys loyall subiects, never contriveing, requireing, or appointing any due or proper meanes of satisfaction for theire many Inuasions, robbories, & murthers comitted vpon vs.

5. For haveing when the Army of English was just vpon the track of those Indians, who now in all places burne, spoyle, murther & when we might with ease have distroyed them who then were in open hostillity, for then haveing expressly countermanded, & sent back our Army, by passing his word for the peaceable demeanour of the said Indians, who imediately p'secuted theire evill intentions, comitting horred murthers & robberies in all places, being p'tected by the said ingagement & word past of him the said Sir Wm Berkeley, haveing ruined & laid desolate a greate part of his Majestys Country, & have now drawne themselves into such obscure & remote places, & are by theire success soe imboldned & confirmed, by theire confederacy soe strengthned that the cryes of blood are in all places, & the terror, & constirnation of the people soe greate, are now become, not onely a difficult, but a very formidable enimy, who might att first with ease haue beene distroyed.

6th. And lately when vpon the loud outcryes of blood the Assembly had with all care raised & framed an Army for the preventing of further mischiefe & safeguard of this his Majestys Colony.

7th. For haveing with onely the privacy of some few favorites, without acquainting the people, onely by the alteration of a figure, forged a Comission, by we know not what hand, not onely without, but even against the consent of the people, for the raiseing & effecting civill warr & destruction, which being happily & without blood shed prevented, for haveing the second time attempted the same, thereby calling downe our forces from the defence of the fronteeres & most weekely exposed places.

8. For the prevention of civill mischeife & ruin amongst ourselues, whilst the barbarous enimy in all places did invade, murther & spoyle vs, his majestys most faithfull subiects.

Edward Hill Explains His Opposition to Nathaniel Bacon

Colonel Edward Hill, a Berkeley loyalist, vigorously suppressed the rebellion in Charles City County where he lived. When other planters in the area criticized his brutality, he countered with a description of the treatment he and his family received from the rebels, which he clearly believed justified his own actions. The following excerpt is taken from the Virginia Magazine of History and Biography, *3 (1895–1896): 250.*

I must with trouble and sorrow say that I am grieved to see the spirit of rebellion soe strong and fresh in the hearts of these people that would make it a grievance of the County for to obey those just comands which I received from his honor [the governor], and I should think theire true grievance should be that they were soe active and mischievous as they were from the beginning of the rebellion to the end thereof, and were the first that against the King's Governor's comands went out upon the Occaneechees, were the very men to help Bacon to force his comission, and marched a hundred miles out of theire own country [county] as low as Lower Norfolk to fight the king's loyall subjects, and over into Gloucester, and indeed all over the country, and in fine were the first in armes, and the laste that opposed and faced the King's Governor's power, yet these noe grievances, And I bless God, and truely rejoice in the great goodness and mercey of our most gracious king that they are pardoned; but me thinks with modesty they mought [might] have given me leave to have had my grievances that my house was plundered of all I had, my sheep all destroyed, my hoggs and cattle killed, all my grain taken and destroyed, wheat, barley, oates, & Indian graine, to the quantity of seven, or eight hundred bushels, and to compleat theire jollity draw my brandy, Butts of wyne and syder [cider, a mildly alcoholic beverage] by payles full, and [toasting] to every health instead of burning theire powder [shooting off their guns], burnt my writings, bills, bonds, acc'ts to the true value of forty thousand pounds of tobacco and to finish theire barbarism, take my wife bigg with child [pregnant] prisoner, beat her with my Cane, tare [tore] her childbed linen out of her hands, and with her ledd away my children where they must live on corne and water and lye on the ground.

Indentured Servants and Slaves Resist Surrender

Along with poor freemen, indentured servants and slaves who had deserted their masters formed a large part of Bacon's army. As the rebellion collapsed, they still held the fort at West Point. As the passage below indicates, Berkeley and his supporters were not above lying to trick such people into putting down their arms. Thomas Grantham was a ship captain who helped Berkeley suppress the uprising. From "A Narrative of the Indian and Civil Wars in Virginia . . .," in Tracts and Other Papers . . ., *ed. Peter Force, 1:44–45.*

What number of soulders was, at this time, in Garrisson at West Point, I am not certaine: It is saide about 250, sumed up in freemen, sarvants and slaves; these three ingredience being the compossition of Bacons Army, ever since that the Governour left Towne. These was informed (to prepare the way) two or three days before that Grantham came to them, that there was a treaty on foote betwene there Generall, and the Governour; and that Grantham did manely promote the same, as he was a parson [person] that favoured the cause, that they were contending for.

When that Grantham arived, amongst these fine fellowes, he was receved with more then an ordnary respect; which he haveing repade, with a suteable deportment, he acquaints them with his commission, which was to tell them, that there was a peace concluded betwene the Governour and their Generall; an since himself had (in some measure) used his indeviours, to bring the same to pass, hee begged of the Governour, that he might have the honor to com and acquaint them with the terms; which he saide

87

was such, that they had all cause to rejoyce at, than any ways to thinke hardly of the same; there being a compleate satisfaction to be given (by the Articles of agreement) according to every ones particuler intress; which he sumed up under these heads. And first, those that were now in Arms (and free men) under the Generall, were still to be retained in Arms, if they so pleased, against the Indians. Secondly, and for those who had a desire for to return hom, to their owne abodes, care was taken for to have them satisfide, for the time they had bin out, according to the alowance made the last Assembley. And lastly, those that were sarvants in Arms, and behaved themselves well, in their imployment, should emediately receve discharges from their Indentures, signed by the Governour or Sequetary of State; and their Masters to receve, from the publick, a valluable satisfaction, for every sarvant, so set free (marke the words) proportionably to the time that they have to sarve.

Upon these terms, the soulders forsake West Point, and goe with Grantham to kiss the Governours hands (still at Tindells point) and to receve the benefitt of the Articles, mentioned by Grantham; where when they came (which was by water, themselves in one vessill, and their arms in another; and so contrived by Grantham, as he tould me himselfe, upon good reason) the sarvants and slaves was sent hom to their Masters, there to stay till the Governour had leasure to signe their discharges; or to say better, till they were free according to the custom of the countrey [which meant finishing their indentures, plus serving extra time for being runaways], the rest was made prissoners, or entertained by the Governour, as hee found them inclined.

Mrs. Cheisman's Attempt to Save Her Husband

Mrs. Cheisman's husband was an officer in Bacon's army who was captured at the end of the rebellion. The selection below describes her effort to protect her husband from a death sentence by claiming responsibility for his rebellious actions. Assuming she honestly stated her views in this interview, she stands as one of the female supporters of the rebellion whom we can identify. If this account had not been recorded by an anonymous participant, we would not know today that Mrs. Cheisman existed (and we shall probably never know her first name). Her husband was never tried for his crime, dying in prison of "feare, griefe, or bad useage," as the author of this narrative put it. Excerpted from "A Narrative of the Indian and Civil Wars in Virginia . . .," in Tracts and Other Papers . . ., *ed. Peter Force, 1:34*

There is one remarkable passage reported of this Major Cheismans Lady [or wife], which because it sounds to the honor of her sex, and consequently of all loveing Wives, I will not deny it a roome in this Narrative.

When that the Major was brought into the Governours presence, and by him demanded, what made him to ingage in Bacons designes? Before that the Major could frame an answer to the Governours demand; his Wife steps in and tould his honour that it was her provocations that made her Husband joyne in the cause that Bacon contended for; ading, that if he had not bin influenced by her instigations, he had never don that which he had done. Therefore (upon her bended knees) she desired of his honour, that since what her husband had done, was by her meanes, and so, by consequence, she most guilty, that she might be hanged, and he pardoned. Though the Governour did know, that what she had saide, was neare to the truth, yet he said litle to her request.

Thomas Hansford's Execution

Thomas Hansford, who was a colonel in Bacon's army, was captured by Berkeley supporters as the rebellion collapsed. The excerpt below, describes his capture and death. Taken from the same anonymous "A Narrative of the Indian and Civil Wars in Virginia . . .," printed in Tracts and Other Papers . . ., *ed. Peter Force, vol. 1:33.*

[P]resently after that he [Thomas Hansford, a soldier] came to Accomack, he had the ill luck to be the first Verginian borne that dyed [meaning the first person of English descent born in Virginia to die] upon a paire of Gallows. When that he came to the place of

Execution (which was about a mile removed from his prison) he seemed very well resolved to undergo the utmost mallize [malaise] of his not over kinde Destinies, onely complaineing of the maner of his death. Being observed neather at the time of his tryall (which was by a Court Martiall) nor afterwards, to supplicate any other faviour, than that he might be shot like a soulder, and not to be hanged like a Dog. But it was tould him, that what he so passionately petitioned for could not be granted, in that he was not condemned as he was merely a soldier, but as a Rebell, taken in Arms, against the king, whose laws had ordained him that death. During the short time he had to live after his sentence he approved to his best advantage for the wellfare of his soul, by repentance and contrition for all his sins, in generall, excepting his Rebellion, which he would not acknowledge; desireing the people at the place of execution, to take notis that he dyed a loyal subject, and a lover of his countrey; and that he had never taken up arms, but for the destruction of the Indians, who had murthered so many Christians.

Questions

---

1. *Why did Berkeley believe it significant that only "the lowest of the people" supported Bacon?*
2. *Do you think that Bacon was really speaking on behalf of the "people" when he issued the "Declaration"?*
3. *What motivated the various individuals whose actions are described or whose words are quoted in these documents?*
4. *Do you think there was one rebellion or several rebellions, according to the accounts you have read?*
5. *How did the rebellion appear from the perspective of various Native American groups who fought against or refused to fight against Bacon?*

FURTHER READING

Thomas Wertenbaker's Torchbearer of the Revolution: The Story of Bacon's Rebellion in Virginia *(Princeton, 1940) and Wilcomb Washburn's* The Governor and The Rebel: A History of Bacon's Rebellion in Virginia *(Chapel Hill, 1957) are still the two most important full-length books on Bacon's Rebellion.* 1676: The End of American Independence *(New York, 1984), written by Stephen Saunders Webb, connects Bacon's Rebellion with other developments in English-Indian relations on the North American continent that occurred simultaneously. Warren M. Billings has re-explored the long-term economic and political conditions that led to the conflict in "The Causes of Bacon's Rebellion: Some Suggestions," an article in the October 1970 issue of the* Virginia Magazine of History and Biography. *Martha W. McCartney examines in detail the Queen of Pamunkey and her role in Virginia politics before, during, and after Bacon's Rebellion in "Cockacoeske, Queen of Pamunkey: Diplomat and Suzerain," an essay in* Powhatan's Mantle: Indians in the Colonial Southeast, *ed. Peter H. Wood, Gregory A. Waselko, and M. Thomas Hatley (Lincoln, Nebraska, 1989).*

The Radicalism of the American Revolution

Saul Cornell

INTRODUCTION

Americans have debated the meaning of the Revolution for more than two hundred years. Was the Revolution "a war for home rule, or a war for who should rule at home?" For those scholars who believe that the break with Britain was merely a colonial war for independence, the Revolution has been portrayed as hardly revolutionary. In the case of those scholars who believe that the challenge to British authority was part of a broader social and political transformation, the Revolution appears as a distinctly revolutionary event.

Historians have explored many different aspects of the Revolution. The political and constitutional ideas of the Revolution have been analyzed in great detail. The Revolution has also produced a large body of scholarship devoted to exploring "history from the bottom up." In contrast to traditional political and constitutional history, history from the bottom up focuses on the experience of non-elite groups, including artisans, farmers, women, and slaves. The Revolution did not mean the same thing to all Americans. Nor did the Revolution have the same impact on all groups in American society. Given the complexity of the revolutionary experience, it is easy to understand why scholars would be divided when asked to assess the radicalism of the Revolution.

RADICALISM OF THE AMERICAN REVOLUTION

Historical debate over the meaning of the Revolution has been dominated by the question first posed by the Progressive historian Carl Becker—Was the Revolution "a war for home rule, or a war for who should rule at home?" For historians interested in the political and constitutional ideas of the Revolution, the achievements of the American Revolution are impressive. The right of revolution, the idea of limited government, and the beginnings of a new, more democratic conception of politics are among the most important examples of the profound changes wrought by the Revolution. Social historians, by contrast, have been more interested in documenting how the Revolution changed the lives of Americans. When viewed from the perspective of social history, the legacy of the Revolution is more complicated. The experience of African slaves and back-country farmers was quite different. The selections in this section explore the meaning of the Revolution from a variety of different viewpoints. The ideas of the revolutionaries, the governments they created, and the fortunes of Americans from all walks of life have been examined by scholars. How we assess the radicalism of the Revolution ultimately depends as much on the criteria we use as on the events of 1776.

Forming New Governments

Political scientist Donald Lutz focuses on the constitutional documents drafted by Americans. The period between the Revolution and the ratification of the federal Constitution was a period of lively political experimentation. For Lutz, the meaning of the Revolution can best be understood by analyzing the kinds of governments Americans created after independence. Abridged from Donald S. Lutz, "State Constitution-making, Through 1781," in The Blackwell Encyclopedia of the American Revolution, *ed. Jack P. Greene and J. R. Pole (Cambridge, Massachusetts, 1991), 278-81, 287-88.*

MASSACHUSETTS, NEW HAMPSHIRE, AND SOUTH CAROLINA

The first state constitution put into effect was that of Massachusetts. On 16 May 1775 the Provincial Congress of Massachusetts suggested that the Continental Congress write a model constitution for it and the other colonies. Afraid of alarming those who still hoped for reconciliation with Britain, the Continental Congress did not oblige. But on 2 June 1775 it did suggest that Massachusetts consider its charter of 1691 as still in force and the offices of governor and lieutenant-governor as temporarily vacated. It also recommended that new elections be held and a new governor's council be elected by the Provincial Congress. On 19 June 1775 the Massachusetts Congress elected a 28-member council that replaced the governor as executive. With this one alteration, the replacement of the governor with an executive council, the Massachusetts Charter of 1691 became the first state constitution. It was replaced in 1780 but in the meantime constituted, along with the Connecticut and Rhode Island charters, the most obvious link between colonial and statehood political institutions.

On 18 October 1775 New Hampshire put to the Continental Congress the same question that Massachusetts had asked the previous May. The intent of the request was to press the issue of

---

"State Constitution-making, Through 1781" by Donald S. Lutz from *The Blackwell Encyclopedia of the American Revolution*, Jack P. Greene and J.R. Pole, eds. Copyright © 1991 by Blackwell Publishers.

independence, since a recommendation to frame a state constitution would be regarded by many as a declaration of independence. There was no functioning colonial charter which the Continental Congress could use to dodge the issue, so it advised the New Hampshire provincial congress to "establish such a government, as in their judgment will best produce the happiness of the people." The letter to the New Hampshire Provincial Congress added, however, that such reorganization should endure only until the conflict with Britain was over. In the face of this ambiguous recommendation, on 21 December 1775 the New Hampshire Provincial Congress met to draft a document. Prominent during these proceedings were Matthew Thornton, Meshech Weare, John Langdon, and John Sullivan. On 5 January 1776 New Hampshire became the first state to write a new constitution. As in Massachusetts, the major change from colonial practice was the election of a council by the House of Representatives. The council, the upper house in what was now a bicameral legislature, in turn elected a president who replaced the Crown-appointed governor.

South Carolina received the same recommendation from the Continental Congress on 4 November 1775. Prominent figures during the proceedings included John Rutledge, Christopher Gadsden, Henry Laurens, Charles Pinckney, and Rawlins Lowndes. As elsewhere, there was great hesitation to break openly with Britain, and the document approved on 26 March 1776 by the provincial congress of South Carolina amounted only minimally to a constitution. Designed to be in effect only until hostilities with Britain were over and passed as a normal piece of legislation by a legislature that underwent no special election to frame such a document, the "constitution" did not carry enormous authority and would be replaced in 1778. The indeterminate nature of the constitution reflected the position of the South Carolina Congress that wrote and adopted it. When it wrote the document, this body was simultaneously the old revolutionary legislature, the constitutional convention, and the new legislature created by the old legislature. During the morning of 25 March 1776, the men in this group acted in the first two capacities; in the afternoon of the same day they acted as an Assembly under the new government and elected the Council, which became the new upper house in the new bicameral legislature.

These first three state constitutions had a half-hearted quality to them. Rather short and incomplete as foundation documents, written and adopted by a sitting legislature in a manner indistinguishable from normal legislation, and bearing the marks of compromise between proponents for independence and supporters of reconciliation, they could in truth be viewed either as temporary expedients implying no significant alteration in colonial status or as manifestations of the intent to break with Britain. If the American Revolution had not been successful, perhaps history would have recorded them as the former. However, since the Revolution did conclude successfully and no other constitutional action was necessary for Massachusetts, New Hampshire, and South Carolina to assert their independence, we can view these three documents as being the constitutions of states establishing their independence. Still, their transitional status is clearly reflected in the fact that, by the time the United States Constitution was written in 1787, only these three states of the original 13 felt the need to write and adopt a second state constitution—South Carolina in 1778, Massachusetts in 1780, and New Hampshire in 1784.

VIRGINIA AND NEW JERSEY

There was no half-heartedness about the next constitution. The Virginia Provincial Congress had its share of reluctance about writing a state constitution, since such an action was viewed as equivalent to a declaration of independence. However, by 15 May 1776 the Virginia Congress had instructed its delegates at the Continental Congress to vote for independence. Thus, when Virginia turned to writing a declaration of rights and a state constitution, there was no doubt in the minds of the delegates about what they were doing. Although a committee of the provincial congress was charged with the task, George Mason was largely responsible for both the Declaration of Rights adopted on 27 May 1776 and the new constitution adopted unanimously on 29 June 1776. The similarity in wording between Virginia's Declaration of Rights and that found in the first two paragraphs of the Declaration of Independence can probably be accounted for by the close juxtaposition in time between the two documents, and Mason's close connections with his fellow Virginian Thomas Jefferson. Many of Virginia's most visible leaders were not available. George Washington was leading the army, and Jefferson was away serving in the Continental Congress, as were Richard Henry Lee and George Wythe. However, Virginia was blessed with a host of good minds, and among these Edmund Pendleton, Richard Bland, James Madison, Patrick Henry, Edmund Randolph, and Mason were in attendance and prominent in debates.

The New Jersey Provincial Congress barely missed beating Virginia. Although it did not start drafting a document until 21 June 1776, it was able to adopt a new constitution on 2 July 1776, only nine days after starting. The Virginia Congress had put in very long hours to write its document in 45 days, so one might conclude that the New Jersey Congress either worked around the clock, or, as is likely, was not scrupulously concerned about its new document. It is doubtful that such speed would have been possible in either Virginia's or New Jersey's case if there had not been a long colonial experience upon which to draw and an existing form of government successful enough to warrant close approximation. That New Jersey's hastily framed and adopted constitution lasted 44 years before being replaced is testimony to the utility of having an existing political system upon which to model a new constitution. Prominent in New Jersey's deliberations were the Reverend Jacob Greene, John Cleves Symmes, Lewis Ogden, Jonathan D. Sergeant, and Theophilus Elmer. Greene was the most influential and is reputed to have received considerable help from another cleric, the famous John Witherspoon.

PENNSYLVANIA AND DELAWARE

Thus, by the time the Declaration of Independence was adopted, seven fully constituted states were already in existence, counting Connecticut and Rhode Island. Almost three months elapsed before another group of state constitutions appeared, during late 1776. The brief hiatus allowed enough time for experience and evolving constitutional theory to support a number of innovations. The first of these was to use a specially elected rather than an already sitting legislature to write a constitution. Pennsylvania initiated the innovation, but Delaware, copying its neighbor, was the first to finish a constitution using the method.

Among proponents for independence there were two viewpoints concerning the method for writing new state constitutions. On the one hand were those who wished to emphasize the continuity between colonial and statehood institutions in service of the basic premise that Americans were breaking with Britain in order to preserve their constitutional tradition. The provincial congresses were the bearers of that continuity and thus were the bodies that should write constitutions. Also, during the colonial era constitution-like documents had occasionally been adopted by the legislature.

On the other hand, there were those who felt that the American commitment to popular sovereignty and the need to engage as many people as possible in support of the legitimacy of the new governments required both a distinction between constitutions and normal legislation and a more direct linkage with popular sentiment. Since masses of people could not directly write a constitution, the best alternative seemed to be a body elected specifically for the purpose. The second group gradually won its point as constitution-writing progressed. Americans would eventually move a step further and require that constitutions written by a special convention also be approved by the people at large in a referendum. As logical as this next step was, it was not taken until 1780, in the fifteenth state constitution adopted.

Delaware was slow in moving from a colonial assembly to a provincial congress, and did so only on 15 June 1776, when all public officials were requested to continue their power from that date forward in the name of the people of specific counties rather than in the name of the King. On 27 July 1776 elections were called for a legislature that was first to sit as a constitutional convention. This specially elected legislature convened on 2 September 1776 and adopted a declaration of rights nine days later. The process was speeded along by copying much of Pennsylvania's declaration. The convention adopted a constitution on 20 September 1776, with both George Read and Thomas McKean being mentioned as the document's primary authors. Despite the haste, the document would not be replaced for 39 years.

Pennsylvania's new state constitution was interesting for far more than its being written by a specially elected legislature sitting as a constitutional convention. More than any other state until that of Massachusetts in 1778-80, Pennsylvania worked at developing a constitution that would reflect the latest in constitutional theory. The result was the most radical document of the era, certainly the most innovative, and until the adoption of the 1780 Massachusetts document the primary contender as a model for future state constitutions. It was at least partially adopted by several states.

Like Delaware, Pennsylvania was slow to move to provincial status, and for the same reason—there were many who did not wish to replace the old government. The legal assembly proved unwilling to act, and the election of 1 May 1776 failed to alter significantly the make-up of the legislative assembly. The proponents for independence absented themselves from the legislature, thereby denying the assembly its quorum and rendering it impotent. Then a convention of county committees of inspection was called by the Philadelphia Committee of Inspection in an attempt to bypass the legal assembly. This convention met for a week in Philadelphia, and its 108 delegates in June scheduled an election for 8 July 1776. Ninety-six men were elected by an electorate that was potentially broader than usual, since the normal property requirements were waived, but was in fact narrower than usual, since it excluded from voting anyone who did not attest to their support for independence. These men became a legislature parallel to the legal one, but they first assembled as a constitutional convention and met across the street from the Continental Congress in Philadelphia.

The Pennsylvania Constitutional Convention was dominated by pro-independence men, and several of its more radically democratic members were prominent in writing the new constitution. Benjamin Franklin had a considerable impact on the document, but James Cannon, Timothy Matlack, and Cannon's good friend George Bryan (who was not a delegate but worked closely with Cannon nonetheless) were the primary authors.

Pennsylvania's Declaration of Rights owed much to Virginia's, although Pennsylvania's was both longer and more far reaching. The resulting constitution, adopted along with the Declaration of Rights on 28 September 1776, was distinguished by creating a unicameral legislature, an extremely broad electorate, and a set of institutions designed to make the government as responsive to popular consent as possible. For example, in order to become a law a bill had to be passed in two consecutive sessions of the legislature. Since Pennsylvania had what became the standard American practice of annual elections, and bills approved the first time had to be published for public perusal, legislators were subject to explain their past and future votes between elections. Also, the constitution established a state-wide grand jury, called a Council of Censors, which was to be elected every seven years to review and evaluate all aspects of governmental action. Vermont would later copy most of this constitution, including its

101

council of censors, and Georgia would emulate its unicameral legislature. Indeed, during the 1820s, 1830s, and 1840s the next generation of state constitutions would bring to widespread fruition many of the potentially highly democratic aspects of Pennsylvania's 1776 constitution. . . .

THE COMMON POLITICAL CULTURE OF THE COLONIES

What is striking about the early state constitutions as a group is that, despite some institutional diversity, there were strong similarities among them that reflected a common political culture. That is, the political institutions developed in relative isolation by each colony converged over time, and during the revolutionary era the similarities became even stronger. To a certain extent this can be explained by the common practice of borrowing from other state constitutions, but it is doubtful that such borrowing would have been likely, or so successful, unless fundamental similarities had not already existed.

A general look at the 15 state constitutions adopted between 1775 and 1781 reveals the following patterns. All but two states used a bicameral legislature. Georgia went bicameral when it replaced its 1777 document in 1789, and Pennsylvania did so when it replaced its 1776 document in 1790. In all 15 constitutions the lower house was elected directly by the people. Although the percentage of white adult males enfranchised varied from state to state, on average the percentage was at least four times larger than it was in Britain.

Of the 13 constitutions creating bicameral legislatures, all but one had the upper house (senate) elected directly by the people, usually using the same electorate for both houses. Maryland, the one exception, used an electoral college to elect its senate. With only one exception, 1776 South Carolina, all constitutions provided for annual elections for the lower house. Of the 13 bicameral states, eight had annual elections for the senate, two had biennial elections, and three had staggered, multi-year elections.

In nine of the constitutions the executive was elected by the legislature, three used a popular election, and three used a popular election to identify the major candidates from among whom the legislature picked the governor. Eleven constitutions provided for annual elections for the governor, two for biennial elections, and two for triennial elections. Twelve of the constitutions

102

required voters to own property, usually about 50 acres or the equivalent, and three required voters to have paid taxes. Of the 13 bicameral legislatures, ten had the same property requirement to vote for the upper house as for the lower house. Of the nine states that involved the people in selecting the governor, eight used the same property requirement to vote for the governor as was required to vote for the lower house. All but one of the constitutions had property requirements to run for office, and nine [of the constitutions] for the 13 bicameral legislatures required more property to run for the upper house than for the lower house.

Ten of the early state constitutions included bills of rights. These bills of rights varied in length and detail, but generally had similar content. Virtually all rights later found in the United States Bill of Rights could be found in an earlier state constitution, usually in several.

Fourteen of the 15 constitutions were written and adopted by the respective state legislature, usually after an election where it was made clear that the new legislature would also write a new constitution.

Far from exhausting the similarities, the ones listed here indicate that, despite differences resulting from colonial experiences, regionalism, size, diversity, or degree of radicalism, there was a coherent shared political culture underlying the early state constitutions. Perhaps most obvious is the manner in which they produced political systems dominated by a bicameral legislature. The executive was invariably quite weak and a creature of the legislature. This was in keeping with both the colonial tendency to focus upon the legislature as the embodiment of the people, and the colonial distrust of executives and executive privilege.

Typical provisions in state constitutions towards this end, in addition to having the legislature elect the executive, included the requirement that the legislature approve executive appointments, the creation of a small body drawn from the legislature to assist the governor in giving executive approval to legislation, granting pardons, or just generally telling him what to do. The extent to which separation of powers was actually found in state constitutions, aside from the 1780 Massachusetts document, it was limited to a prohibition on anyone holding simultaneously a position in the legislative and executive branches.

In this regard, the United States Constitution built upon and evolved out of state constitutionalism. The national executive was stronger than state executives, although only somewhat more so than the Massachusetts governor. The movement away from the radical model of direct, popular consent was also only a matter of degree with respect to the Massachusetts constitution. When taken together, some believe, the state constitutions and the political process that produced them shows [show] the extent to which the national constitution was in most respects a logical development out of, or deflection from, what had come before rather than a radical departure or a conservative reaction. Regardless, the early state constitutions were the American laboratory for liberty, the base upon which the Continental Congress rested as it successfully prosecuted the war of independence and the first true written constitutions in world history. Even those who prefer to minimize the impact of these documents upon the United States Constitution admit the importance of the early state constitutions in these other respects.

Popular Radicalism

For historians interested in writing "history from the bottom up," it is important to distinguish the views of commonfolk from those of the elite. The most important spokesman for this radical tradition was Thomas Paine. His pamphlet, **Common Sense,** *expressed the more egalitarian and democratic ideals of commonfolk. In the view of historian Edward Countryman, the popular voice of the Revolution was distinctly radical. Popular radicalism contrasted sharply with the conservative views of the men who led the revolutionary movement. Taken from Edward Countryman, "Social Protest and the Revolutionary Movement, 1765-1776," in* The Blackwell Encyclopedia of the American Revolution, *ed. Jack P. Greene and J. R. Pole (Cambridge, Massachusetts, 1991), 193-96.*

REVOLUTION AND RADICALISM IN PHILADELPHIA

As the independence movement gained strength, social protest and political experience began combining to create new public identities. The case of Philadelphia shows the process particularly well. Pennsylvania's capital took little part in the great uprisings of the Stamp Act period; its stamp distributor resigned with little ado and there was virtually no rioting. But by the end of the 1760s relations within the city were growing tense. The issue was the non-importation movement with which the colonies had responded to Parliament's Townshend Duties of 1767. These were an attempt to meet the supposed colonial objection to "internal" taxes, such as the Stamp Tax, by imposing "external" duties on colonial imports. The colonials had long accepted Parliament's right to impose duties in order to control their behavior, such as the Molasses Act of 1733. By and large they were even paying the duties imposed by the Sugar Act of 1764. It seemed to the British that they had made the external-internal distinction themselves. On all counts, it looked as if Parliament had found a way of taxing the colonials that the colonials would accept.

They did not accept it. Instead, they agreed to boycott British commerce until the taxes were repealed. To the merchants of the great ports it was a disagreeable necessity: they would not accept Parliament's right to tax them, but transatlantic commerce was their life. But to Philadelphia's artisans it was another matter. Like New Yorkers and Bostonians, Philadelphians were enduring the depression that had settled on the colonies at the end of the Seven Years' War. It seemed to the artisans that nonimportation offered a chance to bring prosperity back. Without British imports there would be more of a market for their own goods. But when Parliament repealed four of the five Townshend Duties in 1770, leaving only the duty on tea in place, nonimportation began to collapse.

To the merchants the issue was simple: they were the traders and they had the right to decide whether to import or not. But to one Philadelphia "tradesman" the "consent of the majority of the tradesmen, farmers and other freemen . . . should have been obtained." A "lover of liberty and a mechanic's friend" wrote that a "good mechanic" was "one of the most serviceable, one of the most valuable members of society" but that merchants were only "weak and babbling boys—clerks of yesterday." "Brother Chip" asked Philadelphia artisans whether they did not have "an equal

---

"Social Protest and the Revolutionary Movement, 1765–1776" by Edward Countryman from *The Blackwell Encyclopedia of the American Revolution*, Jack P. Greene and J.R. Pole, eds. Copyright © 1991 by Blackwell Publishers.

right of electing or being elected. . . . Are there no . . . men well acquainted with the constitution and laws of their country among the tradesmen and mechanics?"

The issue was one of social and political consciousness more than it was one of overt social conflict. The Philadelphia artisans wanted an equal voice in the making of their community's major decisions. But in their self-assertion they were also redefining the terms of their membership in the community. In the colonial period they may have accepted that their political position and their social rank were inferior. Now they were casting such beliefs aside and developing instead the ideology of equal rights which would become dominant in American political culture.

From its slow start in 1765, Philadelphia went on to become the most radical urban center in revolutionary America. Politically the culmination came in June 1776, when the old provincial government was forcibly overthrown. One element in the coalition that overthrew it was the militant members of the Continental Congress, who were determined to have independence and who recognized that the Pennsylvania Assembly formed the last major obstacle to it. But they were joined by Pennsylvanians whose vision of America demanded transformation as well as independence. Many of them were master artisans, the people who had asserted their right to an equal political voice in 1770. But now they were joined by lesser men, most notably the journeymen and laborers who formed the bulk of the city's revolutionary militia. The artisans had found the means to express themselves in the city's committee of safety. Like similar committees elsewhere this had begun to take shape in the aftermath of the Boston Tea Party, and by 1776 its voice was dominant in the city's popular politics. The emergence and triumph of such committees was the surest possible sign that a full political revolution was underway. The spread of their membership to include men who would never have had such a voice in running the old order was as sure a sign that the Revolution had a profound social dimension.

But Philadelphians took it further. They met the final crisis as a bitterly divided people. For reasons of both religion and self-interest the city's old elite of Quaker and Anglican merchants were rejecting the revolution. The non-Quaker patriot elite, typified by the lawyer and pamphleteer John Dickinson, proved unwilling to accept the consequences of what they had helped to begin. In 1768 Dickinson's own *Letters From a Farmer in Pennsylva-*

nia had been enormously influential in rousing opposition to the Townshend Duties and his "Liberty Song" had been sung from New Hampshire to Georgia. In it he had urged, "Come join hand in hand, brave Americans all, and rouse your bold hearts at fair liberty's call," but now his own heart was timid and he held back from joining his own hand to the cause of independence. It was Dickinson and his like, not open loyalists, who were using the old provincial assembly to put the moment of independence off, and it was their power that dissolved when the popular committee and the Continental Congress joined their own hands to bring the assembly down.

Meanwhile another group had also taken on shape and consciousness: the privates of the city's militia. Philadelphia's Quaker pacifist heritage meant that it had no military tradition, which meant that there were no established lines of military authority. When a militia became necessary its officers were drawn from the better and middling sorts, and the privates came from the city's journeymen, apprentices, laborers, and servants. But the terms of the militia law were lenient, and a man who had conscientious objections could easily avoid service. To the city's Quakers it was a matter of religious belief. But to the militiamen liability to military service became a matter of political principle.

The consequence was that the militiamen established their own committee and formulated their own program for the Revolution. Equal liability to service was only one of the points they put forward. They scorned the paternalistic willingness of some of their officers to equip the troops they commanded; instead they wanted officers and men alike to be uniformed in simple hunting shirts. They wanted to elect their officers themselves, rather than serve under men appointed by higher authority. Their demands found echoes elsewhere. Hunting shirts became the costume of revolutionary commitment in Virginia. A committee of artisans took shape in New York City, and in May 1776 it issued a strident set of demands to the "elected delegates" in the province's provincial congress. One of those demands was that under the new order the system of popular committees that had taken power during the final crisis be able to reconstitute itself whenever the people might choose.

The need for governmental simplicity and responsiveness became one of the dominant themes in popular political discourse. No one put the point more clearly than the pamphleteer

Thomas Paine. His first great piece in a long career of radical political writing was *Common Sense*, published in Philadelphia in January 1776. Paine was a former corset-maker and British customs official, and he had migrated from England only in 1774. He had known Benjamin Franklin there, and through the famous former printer he found an entrée to the artisan community just at the point when it was awakening to political consciousness.

Paine set himself three distinct projects in *Common Sense*. One, after nine inconclusive months of war, was to convince Americans that reconciliation was impossible. Full independence was the only course worth following: "the weeping voice of nature cries 'tis time to part." The second was to argue the case for simple republicanism: "let the assemblies be annual, with a president only." The third was to put his case in a political language that would be sophisticated but also simple. Paine's predecessors in the Revolution's pamphlet literature had been gentlemen and they had written for other gentlemen. Paine's own roots were plebeian, and he wrote for people like himself

His impact was enormous. *Common Sense* sold some 150,000 copies and was read and discussed from one end of the 13 provinces to the other. People had been waiting for an unequivocal call for independence. Artisans and farmers were ready for a major piece of political writing that was neither beyond them nor condescending to them. Paine had made himself the voice of these people. The power with which he spoke for them was a measure of their own importance to the revolutionary movement. It was also a measure of how much their consciousness and situation had changed over the decade since the crisis first began. His call for republican institutions of the simplest sort, directly responsive, open to anyone's participation, devoid of the complications and balances of the old order, expressed the conclusions that the people who devoured *Common Sense* were drawing from their experience in the revolutionary movement.

LATER DEVELOPMENTS

The fullest measure of social protest in revolutionary America came after 1776, and it is beyond the main scope of this article. Independence brought the collapse of existing political institutions, and the collapse provided opportunity for many sorts of Americans to try to change their situations. Paine's people—white working men–pressed for institutional settlements of the sort he sketched in *Common Sense*. Their fullest opportunity came in Pennsylvania itself, where the patriot wing of the old elite gave way to panic and lost control. The result was the state's radical constitution of1776, and its provisions found echoes elsewhere. It was copied directly in the Green Mountains, where the New England settlers seized the moment and cut themselves free of New York. Their choice of the Pennsylvania model suggests the political mentality of revolutionary rural America. So does the equally simple New England proposal called *The People the Best Governors*. Following Paine, the Pennsylvanians repudiated the whole idea of a governorship, appointing a "president only" to see to public business. The title bore none of the quasi-regal meaning it would later take on in American political culture, and others proposed it as well: South Carolina, Delaware, and New Hampshire in their first constitutions and New York in a constitutional proposal of 1776.

All of these changes took place among white men. [Historians] Mary Beth Norton, Linda Kerber, and Ira Berlin have pointed the way for understanding the terms on which women and African-Americans confronted the Revolution, entered it, and tried to take advantage of the possibilities it presented.... Enough here to make four points. The first is that they started from situations far less privileged than those of any white males. The second, springing from the first, is that neither women nor Blacks found themselves in a position to claim full political equality or direct political power. The third is that members of each group were to at least some extent actors in the main events between 1765 and 1776. The most notable case is that of Crispus Attucks, who was black and who was one of the five Bostonians slain in the King Street Riot in 1770. The fourth is that some members of both groups did make the most they could of the political and the ideological opportunities that the Revolution presented.

The American Revolution does not, perhaps, fit a mechanistic model of a social revolution. But that is not to say that the Revolution did not have a profound social dimension, both in its origins, to which this article has referred, and in its short-term and long-term consequences. One starting point for the people who made the Revolution was their common membership in a dependent, colonial yet British society. The other was their many different situations within that society and their relations with one another. During the political crisis with Britain they found themselves confronting their own social situations and relationships as well as the large imperial issues. The process and the great transformations of the Revolution grew from its domestic and social aspects as well as from its imperial and political ones.

African Americans and the Revolution

In the following selection, Sylvia Frey explores the experiences of African Americans during the Revolution. The ideology of the Revolution contributed to the emergence of an anti-slavery movement in both the middle Atlantic colonies and New England. The impact of the Revolution on anti-slavery in the South was more modest. Frey concludes that the legacy of the Revolution was ambiguous for African Americans. Abridged from Sylvia R. Frey, "Slavery and Anti-Slavery," in The Blackwell Encyclopedia of the American Revolution, *ed. Jack P. Greene and J. R. Pole (Cambridge, Massachusetts, 1991), 385-90.*

[T]he roots of anti-slavery sentiment were religious in origin. The first explicit religious condemnation of slavery in America was the 1688 Germantown petition of the Mennonites, a sect similar to the Quakers. The mildly worded Germantown Protest, which argued from the golden rule, went unheeded. It was soon followed, however, by more elaborate, distinctly religious anti-slavery literature, most of it written by Quakers such as George Keith, John Hepburn, Ralph Sandiford, and Benjamin Lay. At least one New England Puritan, Judge Samuel Sewell, was among the anti-slavery pioneers. Sewell's tract *The Selling of Joseph* (1701) attacked the Biblical arguments traditionally used to justify slavery and advanced the opinion that, as children of God, blacks had "equal Right unto Liberty," an original right which could not be forfeited either by consent or by captivity in war.

"Slavery and Anti-slavery" by Sylvia R. Frey from *The Blackwell Encyclopedia of the American Revolution*, Jack P. Greene and J.R. Pole, eds. Copyright © 1991 by Blackwell Publishers.

No practical results came of any of these early efforts until the evangelical upsurge known as the Great Awakening swept through New England and the middle colonies, beginning in the 1740s. The frenzy of religious revivalism associated with it reinvigorated the Quaker anti-slavery tradition and produced a flood of anti-slavery tracts, the most influential of which were written by Anthony Benezet and John Woolman. Benezet, a Quaker schoolmaster in the Friend's English School in Philadelphia, wrote nine tracts between the late 1750s and his death in 1784. The three which are considered most important are *A Short Account of That Part of Africa, Inhabited by the Negroes* (1762), *A Caution and Warning to Great Britain and her Colonies* (1766), and *Some Historical Account of Guinea* (1771). The practical issue of Benezet's tracts, which were directed at the suppression of the slave trade, were apparent on both sides of the Atlantic. His *Short Account* apparently influenced the great English barrister Granville Sharp, who in 1772 led the successful court battle to free James Somerset, a slave in England. His *Historical Account* attracted the attention of Thomas Clarkson, who directed the successful fight to abolish the British slave trade in 1807. At Benezet's urging the prominent Philadelphia physician Benjamin Rush published his influential *An Address to the Inhabitants of the British Settlements in America, Upon Slave-Keeping* (1773). Although Benjamin Franklin's *Observations Concerning the Increase of Mankind* (1751) represented the first American attack on slavery from an economic and demographic perspective, Franklin too was influenced by the moral arguments of Benezet.

Woolman's efforts were directed at the Quaker community. For a quarter of a century Woolman traveled from Quaker meeting to meeting, trying to persuade his fellow Quakers to free their slaves. His extended tours of Maryland, Virginia, and North Carolina in 1746 and again in 1757 gave him first-hand experience with slavery and powerfully influenced his essay *Some Considerations on the Keeping of Negroes*, the first part of which appeared in 1754, the second in 1762. In it Woolman laid down the basic tenets of religious anti-slavery thought: the brotherhood of all God's children as partakers of the Inner Light; liberty as the gift of God to all his children; the entitlement of all God's children to "treatment according to the Golden Rule." Woolman's work had a notable impact among Quakers. In 1754 the Philadelphia Yearly approved a resolution written by him advising members of constituent meetings against purchasing slaves. In 1755 the Yearly advised monthly meetings to admonish any friend who persisted in the practice of buying slaves. In 1758 the Woolmanites scored a major victory with the adoption by the Yearly of the 1758 minute enjoining Friends to free their slaves or face discipline from the monthly meetings. The Philadelphia example spread through New England and New York, whose yearly meetings also approved minutes outlawing slavery. In New England, where the slave population was small and assimilable, and in Pennsylvania and New York, where Quaker influence was strong, slavery was practically abandoned by the Quakers before the Revolutionary War. Outside the Society of Friends, the religious movement did not produce important results until the revolutionary era, when the religious and moral movement began to converge with new political and economic ideas to produce a searing intellectual indictment of slavery.

The tradition of religious anti-slavery in New England and the middle colonies intersected with two independent but parallel systems of thought and culminated eventually in a powerful secular anti-slavery movement. The first developed out of the writings of John Locke, the seventeenth-century English philosopher whose ideas were formulated in opposition politics under Charles II. In their struggle with Britain over imperial policies, revolutionary leaders relied upon a popularized version of Lockean philosophy, which affirmed the existence of immutable laws of nature and the doctrine of natural rights, whose guiding values of liberty and equality found resonance in the religious principles of the spiritual equality of all God's children and liberty as His special gift to each of them equally. Although Locke himself had justified slavery, the French philosopher Montesquieu, in his *Spirit of the Laws* (1748), was the first to expound the theory that slavery was forbidden by natural law, an argument later vaguely made by Woolman and by Benezet, whose *A Caution and Warning . . .* quoted from the writings of Montesquieu. The rising tide of anti-slavery thought was supported by the publication in 1776 of Adam Smith's *Wealth of Nations*, whose utilitarian arguments that slavery was the "dearest of any" form of labor seemed to fit the economic realities of the late eighteenth century.

The three convergent, often interlocking, movements produced a fundamental intellectual reorientation, whose leading religious or moral, political and economic motifs raised questions about the obvious contradictions between society's professed values, religious and secular, and the existence of chattel slavery. Although most Americans drew back from the logic of their own arguments when it came to Blacks, the Boston Revolutionary James Otis did not. In *The Rights of the British Colonies Asserted and Proved* (1764), essentially an argument against the British writs of assistance, Otis bluntly asserted that "The Colonists are by the law of nature free born, as indeed all men are, white or black." During the controversy over the Stamp Act, anti-slavery literature began to proliferate. Produced by a diverse group of ministers, lawyers, merchants, and schoolteachers, it appealed to both religious sanctions and natural law. Among the anti-slavery advocates were Blacks themselves, including the poet Phillis Wheatley, whose work gained international recognition, and the one-time slave Caesar Sarter, whose essay on slavery appeared in the *Essex Journal*. "Freedom suits" brought by slaves against their masters in New England courts gave practical application to the ideas of anti-slavery writers, as did the wartime flight of thousands of slaves to the British Army.

EMANCIPATION IN THE NORTH

The practical issue of the intellectual anti-slavery movement was a trend in the northern states towards gradual emancipation, the preliminary to which was the passage of slave-trade legislation. In 1766, the year of the repeal of the Stamp Act, Boston instructed its representatives to "move for a law, to prohibit the importation and purchasing of slaves for the future." A number of New England towns approved similar instructions, and in 1767 the General Court debated but declined to take action on several bills prohibiting or restricting the slave trade. In 1771 a prohibitory bill passed the House and Council, but Governor Thomas Hutchinson refused to sign it. Although Massachusetts did not succeed in prohibiting the slave trade until 1788, Pennsylvania (1773), Rhode Island (1774), and Connecticut (1774) all passed prohibitory acts, and the general Articles of Association adopted by the first Continental Congress in 1774 contained a slave-trade clause which pledged the Association "neither [to] import nor purchase any slave imported after the first day of December next," after which time it agreed "wholly [to] discontinue the slave trade" and "neither [to] be concerned in it ourselves" nor to "hire our vessels, nor sell our commodities or manufacturers to those who are concerned in it."

113

Efforts to remove restraints on manumission, which existed in many states, were the next steps on the road to emancipation. Encouraged by petitions from Quakers and local abolitionist societies, several northern states adopted measures to facilitate voluntary manumission. Delaware approved a measure permitting manumission by will or other instrument (1787), and similar acts were passed in New Jersey (1786, 1798), New York (1785, 1788), Kentucky (1798, 1800), and Tennessee (1801). Concern that the freedmen might become a public charge led most states to establish age limitations and impose restrictions, including the requirement that the manumittor provide some form of maintenance for freedmen. During the Revolutionary War years, all of the northern states except New York and New Jersey took steps to abolish slavery.

Actual emancipation in the northern states was achieved by a variety of means: direct legislative action, direct constitutional provision, and the judicial process as supplementary to the Constitution. Early attempts at legislative emancipation in New England and New Jersey failed, but in 1780 the Pennsylvania Assembly enacted the first gradual emancipation law in American history. In New York and New Jersey, where slavery was more deeply entrenched, gradual emancipation legislation was not adopted until 1799 and 1804 respectively, New Jersey being the last state to do so before the Civil War. Both states made emancipation contingent upon the inclusion of abandonment clauses, which permitted owners of negro children freed by the act to abandon them a year after birth, after which time they were considered paupers and therefore subject to be bound out to service by the overseers of the poor. Since the law did not prohibit overseers from binding out children to the very masters who had abandoned them, masters were entitled to receive reimbursement from the towns for the support of the children they had abandoned.

Although the doctrine of natural rights was the foundation upon which all states constructed their new state constitutions, only that of Vermont provided for the total prohibition of slavery. It, however, established the precedent for similar action in the new states formed from the Northwest Territory. In Massachusetts and New Hampshire emancipation was accomplished by constitutional provision supplemented by judicial action. After petition campaigns waged by slaves in both states failed to achieve legislative emancipation, slaves, aided by anti-slavery lawyers, began suing for freedom in the courts. In the 1781 case of *Brom and Bett v. John Ashley*, heard in the Inferior Court of Common Pleas, Great Barrington, Massachusetts, Elizabeth Freeman, or "Bett," argued that the phrase in the new Massachusetts constitution of 1780 declaring all individuals were "born free and equal" applied to black as well as white Americans. Bett's claim to a share in the heritage of the Revolution established the precedent for a series of court decisions which effectively destroyed slavery in Massachusetts.

ENTRENCHMENT AND EXPANSION IN THE SOUTH

Although the northern record of emancipation was sullied by the general refusal to offer to freed Blacks full membership in the political community or to alter in any way their degraded social status, by a slow, often tortuous process, slavery was gradually abolished in all of the northern states. In the southern states it emerged from the Revolution as a firmly entrenched sectional institution, thus foreshadowing conflict at some remoter date. There are several reasons for these divergent developments, including the lack of economic dependence on slavery in the northern states, and the fact that the major intellectual tradition of religious radicalism reinforced by revolutionary ideology, which gave impetus to the anti-slavery movement in New England and the middle colonies, was largely absent in the South. The period of intense religious revivalism known as the First Great Awakening was also experienced in the South, but its geographic strength was limited to a few counties in Virginia's piedmont and the upper tidewater. Before the tradition of religious anti-slavery could become very deeply rooted, popular attention was preoccupied with the events of the imperial conflict.

White southerners also had a different conception of revolutionary ideology. Although they embraced the ideology of republicanism, which espoused the notions of liberty and equality, they had built a social order upon the contrary ideal of inequality. The ideal of equality, which captivated so many of their northern countrymen, held no allure for a people committed to slavery, for it was identified by them with racial anarchy and barbarism. From the white southern perspective, an ordered inequality was the best safeguard of harmony and peace. Unable to identify fully with the values of equality and liberty that were projected by the language of republicanism, white southerners fastened upon the rights of property as the focal point of their attachment to republican thought.

The experience of the Revolutionary War reinforced these ideas. Years of military occupation, continuous naval assaults, and bitter internecine warfare produced massive damage and overwhelming chaos in the South. British efforts to use slavery as a matter of tactics threatened to shatter social cohesion and to destroy the existing social order. The flight of thousands of slaves to the British Army or to sanctuaries in the developing Southwest and in Florida contributed to the devastation of southern plantation economies and to the severe depletion of the slave labor force. Faced with the disintegration of their society and the forfeiture of their material power, southerners emerged from the war, not persuaded to end slavery, but convinced that its restoration was the indispensable condition for the economic rehabilitation of the entire region.

The result was the further entrenchment of slavery everywhere in the South except Maryland, and its expansion westwards: into the southside and transmontane areas of Virginia and the back country of Georgia and South Carolina; across the Allegheny Mountains into Kentucky and Tennessee; and southwest to frontier plantations in Mississippi and Alabama. During and after the Revolution, Maryland's slave population grew slowly. A small state with no hinterland for expansion, in 1783 Maryland removed restraints on manumission, and by 1810 more than 20 per cent of the state's black population was free. By contrast, neighboring Virginia's slave population nearly doubled between 1755 and 1782, most of the growth owing to natural increase. Left by the transition from tobacco to wheat with a superfluity of slaves, tidewater planters resorted to the manumission, transfer, and sale of the surplus. In 1782 Virginia revised the slave code to permit individual manumission, and some 10,000 slaves were subsquently freed. During the 1790s and 1800s many times that number were taken into Kentucky and Tennessee by the hundreds of small, middling, and large planters fleeing the depression-ridden tidewater, or were marketed in slave-hungry Georgia and South Carolina. When that source of supply proved inadequate to meet the insatiable demand, planters from the lower South began importing slaves from Africa. Between 1783 and1807 an estimated 100,000 Africans were imported into Savan-

116

nah and Charleston to meet frontier demands in the back country. By 1790 Georgia's slave population was almost 30,000, nearly double the prewar figure. South Carolina, which lost an estimated one-quarter of its slave force during the war, imported almost 20,000 Africans before 1800, and between 1800 and 1807, when the slave trade was closed by federal law, another 39,075. The closing of the international trade accelerated the domestic trade, and between 1810 and 1820 approximately 137,000 slaves from the Chesapeake were marketed in Mississippi, Alabama, and the developing area west of the Mississippi River.

By the time the postwar anti-slavery movement was launched in the South, slavery was the pivotal institution of southern society. The catalyst for the short-lived crusade was the Second Great Awakening, which broke out on the banks of the James River in 1785 and erupted intermittently thereafter until 1820. Unorganized and generally confined to a handful of European evangelical leaders and northern itinerant preachers, the movement was inaugurated by Methodist conferences in 1780, 1783, and 1784, the last the Baltimore "Christmas" Conference, which directed members of the Society to manumit their slaves or face excommunication. When the English churchmen Thomas Coke, the first superintendent of the church in America, and Francis Asbury, ordained a superintendent by Coke, attempted to enforce the injunction among Virginia Methodists they met with bitter hostility and open threats of violence. As a consequence, the so-called Slave Rule was suspended in 1785, barely six months after it was adopted. Coke and Asbury then launched a petition campaign for the general emancipation of Virginia slaves. Although a number of the great Virginians of the revolutionary generation, including Washington, Jefferson, Madison, and Mason, were philosophically opposed to slavery, none was willing publicly to support the anti-slavery movement. The petition campaign was rejected by the Virginia Assembly and stirred a pro-slavery attack. Methodist efforts to achieve gradual emancipation continued intermittently until 1808, when the denominational effort was abandoned in favor of spiritual salvation of the slave population of the South.

The congregational organization of the Baptist polity militated against an organizational anti-slavery effort. In Virginia, the center of southern Baptist strength, the Baptist General Committee of the state adopted a resolution drafted by John Leland, a Massachusetts native, condemning slavery, but it failed to win

117

support in the associations. Advised by the Roanoke and Strawberry associations against further interference with the institution of slavery, the General Committee decided in 1793 to drop the divisive issue on the grounds that it was a matter more appropriately decided by the state. David Barrow, a native of Virginia, led a short-lived but significant antislavery movement in Kentucky. Finding no anti-slavery sentiment in the regular Baptist associations, Barrow formed the Licking-Locust Association, Friends of Humanity, and through it preached emancipationism. After Barrow's death in 1819 the movement rapidly disintegrated, however. Although Baptist churches in the lower South contained thousands of black members, there was no Baptist anti-slavery sentiment outside Virginia and Kentucky.

The American Revolution produced an ambiguous legacy. It created the illusion of a young nation united on the principles of liberty and equality, when in fact from the very inception there were invidious divisions along geographical, demographic, and ideological lines. Building upon the revolutionary ideal of political freedom, the "commercial" states of the North moved towards the gradual extinction of slavery. Driven by a different set of imperatives, the "plantation" states of the South entrenched and extended slavery, the very antithesis of freedom. The federal Constitution, which banned the slave trade after 1808 but implicitly recognized the existence of slavery, preserved the moral contradictions present in the situation and passed on to another generation the problem of creating the "more perfect union."

Women and the Revolution

Abigail Adams implored her husband John to "remember the ladies" and reminded him that "all Men would be tyrants if they could." The experience of war and the ideological struggle waged against Britain had important consequences for women's lives. Historian Betty Wood explores the mixed legacy that the Revolution bequeathed to women. Taken from Betty Wood, "The Impact of the Revolution on the Role, Status, and Experience of Women," in The Blackwell Encyclopedia of the American Revolution, *ed. Jack P. Greene and J. R. Pole (Cambridge, Massachusetts, 1991), 404-7.*

Examples of the female commitment to the patriot cause, and the support given by women to that cause both before and during the War for Independence, are manifold. Among the best known is the Edenton resolution. In October 1774, 51 women from Edenton, North Carolina, signed a statement in which they declared their unwavering commitment to the patriot cause and their intent to do all that they could to further the same. Equally well known are the 36 women in Philadelphia who in 1780 launched what was to prove an immensely successful campaign to raise money to help equip American troops. Within a matter of weeks they managed to collect around $300,000.

In Edenton and Philadelphia, and elsewhere on the mainland also, some women were taking the initiative. But there was a very real sense in which women were participating in a political campaign devised and orchestrated by men. And those men had fairly explicit ideas about the most appropriate ways in which women could help them. During the 1760s and early 1770s male patriots freely acknowledged that the success of the most important weapon in their political armoury, the boycotting of British goods, depended upon the cooperation of women, upon their willingness to change their patterns of consumption. It is abundantly clear that many women in all social classes were willing to do precisely that. However, male patriots went on to suggest that women could express their support for the American cause not only by wearing homespun clothes but also by making them. It was in their homes, in an essentially domestic context, sitting at their wheels and looms, that women could most appropriately assist their menfolk. And, it must be said, that is precisely what many women from all walks of life did, often with great gusto and enthusiasm. Patriot men were concerned to ensure that the horizons of women did not extend very far beyond their wheels and looms.

"The Impact of the Revolution on the Role, Status, and Experience of Women" by Betty Wood from *The Blackwell Encyclopedia of the American Revolution,* Jack P. Greene and J.R. Pole, eds. Copyright © 1991 by Blackwell Publishers.

In a purely practical sense, the War for Independence, when it came, was to have essentially similar consequences for women as had all previous colonial wars. Out of necessity, women were required to fill various economic roles often closed to them in peacetime. As their fathers, husbands, sons, and brothers went off to fight, for whichever side, so many women found themselves left to run the family farm or business. For those who had worked alongside the men in their family and in the process acquired invaluable knowledge and expertise, this might have been an unwelcome prospect, but was certainly not daunting. It was a rather different proposition for women whose husbands and fathers had effectively denied them any detailed knowledge of their business affairs. But in either case, the assumption was that when men returned from the war they would resume their usual role and responsibilities in the family. And more often than not that is exactly what did happen. But of course many men did not return from the war. For their wives this meant not only the trauma of bereavement but also the psychological and sometimes material problems of adjusting to widowhood.

It would seem reasonable to suggest that, in the longer term at any rate, the War for Independence *per se* did not result in any significant or permanent changes in the status, roles and daily lives of most white women. However, the dislocations of war, especially in the southern theater, did offer possibilities of escape and flight to black women. An unknown number of slave women did run away, but their freedom was often to prove both precarious and temporary.

In some respects it was patriot ideology rather than the War for Independence *per se* which seemed to hold out the best prospect of freedom, if not complete equality, for black men and women, both in the North and in the South. To some degree, that prospect began to be realized during the 1770s and 1780s, albeit often gradually and grudgingly in the North and, through the device of private manumission, on a limited scale in parts of the South. In the South, however, most black men and women ended the revolutionary era as they had begun it: as chattel slaves. The accommodations and compromises made in Philadelphia in 1787 ruled out the possibility that this situation would change in the foreseeable future.

Many people, on both sides of the Atlantic, had pointed to the apparent inconsistency, if not hypocrisy, of a patriot ideology which demanded freedom, liberty, and equality for white Americans but which denied those self-same things to black Americans. But, with the notable exception of Thomas Paine, no patriot pamphleteer or politician suggested or even hinted that women too might legitimately claim full and equal participation in the political society which men were so busy defining and bringing into existence. Neither did American women make the same claim on their own behalf or, during the 1790s, enthusiastically applaud Mary Wollstonecraft when she did.

THE NEW REPUBLICAN WOMAN

Yet the social and political discourse of the revolutionary era did not, and arguably could not, totally avoid the question of women. In many respects, it was the greater visibility of women in the America of the 1760s and 1770s, the part which they were playing and ought to be playing in the revolutionary movement, that prompted an intense examination of various attitudes and assumptions which previously had been largely taken for granted by both sexes. During the 1780s, with the achievement of American independence, the debate focused on the attributes which made for the "ideal" republican woman, the role of women in the new republic, and how they might best be prepared for that role. The outcome of that debate, in which women participated and with which they by and large concurred, was to return women to the private, domestic sphere from which it seemed by their actions if not by their words they might be trying to escape.

The fact of the matter was, however, that the political upheavals and disruptions of the revolutionary era did not dramatically change the self-perception of American women, or at least of those middle- and upper-class women who committed their thoughts and opinions to paper. Both before, during, and after the War for Independence, these women were arguing vociferously not for a complete redefinition of their role and status which, amongst other things, would have accorded them complete political equality with men, but for the acknowledgment by men of the equal importance and value of the private sphere in which they operated and were content to continue operating. As Abigail Adams put it—and she was by no means atypical of women in her social class—"if man is Lord, women is *Lordess*—that is what I contend for." When she urged the delegates meeting in Philadel-

121

phia to "Remember the Ladies," she was not and probably would not have dreamed of suggesting that Jefferson amend the Declaration of Independence to read "All men and women are created equal." Rather, she was emphasizing the importance of and claiming an equality of status for the private sphere in which women operated. Abigail Adams, and women like her, subscribed to many of the same social attitudes, assumptions, and values as American men.

Abigail Adams would not have dissented from the almost universally held view of the social and moral role, function, and importance of marriage and the family. Virtually every woman of her social class was truly appalled by Paine and Wollstonecraft's critiques of marriage and horrified by the way in which the latter practiced what she preached. The path suggested by Paine and Wollstonecraft pointed, or seemed to be pointing, to a complete breakdown of society—to social chaos, disorder, and anarchy. For women to step from the private to the public sphere, assuming that they had the time to combine the roles of wife, mother, and homemaker with the demands of a public career, would be one step along that infinitely dangerous path. In fact, the vehement denunciation by women such as Abigail Adams of state constitutions and election laws which, with the notable exception of those of New Jersey, explicitly denied women even the possibility of formal participation in political life, would have been more surprising and difficult to explain than their apparently placid acceptance of this state of affairs. Because of a dearth of first-hand written evidence, the perceptions of women further down the social scale are much more difficult to unravel.

If one of the principal concerns and preoccupations of some upper- and middle-class women during the 1780s was with establishing the importance and equality of the private sphere, then another, and one which they shared with some men—most notably perhaps with Benjamin Rush—was defining the attributes of the "ideal" republican woman and determining how girls and women might best be prepared to fulfill their assigned role in the new Republic.

In some ways, the "ideal" republican woman shared many of the same attributes and was required to display many of the same virtues as the "ideal" Roman matron. Her civic duty lay in the benign, almost civilizing, influence which she exerted over her husband and sons in ensuring that they became wise, virtuous, just, and, compassionate members of the body politic and, if called upon, good rulers.

The "ideal" republican woman was not a frivolous, empty headed ornament. On the contrary, she was expected and required to be a competent partner who could engage in serious discourse on a wide range of matters with her husband and sons. The problem was, as Benjamin Rush, Judith Sargent Murray, and others realized, that the traditional modes and methods of educating girls, when they were educated at all, scarcely fitted them for such an awesome responsibility. Girls had to be educated, and suitably educated, if they were ever to live up to the high expectations, of the republican woman. The "ideal" republican woman had to know how to cook and manage an efficient household, but she also had to know something about those subjects which would be of interest and concern to her husband. In what was to be one of the more tangible benefits accruing to women as a direct result of the American Revolution, much greater attention than ever before came to be paid to the formal education of girls and, not least, to the devising of curricula more in keeping with those available to boys.

Comparatively few female lives, black or white, in North or South, town or countryside, remained completely untouched or unaffected by the ideas and events of the American Revolution. But although, because of their commitment and contribution to the revolutionary cause, white women came to be regarded in a rather more positive light during the 1780s and 1790s, these years did not witness a "revolutionary" change in the status, role, and daily lives of American women.

Questions

1. *Compare the experiences of African Americans, women, and common people during the Revolution. Which group experienced the most significant improvement in social position?*

2. *Based on the experiences of these groups, is it persuasive to argue that the American Revolution was "revolutionary"?*

REVOLUTIONARY RHETORIC AND REALITY

One way of measuring the revolutionary character of the events of 1776 is to consider the nature of the social change brought about by Americans. Studies of the American Revolution have used other social upheavals like the English Revolution, the French Revolution, or the Russian Revolution as a yardstick against which the events of 1776 should be judged. In all of these European revolutions there was an ideological challenge to the ideals of aristocracy and monarchy. In each of these historical episodes a revolutionary ideology emerged that championed some form of political and social equality. In all of these revolutions the effort to implement these ideals also resulted in profound and rapid social change.

Another way of exploring the meaning of the Revolution is to consider the relationship between the ideals of the Revolution and the political and economic changes that accompanied the break with Britain. In the Declaration of Independence, Jefferson asserted that:

> *[A]ll men are created equal, that they are endowed by their Creator with certain unalienable Rights, that among these are Life, Liberty, and the pursuit of Happiness—That, to secure these rights, Governments are instituted among Men, deriving their just powers from the consent of the governed,—That whenever any Form of Government becomes destructive of these ends, it is the Right of the People to alter or to abolish it, and to institute new Government. . . .*

To evaluate the degree to which revolutionary rhetoric translated into reality one might begin by asking how radical were Jefferson's claims in the Declaration. The next question that needs to be considered is to what extent did the Revolution fulfill the promise of Jefferson's words. The selections that follow provide several different perspectives on these important questions.

Property and the Right to Vote

Patriot leader John Adams was among the most influential political theorists of the revolutionary generation. His pamphlet, Thoughts on Government, *helped define the principles of republican government for Americans. Adams was an avid and prolific correspondent. Like so many of his generation, he used his personal correspondence to explore important political issues of the day. In his letter to John Sullivan, Adams makes clear the republican idea that ownership of property ought to be a prerequisite for the exercise of the right to vote. Abridged from* Papers of John Adams, *ed. Robert J. Taylor (Cambridge, Massachusetts, 1979), 4:208, 210–12.*

Philadelphia May. 26. 1776

Dear Sir

. . . It is certain in Theory, that the only moral Foundation of Government is the Consent of the People. But to what an Extent Shall We carry this Principle? Shall We Say, that every Individual of the Community, old and young, male and female, as well as rich and poor, must consent, expressly to every Act of Legislation? No, you will Say. This is impossible. How then does the Right arise in the Majority to govern the Minority, against their Will? Whence arises the Right of the Men to govern Women, without their Consent? Whence the Right of the old to bind the Young, without theirs.

But let us first Suppose, that the whole Community of every Age, Rank, Sex, and Condition, has a Right to vote. This Community, is assembled—a Motion is made and carried by a Majority of one Voice. The Minority will not agree to this. Whence arises the Right of the Majority to govern, and the Obligation of the Minority to obey? from Necessity, you will Say, because there can be no other Rule. But why exclude Women? You will Say, because their Delicacy renders them unfit for Practice and Experience, in the great Business of Life, and the hardy Enterprizes of War, as well as the arduous Cares of State. Besides, their attention is So much engaged with the necessary Nurture of their Children, that Nature has made them fittest for domestic Cares. And Children have not Judgment or Will of their own. True. But will not these Reasons apply to others? Is it not equally true, that Men in general in every Society, who are wholly destitute of Property, are also too little acquainted with public Affairs to form a Right Judgment, and too dependent upon other Men to have a Will of their own? If this is a Fact, if you give to every Man, who has no Property, a Vote, will you not make a fine encouraging Provision for Corruption by your fundamental Law? Such is the Frailty of the human Heart, that very few Men, who have no Property, have any Judgment of their own. They talk and vote as they are directed by Some Man of Property, who has attached their Minds to his Interest. . . .

Harrington has Shewn that Power always follows Property. This I believe to be as infallible a Maxim, in Politicks, as, that Action and Re-action are equal, is in Mechanicks. Nay I believe We may advance one Step farther and affirm that the Ballance of Power in a Society, accompanies the Ballance of Property in Land. The only possible Way then of preserving the Ballance of Power on the side of equal Liberty and public Virtue, is to make the Acquisition of Land easy to every Member of Society: to make a Division of the Land into Small Quantities, So that the Multitude may be possessed of landed Estates. If the Multitude is possessed of the Ballance of real Estate, the Multitude will have the Ballance of Power, and in that Case the Multitude will take Care of the Liberty, Virtue, and Interest of the Multitude in all Acts of Government. . . .

The Same Reasoning, which will induce you to admit all Men, who have no Property, to vote, . . . will prove that you ought to admit Women and Children: for generally Speaking, Women and Children, have as good Judgment, and as independent Minds as those Men who are wholly destitute of Property: these last being to all Intents and Purposes as much dependent upon others, who will please to feed, cloath, and employ them, as Women are upon their Husbands, or Children on their Parents. . . .

Depend upon it, sir, it is dangerous to open So fruitfull a Source of Controversy and Altercation, as would be opened by attempting to alter the Qualifications of Voters. There will be no End of it. New Claims will arise. Women will demand a Vote. Lads from 12 to 21 will think their Rights not enough attended to, and every Man, who has not a Farthing, will demand an equal Voice with any other in all Acts of State. It tends to confound and destroy all Distinctions, and prostrate all Ranks, to one common Levell.

The Problem of Women's Suffrage

The logic of Adams's argument excluded women who were not property owners from the vote. But what of widows, the group of women who did own property? In this letter, patriot Richard Henry Lee discusses the possibility of allowing suffrage for widows. In the case of widows the connection between the right to vote and the ownership of property need not have presented a barrier to their participation. This contradiction did not go unnoticed by women at the time, as this letter to Mrs. Hannah Corbin suggests. While female suffrage was hardly common in this period, the state constitution New Jersey adopted enfranchised "all free inhabitants." Women voted in New Jersey until an explicit prohibition on female voting was enacted in 1807. Excerpted from **The Letters of Richard Henry Lee,** *ed. James Curtis Ballagh (New York, 1911), 1:392–93.*

[March 17, 1778]

You complain that widows are not represented. . . . The doctrine of representation is a large subject, and it is certain that it ought to be extended as far as wisdom and policy can allow; nor do I see that either of these forbid widows having property from voting, notwithstanding it has never been the practice either here or in England. Perhaps 'twas thought rather out of character for women to press into those tumultuous assemblages of men where the business of choosing representatives is conducted. And it might also have been considered as not so necessary, seeing that the representatives themselves, as their immediate constituents, must suffer the tax imposed in exact proportion as does all other property taxed, and that, therefore, it could not be supposed that taxes would be laid where the public good did not demand it. This, then, is the widow's security as well as that of the never married women, who have lands in their own right, for both of whom I have the highest respect, and would at any time give my consent to establish their right of voting. . . . When we complained of British taxation we did so with much reason, and there is great difference between our case and that of the unrepresented in this country. The English Parliament nor their representatives would pay a farthing of the tax they imposed on us but quite otherwise. . . . Oppressions, therefore, without end and taxes without reason or public necessity would have been our fate had we submitted to British usurpation.

The Problem of Slavery

During the bicentennial of the U.S. Constitution, Justice Thurgood Marshall, the first African American to serve on the Supreme Court, shocked many when he attacked the Founding Fathers' support for the institution of slavery. Marshall was hardly the first person to notice the inconsistency between the ideals of the Revolution and the existence of chattel slavery. The English literary figure Samuel Johnson mocked the sincerity of the patriot cause when he wrote, "How is it that we hear the loudest yelps for liberty among the drivers of Negroes?" In Massachusetts a number of slaves were inspired by the rhetoric of the revolutionary ferment to petition for their freedom. This document provides a glimpse into how the rhetoric of the Revolution was interpreted by those enslaved, not by the arbitrary acts of Parliament, but by the acts of American citizens. In New England and parts of the middle-Atlantic states the institution of slavery was gradually eliminated after the Revolution. Slavery was abolished in the Vermont Constitution of 1777. In 1780 the Supreme Court of Massachusetts ruled that slavery was incompatible with the state constitution's claim that "all men are born free and equal." Pennsylvania (1780), Connecticut (1784), and Rhode Island (1784) all enacted laws that freed children born to slave parents. In the South, the institution of slavery continued to remain an integral part of the social and political order. Taken from "To his Excellency Thomas Gage . . .," May 25, 1774, Collections of the Massachusetts Historical Society, 5th Series, (Boston, 1877), 3:432–33.

The Petition of a Grate Number of Blackes . . .

Humbly Shewing

That your Petitioners apprehind we have in common with all other men a naturel right to our freedoms without Being depriv'd of them by our fellow men as we are a freeborn Pepel and have never forfeited this Blessing by aney compact or agreement whatever. But we were unjustly dragged by the cruel hand of power from our dearest frinds and sum of us stolen from the bosoms of our tender Parents and from a Populous Pleasant and plentiful country and Brought hither to be made slaves for Life in a Christian land. Thus are we deprived of every thing that hath a tendency to make life even tolerable, the endearing ties of husband and wife we are strangers to for we are no longer man and wife then our masters or mestreses thinkes proper.... Our children are also taken from us by force and sent maney miles from us.... Thus our lives are imbittered to us on these accounts.... We therfor Bage [beg] your Excellency and Honours will give this its deu weight and consideration and that you will accordingly cause an act of the legislative to be pessed that we may obtain our Natural right our freedoms.

A Radical Defense of Democracy

The anonymous author of the following pamphlet articulated one of the most egalitarian defenses of democracy written during the Revolution. The pamphlet attacked the argument that property and the suffrage ought to be linked. Excerpted from Anon., The People the Best Governors: or A Plan of Government Founded on the Just Principles of Natural Freedom *(1776), 9–10.*

The question now . . . arises what it is that ought to be the qualification of a representative? In answer we observe, that fear is the principle of a despotic, honour of a kingly, and virtue is the principle of a republican government.—Social virtue and knowledge, I say then, is the best, and only necessary qualification of the person before us. But it will be said, that an estate of two hundred, four hundred pounds, or some other sum is essential.... [W]hat will then be come of the genuine principle of freedom? This notion of an estate has the directed tendency to set up the avaricious over the heads of the poor, though the latter are ever so virtuous. Let it not be said in future generations, that money was made by the founders of the American states, an essential qualification in the rulers of a free people.

Virginians Assert Their Rights

The 1776 Virginia "Declaration of Rights," drafted in large part by George Mason, served as a model of the bills of rights that were prefaced to a number of state constitutions. The "Declaration of Rights" not only affirms the ideals of liberty but also states in clear terms the essential principles of republicanism upon which American constitutional government would be based. Excerpted from The Papers of George Mason, 1725–1792, ed. Robert A. Rutland (Chapel Hill, 1970), 1:287–89.

A DECLARATION OF RIGHTS made by the Representatives of the good people of VIRGINIA, assembled in full and free Convention; which rights do pertain to (them and their) posterity, as the basis and foundation of Government.

1. That all men are (by nature) equally free and independent, and have certain inherent rights, of which, (when they enter into a state of society,) they cannot, by any compact, deprive or divest their posterity; (namely,) the enjoyment of life and liberty, with the means of acquiring and possessing property, and pursuing and obtaining happiness and safety.

2. That all power is vested in, and consequently derived from, the People; that magistrates are their trustees and servants, and at all times amenable to them.

3. That Government is, or ought to be, instituted for the common benefit, protection, and security of the people, nation, or community;—Of all the various modes and forms of Government that is best which is capable of producing the greatest degree of happiness and safety, and is most effectually secured against the danger of mal-administration;—And that, whenever any Government shall be found inadequate or contrary to these purposes, a majority of the community hath an indubitable, unalienable, and indefeasible right, to reform, alter, or abolish it, in such manner as shall be judged most conducive to the publick weal.

4. That no man, or set of men, are entitled to exclusive or separate emoluments and privileges from the community, but in consideration of publick services; which,

131

not being descendible, (neither ought the offices) of Magistrate, Legislator, or Judge, (to be hereditary).

5. That the Legislative and Executive powers of the State should be separate and distinct from the judicative; and, that the members of the two first may be restrained from oppression, by feeling and participating the burdens of the people, they should, at fixed periods, be reduced to a private station, return into that body from which they were originally taken, and the vacancies be supplied by frequent, certain, and regular elections, (in which all, or any part of the former members, to be again eligible, or ineligible, as the laws shall direct).

6. That elections of members to serve as Representatives of the people, in Assembly, ought to be free; and that all men, having sufficient evidence of permanent common interest with, and attachment to, the community, have the right of suffrage, (and cannot be taxed or deprived of their property for) publick uses without their own consent or that of their Representative (so elected,) nor bound by any law to which they have not, in like manner assented, for the publick good.

7. That all power of suspending laws, or the execution of laws, by any authority, without consent of the Representatives of the people, is injurious to their rights, and ought not to be exercised.

8. That in all capital or criminal prosecutions a man hath a right to demand the cause and nature of his accusation, to be confronted with the accusers and witnesses, to call for evidence in his favour, and to a speedy trial by an impartial jury of his vicinage, without whose unanimous consent he cannot be found guilty, nor can he be compelled to give evidence against himself; that no man be deprived of his liberty except by the law of the land, or the judgment of his peers.

9. That excessive bail ought not to be required, nor excessive fines imposed, nor cruel and unusual punishments inflicted.

10. That (general) warrants, whereby any officer or messenger may be commanded to search suspected places (without evidence of a fact committed,) or to seize any person or persons (not named or whose offence is) not

particularly described (and supported by evidence,) are grievous and oppressive, and ought not to be granted.

11. That in controversies respecting property, and in suits between man and man, the ancient trial by Jury is preferable to any other, and ought to be held sacred.

12. That the freedom of the Press is one of the greatest bulwarks of liberty, and can never be restrained but by despotick Governments.

13. That a well-regulated Militia, composed of the body of the people, trained to arms, is the proper, natural, and safe defence of a free State; that Standing Armies, in time of peace, should be avoided as dangerous to liberty; and that, in all cases, the military should be under strict subordination to, and governed by, the civil power.

14. That the people have a right to uniform Government; and, therefore, that no Government separate from, or independent of, the Government of *Virginia*, ought to be erected or established within the limits thereof.

15. That no free Government, or the blessing of liberty, can be preserved to any people but by a firm adherence to justice, moderation, temperance, frugality, and virtue, and by frequent recurrence to fundamental principles.

16. That Religion, or the duty which we owe to our *Creator*, and the manner of discharging it, can be directed only by reason and conviction, not by force or violence; and, therefore, all men (are equally entitled to the free) exercise of religion, according to the dictates of conscience; and that it is the mutual duty of all to practise Christian forbearance, love, and charity, towards each other.

Changes in Suffrage and Voting Behavior

The information presented in the first set of tables shows the change in property requirements enacted by four states during the revolutionary era. The data in the second table provides information about the economic status of individuals elected to the lower houses of the various states both before and after the Revolution.

Property Requirements for Voting and Officeholding

Virginia

	1762 election law, reaffirmed in 1769	1776 constitution
HOUSE electors	fr. of 25 acres with 12' x 12' house; or fr. of 50 acres unsettled; or town lot with 12' x 12' house *Housekeepers in Williamsburg and Norfolk could also vote if they had served to any trade for 5 years.*	"the right of suffrage . . . shall remain as exercised at present"
candidates		freeholder, or otherwise "duly qualified according to law"

Pennsylvania

	1706 election law	1776 constitution
HOUSE electors	fr. of 50 acres, 12 acres thereof "seated and cleared," or pers. est. worth £50 clear of debts	taxpayer, or son of freeholder
candidates	same as electors	

New York

	1699 election law	1777 constitution
HOUSE electors	fr. worth £40 free of debts, or being a freeman of the corporation of Albany or the city of New York	fr. worth £20, or rented real est. worth 40s. per year
candidates	fr. worth £40 free of debts	

Massachusetts

	1691 charter	1780 constitution
HOUSE electors	fr. worth 40s. per year, or pers. est. worth £40	est. worth £60 or fr. worth £3 per year
candidates		est. worth £200, or fr. worth £100

Adapted from *The First American Constitutions: Republican Ideology and the Making of the State Constitutions in the Revolutionary Era,* by Willi Paul Adams. Translated by Rita and Robert Kimber. Published for the Institute of Early American History and Culture, Williamsburg, Virginia. Copyright © 1980 by The University of North Carolina Press. Used by persmission of the publisher.

134

**Economic Status of Representatives to the Lower House
Before and After the Revolution**

	N.H., N.Y., and N.J.		Md., Va., and S.C.	
	Prewar (percentages)	Postwar (percentages)	Prewar (percentages)	Postwar (percentages)
Wealthy	36	12	52	28
Well-to-do	47	26	36	42
Moderate	17	62	12	30

Adapted from "Government by the People: The American Revolution and the Democratization of the Legislatures," by Jackson Turner Main. Reprinted from The William and Mary Quarterly, 3d. ser., Vol. 23, July 1966, pp. 405.

Questions

1. *Why would men like Adams believe that republican government could not survive if the right to vote was not tied to the ownership of property?*
2. *What do the struggles of women and African Americans tell us about the meaning of the Revolution?*
3. *What, if anything, is radical about the argument of the author of The People the Best Governors?*
4. *Does the information about the changes in suffrage and voting behavior support or refute the claim that the Revolution accomplished a radical change in American government and society?*

135

FURTHER READING

Gordon S. Wood's analysis of revolutionary ideas in The Creation of the American Republic, 1776–1787 *(Chapel Hill, 1969), focuses on changing ideas about republican government in the period between the Revolution and the adoption of the Constitution. Linda K. Kerber explores the impact of republicanism on women's roles in* Women of the Republic: Intellect and Ideology in Revolutionary America *(Chapel Hill, 1980). Ira Berlin and Ronald Hoffman's edited volume* Slavery and Freedom in the Age of the American Revolution *(Charlottesville, 1983), traces the impact of the Revolution on the lives of African Americans, including the experiences of slaves and free men and women. Edward Countryman's synthetic account of the Revolution charts the diverse experiences of Americans, and is especially sensitive to how issues of race, class, and gender influenced people's experiences during this period of American history;* The American Revolution *(New York, 1985). See also Gordon S. Wood,* The Radicalism of the American Revolution *(New York, 1992).*

Andrew Jackson and Cherokee Removal

Paul C. Bowers

INTRODUCTION

In the 1830s, the federal government of the United States forced most of the Native Americans living east of the Mississippi off their homelands. Ostensibly intended to relocate these Indians on sparsely populated and less desirable lands to the west; this massive "removal" resulted in the deaths of many. Because the justification for removal was often framed in terms of savage Indians and civilized whites, the forced migration of the Cherokee people earned the most attention at the time and since. Of the Native American people who were finally forced to leave their lands and migrate across the Mississippi River—Choctaw, Cherokee, Creeks, and others—the Cherokee made the most sustained and successful effort to accommodate to the white man's ways. They aided Andrew Jackson in his victory over the Creeks at the pivotal Battle of Horseshoe Bend, 27 March 1814. They made rapid advancement in agriculture, education, and adoption of the Christian religion. In 1827, the Cherokee adopted a written constitution patterned after the Constitution of the United States and claimed to be a sovereign, independent nation with complete jurisdiction over their territory. Neither the federal nor state governments recognized that claim. Ultimately, their efforts to retain their land and freedom were to no avail.

Soon after the Cherokee adopted their constitution, the states in which they resided, especially Georgia, stepped up efforts to gain control of their land. When Andrew Jackson became president of the United States in 1829, he initiated the first major federal effort to relocate Native American populations. His policy, consonant with that of Georgia and other southern states and reflecting the opinions and desires of most white Americans, was to clear the lands east of the Mississippi River for settlement and exploitation by whites.

Jackson's policy was a success. By the Treaty of New Echota, 29 December 1835, a small group of Cherokee leaders ceded the nation's land east of the Mississippi River to the United States for the sum of $5 million and a promise of sufficient land for their resettlement in the west. The treaty bitterly divided the Cherokee into pro- and anti-removal parties and led to the murder, or execution, of John Ridge, Elias Boudinot, and Major Ridge, who favored the treaty, by members of their own nation.

In 1830, Congress passed the Indian Removal Act, which enabled President Jackson to exchange land west of the Mississippi River for tribal territory in the southeastern states. Almost sixteen thousand Cherokee were forced to emigrate, and, according to one estimate, about one-fourth of them died in concentration camps or along the "Trail of Tears," the Cherokee name for the terrible trek west.

How shall we understand what happened to the Cherokee, and indeed to all Native Americans, following the advent and expansion of Europeans in their land? Andrew Jackson has been accused of genocide, as have, of late, Christopher Columbus and all Europeans who invaded, settled, and conquered the Americas.

What is genocide? Webster's New World Dictionary defines it as: "first applied to the attempted killing or extermination of a whole people or nation." You see the key words: "killing," "extermination," "whole people or nation." Was that Andrew Jackson's intent? Or, if not his intent, was it in any case the result of his policy, abetted by the majority of white Americans? If not, why did what happened happen? Jackson himself believed that what happened was tragic but inevitable. So did many of his contemporaries, and so do many today. Jackson believed the removal and deaths of so many Cherokee was the result of the often-repeated clash between civilization and savagery; between a dynamic, superior culture and a backward, inferior one.

Was there no other, better, way? You decide.

JUDGING JACKSON: PRAGMATIC POLITICIAN OR SCHEMING HYPOCRITE?

Following are two views of Andrew Jackson's removal policy. They present differing, often conflicting interpretations of Jackson as a man and as a political leader, of the complex issues involved in Indian removal, and of the results of Jackson's policy and the related actions of Georgia and other southeastern states in relocating Native Americans west of the Mississippi River.

The first selection is an article written by Francis Paul Prucha, a professor at Marquette University. Perhaps no other scholar has published so extensively on Jackson and Indian removal as Prucha. This early article, published in 1969, clearly explains the position that Prucha has since maintained: that Jackson did not hate Native Americans, that he had no intent to destroy them, that he had the best interests of Native Americans at heart, although he firmly believed that America—the United States—was a white man's country. Edward Pessen, author of the second selection, takes a different view of Jackson's policy. He argues that Jackson zealously worked to bring about removal, regardless of the costs. Pessen questions Jackson's claims to have the best interests of the Cherokee at heart, claims which Prucha accepts at face value.

Jackson as a Pragmatic Statesman

Francis Paul Prucha argues that Jackson's policy toward the Native Americans was dictated primarily by considerations of national secu-

143

rity. In the following excerpt Prucha asserts that Jackson actually upheld the rights of Native Americans who lived peaceably with whites. Taken from F.P. Prucha "Andrew Jackson's Indian Policy: A Reassessment," The Journal of American History 56 *(December 1969):527–28, 534–36.*

A GREAT many persons—not excluding some notable historians—have adopted a "devil theory" of American Indian policy. And in their demonic hierarchy Andrew Jackson has first place. He is depicted primarily, if not exclusively, as a western frontiersman and famous Indian fighter, who was a zealous advocate of dispossessing the Indians and at heart an "Indian-hater." When he became President, the story goes, he made use of his new power, ruthlessly and at the point of a bayonet, to force the Indians from their ancestral homes in the East into desert lands west of the Mississippi, which were considered forever useless to the white man.

This simplistic view of Jackson's Indian policy is unacceptable. It was not Jackson's aim to crush the Indians because, as an old Indian fighter, he hated Indians. Although his years in the West had brought him into frequent contact with the Indians, he by no means developed a doctrinaire anti-Indian attitude. Rather, as a military man, his dominant goal in the decades before he became President was to preserve the security and well-being of the United States and its Indian and white inhabitants. His military experience, indeed, gave him an overriding concern for the safety of the nation from foreign rather than internal enemies, and to some extent the anti-Indian sentiment that has been charged against Jackson in his early career was instead basically anti-British. Jackson, as his first biographer pointed out, had "many private reasons for disliking" Great Britain. "In her, he could trace the efficient cause, why, in early life, he had been left forlorn and wretched, without a single relation in the world." His frontier experience, too, had convinced him that foreign agents were behind the raised tomahawks of the red men. In 1808, after a group of settlers had been killed by the Creeks, Jackson told his militia

"Andrew Jackson's Indian Policy: A Reassessment," by F.P. Prucha, as it appeared in *The Journal of American History* (formerly *The Mississippi Valley Historical Review)*, Vol. LVI, No. 3, December 1969. Copyright © 1969 by the Organization of American Historians.

troops: "[T]his brings to our recollection the horrid barbarity committed on our frontier in 1777 under the influence of and by the orders of Great Britain, and it is presumeable that the same influence has excited those barbarians to the late and recent acts of butchery and murder... ." From that date on there is hardly a statement by Jackson about In-

President Andrew Jackson (Courtesy of The Library of Congress.)

dian dangers that does not aim sharp barbs at England. His reaction to the Battle of Tippecanoe was that the Indians had been "excited to war by the secrete agents of Great Britain." . . .

The removal policy, begun long before Jackson's presidency but wholeheartedly adopted by him, was the culmination of these views. Jackson looked upon removal as a means of protecting the process of civilization, as well as of providing land for white settlers, security from foreign invasion, and a quieting of the clamors of Georgia against the federal government. This view is too pervasive in Jackson's thought to be dismissed as polite rationalization for avaricious white aggrandizement. His outlook was essentially Jeffersonian. Jackson envisaged the transition from a hunting society to a settled agricultural society, a process that would make it possible for the Indians to exist with a higher scale of living on less land, and which would make it possible for those who adopted white ways to be quietly absorbed into the white society. Those who wished to preserve their identity in Indian nations could do it only by withdrawing from the economic and political pressures exerted upon their enclaves by the dominant white settlers. West of the Mississippi they might move at their own pace toward civilization.

145

Evaluation of Jackson's policy must be made in the light of the feasible alternatives available to men of his time. The removal program cannot be judged simply as a land grab to satisfy the President's western and southern constituents. The Indian problem that Jackson faced was complex, and various solutions were proposed. There were, in fact, four possibilities.

First, the Indians could simply have been destroyed. They could have been killed in war, mercilessly hounded out of their settlements, or pushed west off the land by brute force, until they were destroyed by disease or starvation. It is not too harsh a judgment to say that this was implicitly, if not explicitly, the policy of many of the aggressive frontiersmen. But it was not the policy, implicit or explicit, of Jackson and the responsible government officials in his administration or of those preceding or following his. It would be easy to compile an anthology of statements of horror on the part of government officials toward any such approach to the solution of the Indian problem.

Second, the Indians could have been rapidly assimilated into white society. It is now clear that this was not a feasible solution. Indian culture has a viability that continually impresses anthropologists, and to become white men was not the goal of the Indians. But many important and learned men of the day thought that this was a possibility. Some were so sanguine as to hope that within one generation the Indians could be taught the white man's ways and that, once they learned them, they would automatically desire to turn to that sort of life. Thomas Jefferson never tired of telling the Indians of the advantages of farming over hunting, and the chief purpose of schools was to train the Indian children in white ways, thereby making them immediately absorbable into the dominant culture. This solution was at first the hope of humanitarians who had the interest of the Indians at heart, but little by little many came to agree with Jackson that this dream was not going to be fulfilled.

Third, if the Indians were not to be destroyed and if they could not be immediately assimilated, they might be protected in their own culture on their ancestral lands in the East—or, at least, on reasonably large remnants of those lands. They would then be enclaves within the white society and would be protected by their treaty agreements and by military force. This was the alternative demanded by the opponents of Jackson's removal bill—for example, the missionaries of the American Board of Commissioners for Foreign Missions. But this, too, was infeasible, given the political and military conditions of the United States at the time. The federal government could not have provided a standing army of sufficient strength to protect the enclaves of Indian territory from the encroachments of the whites. Jackson could not withstand Georgia's demands for the end of the *imperium in imperio* [an empire within an empire] represented by the Cherokee Nation and its new constitution, not because of some inherent immorality on his part but because the political situation of America would not permit it.

The jurisdictional dispute cannot be easily dismissed. Were the Indian tribes independent nations? The question received its legal answer in John Marshall's decision in *Cherokee Nation* v. *Georgia*, in which the chief justice defined the Indian tribes as "dependent domestic nations." But aside from the juridical decision, were the Indians, in fact, independent, and could they have maintained their independence without the support—political and military—of the federal government? The answer, clearly, is no, as writers at the time pointed out. The federal government could have stood firm in defense of the Indian nations against Georgia, but this would have brought it into head-on collision with a state, which insisted that its sovereignty was being impinged upon by the Cherokees.

This was not a conflict that anyone in the federal government wanted. President Monroe had been slow to give in to the demands of the Georgians. He had refused to be panicked into hasty action before he had considered all the possibilities. But eventually he became convinced that a stubborn resistance to the southern states would solve nothing, and from that point on he and his successors, John Quincy Adams and Jackson, sought to solve the problem by removing the cause. They wanted the Indians to be placed in some area where the problem of federal versus state jurisdiction would not arise, where the Indians could be granted land in fee simple [permanent transference of land without restrictions] by the federal government and not have to worry about what some state thought were its rights and prerogatives.

The fourth and final possibility, then, was removal. To Jackson this seemed the only answer. Since neither adequate protection nor quick assimilation of the Indians was possible, it seemed reasonable and necessary to move the Indians to some area where they would not be disturbed by federal-state jurisdictional disputes or by encroachments of white settlers, where they could develop on the road to civilization at their own pace, or, if they so desired, preserve their own culture.

Jackson as a Scheming Devil

Edward Pessen contends that Jackson's hypocritical policy toward Indian removal, though couched in pious rhetoric, actually was intended to remove the Native Americans from their homelands at any cost. The following argument is taken from Edward Pessen, Jacksonian America: Society, Personality, and Politics *(Homewood, Illinois, 1978), 296–301.*

Jacksonian Indian policy was a blending of hypocrisy, cant, and rapaciousness, seemingly shot through with contradictions. Inconsistencies however are present only if the language of the presidential state papers is taken seriously. "The language of Indian removal was pious," observes [historian] Michael P. Rogin, "but the hum of destruction is clearly audible underneath." In [historian] Ronald Satz's phrase, such language provided a "convenient humanitarian rationale" for a policy of force. When the lofty rhetoric is discounted and viewed for what it was—sheer rationale for policy based on much more mundane considerations—then an almost frightening consistency becomes apparent. By one means or another the southern tribes had to be driven to the far side of the Mississippi. For as [historian] Mary E. Young has pointed out, by 1830 "east of the Mississippi, white occupancy was limited by Indian tenure of northeastern Georgia, enclaves in western North Carolina and southern Tennessee, eastern Alabama, and the northern two thirds of Mississippi. In this 25-million acre domain lived nearly 60,000 Cherokees, Creeks, Choctaws and Chickasaws." The Jacksonians invoked alleged higher laws of nature to justify removal. Thomas Benton [Senator from Missouri] spoke of a national imperative that the land be turned over to those who would use it "according to the intentions

Excerpt from *Jacksonian America: Society, Personality and Politics* by Edward Pessen. Copyright © 1969 and 1978 by The Dorsey Press. Reprinted with permission by Wadsworth Publishing Company.

of the creator." Jackson himself referred to the march of progress and civilization, whose American manifestation was "studded with cities, towns and prosperous farms, embellished with all the improvements which art can devise or industry execute, occupied by more than 12 million happy people and filled with all the blessings of liberty, civilization and religion," before which "forests . . . ranged by a few thousand savages" must give ground.

In Miss Young's laconic words, "such a rationalization had one serious weakness as an instrument of policy. The farmer's right of eminent domain over the lands of the savage could be asserted consistently only so long as tribes involved were 'savage.' The southwestern tribes, however, were agriculturists as well as hunters." The obvious proof that the federal government did not take seriously its own justification for removal is the disinterest it displayed in the evidence that Cherokees, Choctaws, and Chickasaws were in fact skilled in the arts of civilization. That "the people it now hoped to displace could by no stretch of dialectic be classed as mere wandering savages," would have given pause to men who sincerely believed in their own professions that it was the Indians' alleged savagery that primarily justified their removal. There is every reason to think that the Jacksonians were fully aware that their doctrine—specious and arrogant at best, with its implication that a people living a "superior" life had the right to take the lands of "inferiors"—was all the more specious because its assumption of Indian savagery was untrue.

White speculators and politicians in the southern states had little interest in *theories* of removal. They wanted removal, however rationalized, and were not fastidious as to the means used to accomplish it. No issue was more important, certainly not in Mississippi, where "to most residents . . . the most salient event of 1833 concerned neither the tariff nor nullification," but the fact that that autumn "the first public auctions of the Choctaw lands were held." According to Edwin Miles, Mississippians were so "grateful to Old Hickory [i.e. Andrew Jackson] for making these lands available to them [that] . . . they were inclined to disregard differences of opinion that he might entertain on issues of less importance." That happy day came to pass in Mississippi and elsewhere only because of the total cooperation shown by the Jackson administration in helping the southern states separate the tribes from their lands. The federal government had to display tact, cunning, guile, cajolery, and more than a hint of coercion. That it proved more than equal to the task was due in no small measure to Andrew Jackson's dedication to it. His performance was not that of responsible government official deferring to the will of constituents but rather that of a zealot who fully shared their biases and rapacity.

Before Jackson became President he had urged that the tribes not be treated as sovereign nations, and when he assumed the highest office he continued to feel that Indians were subjects of the United States, mere hunters who occupied land under its sufferance. A major difference between Jacksonian Indian policy and that of his predecessors lay in this fact. From Jefferson through John Quincy Adams, while national administrations had *desired* the removal of the southwestern tribes and countenanced threats and unlovely inducements to accomplish it, they had continued to treat the tribes "as more or less sovereign nations and to respect their right to remain on their own lands." And where Secretary of War Calhoun, for example, had hoped to accomplish Choctaw removal by "educating" the Indians to see the need for it, Jackson relied on more forceful means certain to work more quickly. In his first inaugural message he promised Indians a humane, just, and liberal policy, based on respect for Indian "rights and wants." A little more than one year later, Secretary of War Eaton induced the highly civilized Choctaws to sign a treaty removing them from their ancient homeland in Mississippi. Eaton succeeded through the use of hypocrisy, bribes, lies, suppression of critics, and intimidation, in securing approval of a treaty that, according to Colonel George Gaines who was present during the negotiations, was "despised by most of the Indians."

Jackson bypassed William Wirt for John Berrien as Attorney-General because he distrusted Wirt on Indian removal. When Wirt subsequently became the lawyer for the Cherokees, Jackson denounced the "wicked" man. He removed the knowledgeable Thomas L. McKenney as head of the Bureau of Indian Affairs because McKenney, as a "warm friend of the Indians," had to be replaced by someone of sounder feelings. (Among McKenney's other flaws, he had been too close to Calhoun and served the Adams Administration too well.) Jackson regarded the practice of negotiating treaties with Indian tribes as an "absurdity" and a "farce." On more than one occasion the President reverted to the practice of his Indian-fighting days, personally dealing with "reluctant tribes" in order to bring about their acquiescence to an agreement detrimental to their interests. He hated [politician William H.] Crawford in part because the latter had exposed the inequity and fraud in the Creek Treaty Jackson had negotiated in 1814. In the judgment of one modern student, Jackson, prior to the Supreme Court decision in the case of *Cherokee Nation* v. *Georgia* in 1831, "threatened the Supreme Court with a refusal to enforce its decree." The Court in that case sidestepped the issue of the constitutionality of Georgia's Indian laws. But when the following year the Court ruled, in *Worcester* v. *Georgia* that the State of Georgia had no right to extend its laws over the Cherokee nation, the Indian tribes being "domestic dependent nations," with limits defined by treaty, the President refused to enforce this decision. Unfortunately for the Cherokee, some of their best friends in Congress and on the high court now urged them to sign a removal treaty. . . .

The actual procedures used to accomplish the desired end were numerous, ingenious, and effective. Simple force was eschewed, "forbidden by custom, by conscience, and by fear that the administration's opponents would exploit religious sentiment which cherished the rights of the red man." But as Miss Young points out, "within the confines of legality and the formulas of voluntarism it was still possible to acquire the much coveted domain of the civilized tribes." A kind of squeeze was directed against the Indians. On the one hand state governments refused to recognize tribal laws or federally assured rights, bringing Indians under state laws which dealt with them as individuals. Only Indians who chose to become citizens could hold on to what their skill and industry enabled them to accumulate and develop. The federal government continued the earlier policy, begun late in the Madison Administration, of offering reservations or allotments to individual Indians who cultivated their lands and wished to become citizens, while encouraging the trans-Mississippi migration of the others. When a Congressional measure appropriating $500,000 and authorizing the President to negotiate removal treaties with all the eastern tribes was under debate in 1830, even administration critics agreed that the "Indian's moral right to keep his land depended on his actual cultivation of it." In some cases the removal treaties were negotiated after sufficient pressure had been exercised by private individuals or government officials, who resorted to physical threats as well as to more subtle

151

means. Jacksonian emissaries carried money and liquor in ample quantities.

In the case of the Creeks, who refused to agree to emigration, their chiefs were persuaded in March, 1832, to sign an allotment treaty. Ostensibly depriving the tribe of none of its Alabama territories, in fact by allotting most acreage to heads of families, it not only reduced the tribal estate but it made the individual owners prey to thieves and corruptionists in civil or public garb, who took advantage of Indian innocence and ignorance concerning property values and disposal. Advised that speculators were defrauding the Indians, among other ways by simply "borrowing" back the money they had paid for individual allotments without any intention of paying back the "loans," Secretary of War Lewis Cass enunciated the interesting doctrine that the War Department had no authority to circumscribe the Indian's right to be defrauded.

The deception practiced by the government in the Creek Treaty may have been as much self-deception as anything else. Certainly many federal agents were honest. Nor was the government's objective profit through fraud. From the Indians' viewpoint however, as from that of moralistic critics, the federal purpose was even more terrible. Mere corruptionists could have been bargained with; zealous believers in their own superiority and their God-given right to Indian lands, could not. In any case, "the disposal of Creek reserves exhibited an ironic contrast between the ostensible purposes of the allotment policy and its actual operation. Instead of giving the tribesmen a more secure title to their individual holdings, the allotment of their lands became an entering wedge for those who would drive them from their eastern domain."

. . . Probably the worst treatment of all was reserved for the Cherokees. They had balked at moving to a region their own surveyors described as "nothing but mountains and [a] huge bed of rocks." In 1838 General Winfield Scott began their systematic removal, more than 4,000 out of 15,000 of them dying, according to one estimate, in the course of "the Trail of Tears." One judgment is that "at their worst the forced migrations approached the horrors created by the Nazi handling of subject peoples."

Men like Edward Everett and [Ralph Waldo] Emerson [nineteenth-century writers] recoiled in horror, the New England press was sickened at the reproach to our national character in this "abhorrent business." But not Andrew Jackson. In his last message to Congress, he complimented the states on the removal of "the evil" that had retarded their development. He also expressed pleasure that "this unhappy race—. . . the original dwellers in our land—are now placed in a situation where we may well hope that they will share in the blessings of civilization and be saved from the degradation and destruction to which they were rapidly hastening while they remained in the states." This bewildering combination of sentiments seemed to mean, as John W. Ward has observed, that "America would save the Indians for civilization by rescuing them from civilization." Jackson's certainty that "the philanthropist will rejoice that the remnant of that ill-fated race has at length been placed beyond the reach of injury or oppression," may have been warranted although one suspects that this monument of self-deception might have been chagrined to discover philanthropy's estimate as to the true source of Indian oppression.

Henry Clay and other Whigs opposed particular removal treaties on constitutional and humanitarian grounds. And yet the Whig party position should not be misconstrued. For, as Satz observes, while the Whigs "found it expedient to condemn the Jacksonian removal policy when they were struggling to gain political control of the government," once in power they followed the very same policy. The Harrison and Tyler administration did not allow "Indians still east of the Mississippi River to remain there." In 1842 it was to a Whig Administration that the War Department reported that in the North as in the South, there was no more Indian land "east of the Mississippi, remaining unceded, to be desired by us." As was true too of the "spoils system," a policy begun by the one major party was continued by the other. Individual Whigs may have been more sensitive than their Democratic counterparts but the policies of their parties were at times remarkably similar.

Questions

1. *What kinds of evidence and arguments do Prucha and Pessen use to make their cases? Which do you think is the most convincing? Why?*
2. *Jackson's Indian policy has been characterized as wrong, ill-conceived and poorly carried out, inevitable, or tragic. If any of these accusations are true, what, according to these writers, explains the shortcomings of the policy?*
3. *Why was Jackson's policy successful? Why were Native American efforts to resist that policy unsuccessful?*

THE CONTEMPORARY DEBATE

Although a number of historians have used the word "inevitable" to describe the final victory of Jackson's removal policy, it is important to realize that Indian removal was vigorously debated at the time. For over a decade, the white citizens of the United States, the spokespeople for the federal and state governments, and Native Americans bitterly contested every aspect of state and national action regarding removal and every encroachment of whites into territory claimed by Native Americans. The issues involved in this extended debate—among them the status of Native American nations in the polity of the United States; the constitutional division of power between states and the federal government; the binding nature of treaties between the colonies, states, federal government and Native American peoples; and the moral and ethical nature of removal—remain a focus for often emotional, even violent, disagreement. We who live in the United States of America have not escaped or outlived the consequences of what happened to the Cherokee and their kin. The following selections provide an introduction to the range of opinions, the depth of emotion, and the breadth of significance for this country occasioned by Indian removal in the nineteenth century.

A Benevolent Policy

In his second annual message to Congress, on 6 December 1830, Andrew Jackson explained and defended his policy of Indian removal. Excerpted from A Compilation of the Messages and Papers of the Presidents, 1789–1897, *ed. James D. Richardson (Washington, 1896), 2:519–23.*

It gives me pleasure to announce to Congress that the benevolent policy of the Government, steadily pursued for nearly thirty years, in relation to the removal of the Indians beyond the white settlements is approaching to a happy consummation. Two important tribes have accepted the provision made for their removal at the last session of Congress, and it is believed that their example will induce the remaining tribes also to seek the same obvious advantages.

The consequences of a speedy removal will be important to the United States, to individual States, and to the Indians themselves. The pecuniary advantages which it promises to the Government are the least of its recommendations. It puts an end to all possible danger of collision between the authorities of the General and State Governments on account of the Indians. It will place a dense and civilized population in large tracts of country now occupied by a few savage hunters. By opening the whole territory between Tennessee on the north and Louisiana on the south to the settlement of the whites it will incalculably strengthen the southwestern frontier and render the adjacent States strong enough to repel future invasions without remote aid. It will relieve the whole State of Mississippi and the western part of Alabama of Indian occupancy, and enable those States to advance rapidly in population, wealth, and power. It will separate the Indians from immediate contact with settlements of whites; free them from the power of the States; enable them to pursue happiness in their own way and under their own rude institutions; will retard the progress of decay, which is lessening their numbers, and perhaps cause them gradually, under the protection of the Government and through the influence of good counsels, to cast off their savage habits and become an interesting, civilized, and Christian community. These consequences, some of them so certain and the rest so probable, make the complete execution of the plan sanctioned by Congress at their last session an object of much solicitude.

Toward the aborigines of the country no one can indulge a more friendly feeling than myself, or would go further in attempting to reclaim them from their wandering habits and make them a happy, prosperous people. I have endeavored to impress upon them my own solemn convictions of the duties and powers of the General Government in relation to the State authorities. For the justice of the laws passed by the States within the scope of their reserved powers they are not responsible to this Government. As individuals we may entertain and express our opinions of their acts, but as a Government we have as little right to control them as we have to prescribe laws for other nations.

With a full understanding of the subject, the Choctaw and the Chickasaw tribes have with great unanimity determined to avail themselves of the liberal offers presented by the act of Congress, and have agreed to remove beyond the Mississippi River. Treaties have been made with them, which in due season will be submitted for consideration. In negotiating these treaties they were made to understand their true condition, and they have preferred maintaining their independence in the Western forests to submitting to the laws of the States in which they now reside. These treaties, being probably the last which will ever be made with them, are characterized by great liberality on the part of the Government. They give the Indians a liberal sum in consideration of their removal, and comfortable subsistence on their arrival at their new homes. If it be their real interest to maintain a separate existence, they will there be at liberty to do so without the inconveniences and vexations to which they would unavoidably have been subject in Alabama and Mississippi.

Humanity has often wept over the fate of the aborigines of this country, and Philanthropy has been long busily employed in devising means to avert it, but its progress has never for a moment been arrested, and one by one have many powerful tribes disappeared from the earth. To follow to the tomb the last of his race and to tread on the graves of extinct nations excite melancholy reflections. But true philanthropy reconciles the mind to these vicissitudes as it does to the extinction of one generation to make room for another. In the monuments and fortresses of an unknown people, spread over the extensive regions of the West, we behold the memorials of a once powerful race, which was exterminated or has disappeared to make room for the existing savage tribes. Nor is there anything in this which, upon a comprehensive view of the general interests of the human race, is to be regretted. Philanthropy could not wish to see this continent restored to the condition in which it was found by our forefathers. What good man would prefer a country covered with forests and ranged by a few thousand savages to our extensive Republic, studded with cities, towns, and prosperous farms, embellished with all the improvements which art can devise or industry execute, occupied by more than 12,000,000 happy people, and filled with all the blessings of liberty, civilization, and religion?

The present policy of the Government is but a continuation of the same progressive change by a milder process. The tribes which occupied the countries now constituting the Eastern States were annihilated or have melted away to make room for the whites. The waves of population and civilization are rolling to the westward, and we now propose to acquire the countries occupied by the red men of the South and West by a fair exchange, and, at the expense of the United States, to send them to a land where their existence may be prolonged and perhaps made perpetual. Doubtless it will be painful to leave the graves of their fathers; but what do they more than our ancestors did or than our children are now doing? To better their condition in an unknown land our forefathers left all that was dear in earthly objects. Our children by thousands yearly leave the land of their birth to seek new homes in distant regions. Does Humanity weep at these painful separations from everything, animate and inanimate, with which the young heart has become entwined? Far from it. It is rather a source of joy that our country affords scope where our young population may range unconstrained in body or in mind, developing the power and faculties of man in their highest perfection. These remove hundreds and almost thousands of miles at their own expense, purchase the lands they occupy, and support themselves at their new homes from the moment of their arrival. Can it be cruel in this Government when, by events which it can not control, the Indian is made discontented in his ancient home to purchase his lands, to give him a new and extensive territory, to pay the expense of his removal, and support him a year in his new abode? How many thousands of our own people would gladly embrace the opportunity of removing to the West on such conditions! If the offers made to the Indians were extended to them, they would be hailed with gratitude and joy.

And is it supposed that the wandering savage has a stronger attachment to his home than the settled, civilized Christian? Is it more afflicting to him to leave the graves of his fathers than it is to our brothers and children? Rightly considered, the policy of the General Government toward the red man is not only liberal, but generous. He is unwilling to submit to the laws of the States and mingle with their population. To save him from this alternative, or perhaps utter annihilation, the General Government kindly offers him a new home, and proposes to pay the whole expense of his removal and settlement. . . .

It is, therefore, a duty which this Government owes to the new States to extinguish as soon as possible the Indian title to all lands which Congress themselves have included within their limits. When this is done the duties of the General Government in relation to the States and the Indians within their limits are at an end. The Indians may leave the State or not, as they choose. The purchase of their lands does not alter in the least their personal relations with the State government. No act of the General Government has ever been deemed necessary to give the States jurisdiction over the persons of the Indians. That they possess by virtue of their sovereign power within their own limits in as full a manner before as after the purchase of the Indian lands; nor can this Government add to or diminish it.

May we not hope, therefore, that all good citizens, and none more zealously than those who think the Indians oppressed by subjection to the laws of the States, will unite in attempting to open the eyes of those children of the forest to their true condition, and by a speedy removal to relieve them from all the evils, real or imaginary, present or prospective, with which they may be supposed to be threatened.

A Divisive Policy

The Congress of the United States provided a national forum for debate over the Indian Removal Bill of 1830. Here follows an excerpt from written records of debate in the House of Representatives, presenting the views of Wilson Lumpkin, a Democratic Representative from Georgia and an advocate of removal. The following material is taken from The American Indian and the United States: A Documentary History, *ed. Wilcomb E. Washburn (New York, 1973), 2:1071, 1080–81.*

I differ with my friend from Tennessee [Mr. Bell] in regard to Indian civilization. I entertain no doubt that a remnant of these people may be entirely reclaimed from their native savage habits, and be brought to enter into the full enjoyment of all the blessings of civilized society. It appears to me, we have too many instances of individual improvement amongst the various native tribes of America, to hesitate any longer in determining whether the Indians are susceptible of civilization. Use the proper means, and success will crown your efforts. The means hitherto resorted to by the Government, as well as by individuals, to improve the condition of the Indians, must, from the present state of things, very soon be withheld from these unfortunate people, if they remain in their present abodes; for they will every day be brought into closer contact and conflict with the white population, and this circumstance will diminish the spirit of benevolence and philanthropy towards them which now exists. . . .

But, sir, upon this subject, this Government has been wanting in good faith to Georgia. It has, by its own acts and policy, forced the Indians to remain in Georgia, by the purchase of their lands in the adjoining States, and by holding out to the Indians strong inducements to remain where they are; by the expenditure of vast sums of money, spent in changing the habit of the savage for those of civilized life. All this was in itself right and proper; it has my hearty approbation; but it should not have been done at the expense of Georgia. The Government, long after it was bound to extinguish the title of the Indians to all the lands in Georgia, has actually forced the Cherokees from their lands in other States, settled them upon Georgia lands, and aided in furnishing the means to create the Cherokee aristocracy.

Sir, I blame not the Indians; I commiserate their case. I have considerable acquaintance with the Cherokees, and amongst them I have seen much to admire. To me, they are in many respects an interesting people. If the wicked influence of designing men, veiled in the garb of philanthropy and christian benevolence, should excite the Cherokees to a course that will end in their speedy destruction, I now call upon this Congress, and the whole American people, not to charge the Georgians with this sin; but let it be remembered that it is the fruit of cant and fanaticism, emanating from the land of steady habits, from the boasted progeny of the pilgrims and puritans.

Sir, my State stands charged before this House, before the nation, and before the whole world, with cruelty and oppression towards the Indians. I deny the charge, and demand proof from those who make it.

Excerpt from a speech made in Congress regarding the Indian Removal Bill of 1830, by Wilson Lumpkin, as it appeared in *The American Indian and the United States: A Documentary History*, Volume II, Wilcomb E. Washburn, editor, 1973. Copyright © 1973 by Random House, Inc.

A Breakdown of National Law?

Worcester v. Georgia (1832)
In the Worcester v. Georgia (1832) landmark decision the Supreme Court of the United States and Chief Justice John Marshall found that the state of Georgia had acted unconstitutionally in its assertion of control over Cherokee land. Georgia ignored the court's decision; Andrew Jackson ignored it as well. Taken from Reports of Decisions in the Supreme Court of the United States, *ed. B. R. Curtis (Boston, 1855), 10: 214, 240, 242–44.*

A return to a writ of error from this court to a state court, certified by the clerk of the court which pronounced the judgment, and to which the writ is addressed, and authenticated by the seal of the court, is in conformity to law, and brings the record regularly before this court.

The law of Georgia, which subjected to punishment all white persons residing within the limits of the Cherokee nation, and authorized their arrest within those limits, and their forcible removal therefrom, and their trial in a court of the State, was repugnant to the constitution, treaties, and laws of the United States, and so void; and a judgment against the plaintiff in error, under color of that law, was reversed by this court, under the 25th section of the Judiciary Act, (1 Stats. at Large, 85.)

The relations between the Indian tribes and the United States examined. . . .

From the commencement of our government, congress has passed acts to regulate trade and intercourse with the Indians; which treat them as nations, respect their rights, and manifest a firm purpose to afford that protection which treaties stipulate. All these acts, and especially that of 1802, which is still in force, manifestly consider the several Indian nations as distinct political communities, having territorial boundaries, within which their

---

"Worcester v. The State of Georgia," (1832) excerpted from *Reports of Decisions in the Supreme Court of the United States,* Vol. 10, published by Little Brown & Company, 1855.

authority is exclusive, and having a right to all the lands within those boundaries, which is not only acknowledged, but guaranteed by the United States.

In 1819, congress passed an act for promoting those humane designs of civilizing the neighboring Indians, which had long been cherished by the executive. It enacts, "that, for the purpose of providing against the further decline and final extinction of the Indian tribes adjoining to the frontier settlements of the United States, and for introducing among them the habits and arts of civilization, the President of the United States shall be, and he is hereby authorized, in every case where he shall judge improvement in the habits and condition of such Indians practicable, and that the means of instruction can be introduced with their own consent, to employ capable persons, of good moral character, to instruct them in the mode of agriculture suited to their situation; and for teaching their children in reading, writing, and arithmetic; and for performing such other duties as may be enjoined, according to such instructions and rules as the President may give and prescribe for the regulation of their conduct in the discharge of their duties."

This act avowedly contemplates the preservation of the Indian nations as an object sought by the United States, and proposes to effect this object by civilizing and converting them from hunters into agriculturists. Though the Cherokees had already made considerable progress in this improvement, it cannot be doubted that the general words of the act comprehend them. Their advance in the "habits and arts of civilization," rather encouraged perseverance in the laudable exertions still further to meliorate their condition. This act furnishes strong additional evidence of a settled purpose to fix the Indians in their country by giving them security at home. . . .

The Indian nations had always been considered as distinct, independent political communities, retaining their original natural rights, as the undisputed possessors of the soil, from time immemorial, with the single exception of that imposed by irresistible power, which excluded them from intercourse with any other European potentate than the first discoverer of the coast of the particular region claimed; and this was a restriction which those European potentates imposed on themselves, as well as on the Indians. The very term "nation," so generally applied to them, means "a people distinct from others." The constitution, by declaring treaties already made, as well as those to be made, to be the supreme law of the land, has adopted and sanctioned the previous treaties with the Indian nations, and consequently admits their rank among those powers who are capable of making treaties. The words "treaty" and "nation" are words of our own language, selected in our diplomatic and legislative proceedings, by ourselves, having each a definite and well understood meaning. We have applied them to Indians, as we have applied them to the other nations of the earth. They are applied to all in the same sense. . . .

The Cherokee nation, then, is a distinct community, occupying its own territory, with boundaries accurately described, in which the laws of Georgia can have no force, and which the citizens of Georgia have no right to enter, but with the assent of the Cherokees themselves, or in conformity with treaties and with the acts of congress. The whole intercourse between the United States and this nation is, by our constitution and laws, vested in the government of the United States. . . .

. . . If the review which has been taken be correct, and we think it is, the acts of Georgia are repugnant to the constitution, laws, and treaties of the United States.

They interfere forcibly with the relations established between the United States and the Cherokee nation, the regulation of which, according to the settled principles of our constitution, are committed exclusively to the government of the Union.

They are in direct hostility with treaties, repeated in a succession of years, which mark out the boundary that separates the Cherokee country from Georgia, guarantee to them all the land within their boundary, solemnly pledge the faith of the United States to restrain their citizens from trespassing on it, and recognize the preëxisting power of the nation to govern itself.

They are in equal hostility with the acts of congress for regulating this intercourse, and giving effect to the treaties.

163

Tragic Decision

Elias Boudinot was a "civilized" Cherokee who, in terms of education, religion, and aspirations, had come far along the white man's path; or so he believed. He agonized over removal, but finally supported it as a last, desperate means of maintaining the existence of his people. His stand cost him his life. The following selection is from editorials written by Boudinot as editor of the Cherokee Phoenix, *reprinted in* Cherokee Editor: The Writings of Elias Boudinot, *ed. Theda Perdue (Knoxville, 1983), 108–9, 142–43.*

[17 June 1829]

From the documents which we this day lay before our readers, there is not a doubt of the kind of policy, which the present administration of the General Government intends to pursue relative to the Indians. President Jackson has, as a neighboring editor remarks, "recognized the doctrine contended for by Georgia in its full extent." It is to be regretted that we were not undeceived long ago, while we were hunters and in our savage state. It appears now from the communication of the Secretary of War to the Cherokee Delegation, that the illustrious Washington, Jefferson, Madison and Monroe were only tantalizing us, when they encouraged us in the pursuit of agriculture and Government, and when they afforded us the protection of the United States, by which we have been preserved to this present time as a nation. Why were we not told long ago, that we could not be permitted to establish a government within the limits of any state? Then we could have borne disappointment much easier than now. The pretext for Georgia to extend her jurisdiction over the Cherokees has always existed. The Cherokees have always had a government of their own. Nothing, however, was said when we were governed by savage laws, when the abominable law of retaliation carried death in our midst, when it was a lawful act to shed the blood of a person charged with witchcraft, when a brother could kill a brother with impunity, or an innocent man suffer for an offending relative. At that time it might have been a matter of charity to have extended over us the mantle of Christian laws & regulations. But how happens it now, after being fostered by the U. States, and advised

Cherokee Indians depicted along the "Trail of Tears" after expulsion from their native lands. (Painting by Robert Lindneux. Original in Wollaroc Museum, Bartesville, Oklahoma. Courtesy of Corbis-Bettmann.)

by great and good men to establish a government of regular law; when the aid and protection of the General Government have been pledged to us; when we, as dutiful "children" of the President, have followed his instructions and advice, and have established for ourselves a government of regular law; when everything looks so promising around us, that a storm is raised by the extension of tyrannical and unchristian laws, which threatens to blast all our rising hopes and expectations?

There is, as would naturally be supposed, a great rejoicing in Georgia. It is a time of "important news"—"gratifying intelligence"—"The Cherokee lands are to be obtained speedily." It is even reported that the Cherokees have come to the conclusion to sell, and move off to the west of the Mississippi—not so fast. We are yet at our homes, at our peaceful firesides, (except those contiguous to Sandtown, Carroll, &c.) attending to our farms and useful occupations. . . .

[12 November 1831]

. . . But alas! no sooner was it made manifest that the Cherokees were becoming strongly attached to the ways and usages of civilized life, than was aroused the opposition of those from whom better things ought to have been expected. No sooner was

165

it known that they had learned the proper use of the earth, and that they were now less likely to dispose of their lands for a mess of pottage, than they came in conflict with the cupidity and self-interest of those who ought to have been their benefactors—Then commenced a series of obstacles hard to overcome, and difficulties intended as a stumbling block, and unthought of before. The "Great Father" of the "red man" has lent his influence to encourage those difficulties. The *guardian* has deprived his *wards* of their rights—The sacred obligations of treaties and laws have been disregarded—The promises of Washington and Jefferson have not been fulfilled. The policy of the United States on Indian affairs has taken a different direction, for no other reason than that the Cherokees have so far become civilized as to appreciate a regular form of Government. They are now deprived of rights they once enjoyed—A neighboring power is now permitted to extend its withering hand over them—Their own laws, intended to regulate their society, to encourage virtue and to suppress vice, must now be abolished, and civilized acts, passed for the purpose of expelling them, must be substituted.—Their intelligent citizens who have been instructed through the means employed by former administrations, and through the efforts of benevolent societies, must be abused and insulted, represented as avaricious, feeding upon the poverty of the common Indians—the hostility of all those who want the Indian lands must be directed against them. That the Cherokees may be kept in ignorance, teachers who had settled among them by the approbation of the Government, for the best of all purposes, have been compelled to leave them by reason of laws unbecoming any civilized nation—Ministers of the Gospel, who might have, at this day of trial, administered to them the consolations of Religion, have been arrested, chained, dragged away before their eyes, tried as felons, and finally immured in prison with thieves and robbers.

Vain Protest

A delegation of Cherokee leaders who opposed the Treaty of New Echota protested to Congress, but in vain. The following excerpt from the "Memorial and Protest of the Cherokee Nation" of 22 June 1836 appears in House Documents, 24th Cong., 1st sess., *vol. 7, Doc. no. 286, CIS US Serial no. 292, microprint, 2–5.*

If it be said that the Cherokees have lost their national character and political existence, as a nation or tribe, by State legislation, then the President and Senate can make no treaty with them; but if they have not, then no treaty can be made for them, binding, without and against their will. Such is the fact, in reference to the instrument intered into at New Echota, in December last. If treaties are to be thus made and enforced, deceptive to the Indians and to the world, purporting to be a contract, when, in truth, wanting the assent of one of the pretended parties, what security would there be for any nation or tribe to retain confidence in the United States? If interest or policy require that the Cherokees be removed, without their consent, from their lands, surely the President and Senate have no constitutional power to accomplish that object. They cannot do it under the power to make treaties, which are contracts, not rules prescribed by a superior, and therefore binding only by the assent of the parties. In the present instance, the assent of the Cherokee nation has not been given, but expressly denied. The President and Senate cannot do it under the power to regulate commerce with the Indian tribes, or intercourse with them, because that belongs to Congress, and so declared by the President, in his message to the Senate of February 22, 1831, relative to the execution of the act to regulate trade and intercourse with the Indian tribes, &c. passed 30th of March, 1802. They cannot do it under any subsisting treaty stipulation with the Cherokee nation. Nor does the peculiar situation of the Cherokees, in reference to the States their necessities and distresses, confer any power upon the President and Senate to alienate their legal rights, or to prescribe the manner and time of their removal.

Without a decision of what ought to be done, under existing circumstances, the question recurs, is the instrument under consideration a contract between the United States and the Cherokee nation? It so purports upon its face, and that falsely. Is that statement so sacred and conclusive that the Cherokee people cannot be heard to deny the fact? They have denied it under their own

---

Excerpt from the "Memorial and Protest of the Cherokee Nation: Memorial of the Cherokee Representatives," reprinted from House Reports, *24th Cong., 1st sess.,* June 22, 1836, Vol. 7, No. 286.

signatures, as the documents herein before referred to will show, and protested against the acts of the unauthorized few, who have arrogated to themselves the right to speak for the nation. The Cherokees have said they will not be bound thereby. The documents submitted to the Senate show, that when the vote was taken upon considering the propositions of the commissioner, there were but seventy-nine for so doing. Then it comes to this: could this small number of persons attending the New Echota meeting, acting in their individual capacity, dispose of the rights and interests of the Cherokee nation, or by any instrument they might sign, confer such power upon the President and Senate?

If the United States are to act as the guardian of the Cherokees, and to treat them as incapable of managing their own affairs, and blind to their true interests, yet this would not furnish power or authority to the President and Senate, as the treaty making power to prescribe the rule for managing their affairs. It may afford a pretence for the legislation of Congress, but none for the ratification of an instrument as a treaty made by a small faction against the protest of the Cherokee people.

That the Cherokees are a distinct people, sovereign to some extent, have a separate political existence as a society, or body politic, and a capability of being contracted with in a national capacity, stands admitted by the uniform practice of the United States from 1785, down to the present day. With them have treaties been made through their chiefs, and distinguished men in primary assemblies, as also with their constituted agents or representatives. That they have not the right to manage their own internal affairs, and to regulate, by treaty, their intercourse with other nations, is a doctrine of modern date. In 1793, Mr. Jefferson said, "I consider our right of pre-emption of the Indian lands, not as amounting to any dominion, or jurisdiction, or paramountship whatever, but merely in the nature of a remainder, after the extinguishment of a present right, which gives us no present right whatever, but of preventing other nations from taking possession, and so defeating our expectancy. That the Indians *have the full, undivided, and independent sovereignty as long as they choose to keep it, and that this may be forever.*" This opinion was recognised and practised upon, by the Government of the United States, through several successive administrations, also recognised by the Supreme Court of the United States, and the several States, when the question has arisen. It has not been the opinion only of jurists, but of politicians, as may be seen from various reports of Secretaries of War—beginning with Gen. Knox, also the correspondence between the British and American ministers at Ghent in the year 1814. If the Cherokees have power to judge of their own interests, and to make treaties, which, it is presumed, will be denied by none, then to make a contract valid, the assent of a majority must be had, expressed by themselves or through their representatives, and the President and Senate have no power to say what their will shall be, for from the laws of nations we learn that "though a nation be obliged to promote, as far as lies in its power, the perfection of others, it is not entitled forcibly to obtrude these good offices on them." Such an attempt would be to violate their natural liberty. Those ambitious Europeans who attacked the American nations, and subjected them to their insatiable avidity of dominion, an order, as they pretended, for civilizing them, and causing them to be instructed in the true religion, (as in the present instance to preserve the Cherokees as a distinct people,) these usurpers grounded themselves on a pretence equally unjust and ridiculous." It is the expressed wish of the Government of the United States to remove the Cherokees to a place west of the Mississippi. That wish is said to be founded in humanity to the Indians. To make their situation more comfortable, and to preserve them as a distinct people. Let facts show how this *benevolent* design has been prosecuted, and how faithful to the spirit and letter has the promise of the President of the United States to the Cherokees been fulfilled—that *"those who remain may be assured of our patronage, our aid, and good neighborhood."* The delegation are not deceived by empty professions, and fear their race is to be destroyed by the mercenary policy of the present day, and their lands wrested from them by physical force; as proof, they will refer to the preamble of an act of the General Assembly of Georgia, in reference to the Cherokees, passed the 2d of December, 1835, where it is said, "from a knowledge of the Indian character, and from the present feelings of these Indians, it is confidently believed, that the right of occupancy of the lands in their possession should be withdrawn, *that it would be a strong inducement to them to treat with the General Government, and consent to a removal to the west;* and whereas, the present Legislature openly avow that their primary object in the measures intended to be pursued *are founded on real humanity to these Indians,* and with a view, in a distant region, to perpetuate them with their old identity of character, *under the*

169

paternal care of the Government of the United States; at the same time frankly disavowing *any selfish or sinister motives towards them in their present legislation."* This is the profession. Let us turn to the practice of *humanity,* to the Cherokees, by the State of Georgia. In violation of the treaties between the United States and the Cherokee nation, that State passed a law requiring all white men, residing in that part of the Cherokee country, in her limits, to take an oath of allegiance to the State of Georgia. For a violation of this law, some of the ministers of Christ, missionaries among the Cherokees, were tried, convicted, and sentenced to hard labor in the penitentiary. Their case may be seen by reference to the records of the Supreme Court of the United States.

Valuable gold mines were discovered upon Cherokee lands, within the chartered limits of Georgia, and the Cherokees commenced working them, and the Legislature of that State interfered by passing an act, making it penal for an Indian to dig for gold within Georgia, no doubt *"frankly disavowing any selfish or sinister motives towards them."* Under this law many Cherokees were arrested, tried, imprisoned, and otherwise abused. Some were even shot in attempting to avoid an arrest; yet the Cherokee people used no violence, but humbly petitioned the Government of the United States for a fulfilment of treaty engagements, to protect them, which was not done, and the answer given that the United States could not interfere. Georgia discovered she was not to be obstructed in carrying out her measures, *"founded on real humanity to these Indians,"* she passed an act directing the Indian country to be surveyed into districts. This excited some alarm, but the Cherokees were quieted with the assurance it would do no harm to survey the country. Another act was shortly after passed, to lay off the country into lots. As yet there was no authority to take possession, but it was not long before a law was made, authorizing a lottery for the lands laid off into lots. In this act the Indians were secured in possession of all the lots touched by their improvements, and the balance of the country allowed to be occupied by white men. This was a direct violation of the 5th article of the treaty of the 27th of February, 1819. The Cherokees made no resistance, still petitioned the United States for protection, and received the same answer that the President could not interpose.

Questions

1. *What, according to his second annual message to Congress, is Jackson's Indian policy? If you were a Cherokee—or Creek, Choctaw, Seminole—why should you trust, or mistrust, Jackson's message?*
2. *What were the important issues involved in the Supreme Court decision in Worcester v. Georgia and in the congressional debates over the Indian Removal Act of 1830?*
3. *If you were a Cherokee, would you have supported the anti- or pro-removal position among the Cherokee people? Why?*

FURTHER READING

The Great Father: The United States Government and the American Indians, *vol. 1 (Lincoln, Nebraska, 1984), by Francis Paul Prucha, contains the latest full treatment of Jackson's Indian policy by this prolific and generally pro-Jackson scholar. Useful for its detailed coverage is Ronald N.* Satz, American Indian Policy in the Jacksonian Era *(Lincoln, Nebraska, 1975). An excellent bibliography covering the removal period is in Thurman Wilkins,* Cherokee Tragedy: The Story of the Ridge Family and the Decimation of a People. *(New York, 1970). For the many books that are highly critical of Jackson's removal policy see the bibliography in Wilkins. William G. McLoughlin, in* Champions of the Cherokees: Evan and John B. Jones *(Princeton, 1990), considers the Cherokee as heroic in their resistance to a terrible injustice.* Cherokee Removal: Before and After, *edited by William L. Anderson (Athens, Georgia, 1991), has several useful articles on various facets of removal and may be used to supplement the bibliographical information in Wilkins. Jackson's role in removal is treated at length by Robert V. Remini in his laudatory biography,* Andrew Jackson and the Course of American Freedom, 1822–1832, *vol. 2 (New York, 1977). An excellent collection of documents on removal is in* The New American State Papers: Indian Affairs, *vol. 9,* Southeast *(Wilmington, Delaware, 1972).*

Nat Turner and Slave Resistance

Merton L. Dillon

INTRODUCTION

Africans, who were forcefully brought to North America, did not willingly accept enslavement. They used every opportunity to prove to their "owners" that, even though the law considered them slaves, they still were human beings with wills of their own and that there were limits beyond which they would not allow themselves to be pushed. Most slaveowners accepted these limits as the price they had to pay for getting an acceptable amount of work from their labor force and for maintaining order on the plantation. Most slaves, in turn, learned that there also were limits to the degree of resistance that their owners—or the state—would tolerate. Outright defiance of authority or overt rebellion risked such severe punishment that only the bravest or most aggrieved dared undertake them. Thus life on every plantation was marked by tension between the slaves, who were trying to gain advantage in order to create a tolerable life for themselves, and the owners and overseers, who were trying to maintain strict control in order to run a profitable plantation. On rare occasions, this uneasy accommodation broke down, and violence, even revolt, was the result.

Slaves in the West Indies and in South America, like slaves in ancient Greece and Rome, carried out extensive uprisings. In contrast, only three such outbreaks occurred in North America: the Stono revolt in South Carolina (1739), the revolt in Louisiana (1811), and Nat Turner's revolt in Virginia (1831). Of these, Nat Turner's was the costliest in human life, for both races, and the most momentous in its impact on official policy and public opinion. It was also the most difficult for the white population to understand, first, because its leader apparently had been subjected to no unusually cruel treatment and, second, because the revolt was characterized by a messianic quality foreign to the experience of many, if not most, white people at the time.

176

PLACING NAT TURNER'S REVOLT IN CONTEXT

In order to understand a slave revolt such as that led by Nat Turner in 1831, we need to examine the specific events that occurred and to place those events in a larger historical context. The following selections are intended to help you do that.

Nat Turner's Revolt, August 1831

This essay explains the events and influences that led Nat Turner, an otherwise obscure slave, to plan his revolt. Little is known about Turner's life except for the information that he himself disclosed to Thomas Gray in an interview conducted in his prison cell shortly before he was hanged. All accounts, including this one, of the background of the revolt are based on that source. Modern readers will ask themselves, as contemporaries did, whether mistreatment alone accounted for Nat Turner's actions or whether other influences were at work in the revolt. If, as some suspected, his actions resulted from unavoidable aspects of slavery, then others might be expected to follow the same destructive course. Abridged from R. Jackson Wilson et al., The Pursuit of Liberty: A History of the American People *(Glenview, Illinois, 1996), 3d ed., 1:424–439.*

The voice of the spirit had told him the sign would appear in the sky. Now, as Nat Turner looked at the sun on the morning of Saturday, August 13, 1831, he knew this was the signal he had been waiting for. It was a strange phenomenon, one that many people on the east coast of the United States were noticing that day, even though it did not mean to them what it meant to Nat Turner as he worked in the fields of Southampton County, Virginia. First, the sun grew dim in the cloudless sky. Then it began to change colors—turning green, then blue, finally almost white. By the afternoon the sun was looking almost like a silvery mirror. Then, as Nat stared in fascination, on the solar surface appeared a single black spot.

Nat Turner thought he knew exactly what it all meant. The sun had become a mirror of what was about to happen on the earth. Just as a black spot had passed across the sun, so black men would rise up and move across the earth. This was the signal Nat had been waiting for—the signal the spirit had promised him. He knew the time for delay had passed. The massacre must begin. The white people of Southampton County must be killed or put to flight.

Nine days later, fifty-five whites lay slaughtered—forty-two of them women and children. Most were hacked to death with axes. Many had been decapitated. Then vengeful whites struck back. The luckier blacks were captured alive and held for trial; others were simply killed outright by enraged and terrified white men. It was by far the bloodiest uprising in the long history of American slavery. Nat Turner himself managed to evade capture for more than two months, far longer than any of his fellow conspirators. He was finally taken in late October, duly tried and convicted, and publicly hanged on November 11, 1831. . . .

Nat was about thirty years old at the time of the massacre. Even in his earliest years, though, he had felt himself to be no ordinary slave but someone who was marked for greatness—or, as he put it, "called to superior righteousness." Nat had taught himself how to read—his parents were both illiterate—and he seemed to "remember" things that had happened before he was born. Around the farm on which his parents worked, his abilities soon became a "source of wonder." More than once Nat had overheard his mother and father tell each other that he was "intended for some great purpose.". . .

Nat Turner grew up with great expectations and . . . with a determination to make something of himself. He played with the

From *The Pursuit of Liberty: A History of the American People*, Volume I, Third Edition. Copyright © 1996 by HarperCollins College Publishers. Reprinted by permission of Addison-Wesley Educational Publishers, Inc.

Nat Turner's capture; he had managed to evade authorities for over two months.

white children around the farm. His mind was restless. He read every book that came his way. He performed experiments with everyday materials, devising things like paper and gunpowder. When he reached his teens, he decided to adopt a life of "austerity": never to touch alcohol or tobacco, and "studiously" to avoid any kind of carousing with his fellow slaves. Through this program of self-improvement and self-discipline, Nat Turner tried to show others something of his great promise and to prepare himself for the rewards it would bring.

What happened was a bitter disappointment. He hoped to be emancipated at the death of his master. But when Benjamin Turner died, ten-year-old Nat was simply handed on to Turner's son Samuel, who was just setting himself up on a nearby farm of his own. . . . For the first time it occurred to him . . . that he might have to spend his entire life as a field hand. When Nat reached his twenty-first birthday, his future had become clear: "I had arrived to man's estate," he recalled, "and was a slave." The prospect was unbearable.

In his frustration, Nat ran away from his owner. For an entire month he hid in the woods. But for some reason he changed his mind. At the end of the month he voluntarily returned, to resume the drudgery of field work.

But still he held his ambition. It was about this time that Nat discovered his hopes might be fulfilled through religion. His mind fastened on one verse he had read in the Bible: "Seek ye the kingdom of heaven, and all things shall be added to you." The words seemed to promise that if Nat would only concentrate his energy on spiritual matters—the kingdom of heaven—everything else would follow. In order to win the world, he must look to heaven. But what did that involve?

One day, while working alone behind the plow in one of his owner's fields, Nat heard a voice intoning the biblical passage he had been pondering. He was sure the voice was the spirit of God, speaking directly to him as He had spoken ages before to the biblical prophets. From that time on, the divine spirit addressed him regularly. And this confirmed Nat's belief that he was "ordained to some great purpose."

But there were worldly disappointments. About 1822, Nat's young master, Samuel Turner, died, and Nat was sold . . . to a neighboring farmer named Thomas Moore. What made this event even more unsettling was the fact that Nat had recently married a slave woman on Samuel Turner's farm, and the couple was now forced to live apart. All in all, it was a vivid display of Nat's inability to control the ordinary course of his life. But he had decided to focus his attention elsewhere. He fasted, he prayed, and he avoided contact with his fellow slaves. And through it all the spirit continued to talk to him, to reassure him that "something was about to happen that would terminate in fulfilling the great promise that had been made to me."

For the time being, though, Nat did not know just how his "great promise" would be fulfilled, and he awaited further revelations. First, the spirit gave him secret understandings of the natural world around him: "knowledge of the elements, the revolution of the planets, the operation of the tides, and changes of the seasons." In essence, Nat was resuming his old program of self-improvement in the only way still open to him—through mystic revelation instead of white men's books. . . .

One day in 1825, Nat had his first vision of racial violence:

I saw white spirits and black spirits engaged in battle, and the sun was darkened—the thunder rolled in the heavens, and blood flowed in streams. And I heard a voice saying, "Such is your luck, such you are called to see, and let it come rough or smooth, you must surely bear it."

Was race war, then, the "great purpose" for which Nat was chosen? It was a shocking prospect. Nat decided not to tell this terrible vision to his fellow slaves, and for several years he even withdrew from associating with them in order to ponder it, and to understand more fully what he was expected to bear.

Nat looked everywhere for signs—in the sky, in the woods, even in the crops he worked for his master. And slowly, with the aid of his spirit voice, he came to discover strange connections— between heaven and earth, between religious salvation and slave rebellion, between Jesus Christ and Nat Turner.

He learned that what people called the Milky Way was really "the lights of the Savior's hands, stretched forth from east to west, as they were extended on the cross on Calvary for the redemption of sinners." One day, at work in the corn field, Nat found "drops of blood on the corn, as though it were dew from Heaven." And the spirit explained to him that the Milky Way and the blood on the corn were both symbols of Christ's sacrifice:

The blood of Christ had been shed on this earth, and had ascended to heaven for the salvation of sinners, and was now returning to earth again in the form of dew.

Searching the night sky once again, Nat saw that the stars were arranged to form pictures of men in different poses. Then, walking in the woods, he discovered certain leaves that contained the very same pictures, along with mysterious hieroglyphic markings—all marked in blood. Once more the spirit explained the meaning—the ominous meaning—of this strange discovery:

As the leaves on the trees bore the impression of the figures I had seen in the heavens, it was plain to me that the Savior was about to lay down the yoke he had borne for the sins of men—and the Day of Judgment was at hand.

The signs were beginning to become clear. Nat was finally putting together the diverse elements in his life: religion, self-improvement, the promise of greatness, and the bitter, incomprehensible frustration. But what did it all mean for Nat himself? What was his personal role in the tremendous mystery he was coming to unravel? Finally, the answer to that question began to emerge. On May 12, 1828—he would always recall the exact date—Nat heard "a loud noise in the heavens." Then, in fateful language, the spirit spoke again:

> The serpent was loosened [let loose], and Christ had laid down the yoke he had borne for the sins of man, and *I should take it on, and fight against the serpent—for the time was fast approaching when the first should be last, and the last should be first.*

Finally, it was all fitting into place: the patterns in the leaves and the stars, the blood on the corn, the vision of race war, and the abiding question of Nat's own great purpose in life. Christ had not simply laid down his burden of suffering, he had passed it on, to Nat Turner himself. By taking up the cross, Nat would fulfill both Christ's purpose and his own burning ambition.

The "serpent" in Nat's vision was of course the white man, and by doing battle against him, Nat would "redeem" his own black race in both a religious sense and a political one—freeing them simultaneously from the bonds of both sin and slavery. The final result would not be race war but a more just reordering of society—"the first should be last, and the last should be first." Nat himself might die in the struggle, but his death, like Christ's, would only seal his triumph. . . .

The Day of Judgment was nearly at hand. All that now remained was to discover the details. And even these the spirit promised to reveal. . . . The promised signs took almost three years to appear. . . . Finally, in February 1831, there was an eclipse of the sun. Nat determined this to be the promised sign—the sign that removed "the seal from my lips." He now revealed his intentions to four trusted black friends who had fallen under the influence of his personality. The four men soon agreed to participate in his great work. The time had come "to slay my enemies with their own weapons," to plan strategy, to convert a private religious vision into a political and military operation. . . .

Through the spring months of 1831, the five men engaged in long debates and formulated any number of plans. But they could come to no agreement. "The time passed," Nat later recalled, "without our coming to any determination how to commence." Nat himself was so disturbed by this turn of events that he fell ill.

. . . The conspirators were "still forming new schemes and rejecting them." It was at this confused and discouraged point, on August 13, that Nat was finally jolted into action by a sign too clear to be ignored: This was, of course, the day the sun grew dim and changed colors, and the black spot appeared on its surface. Now Nat knew that the Day of Judgment could be delayed no longer.

Eight days later, on Sunday, August 21, Nat's four associates gathered at a secluded pond in the neighborhood: Hark, Nelson, Sam, and Henry. Hark (his full name was Hercules) brought a pig he had filched from his master. Henry brought some brandy. There were also present two new conspirators, slaves who had not previously been part of the group. Both were well known to the original four. The pig was killed and cooked.

Nat himself did not join this last meal until the middle of the afternoon. The seven men ate and drank (though Nat himself, true to his temperance principles, refused to touch the brandy). After the food was finished, the group continued to sit around the pond and debate their plans—for even at this late hour they had not formulated any clear strategy. There was, however, general agreement that the group could delay no longer—that very night they had to rise up and "kill all the white people." . . .

Nat was determined above all to maintain secrecy. Until the moment of the actual onslaught, only seven men knew what was going to happen. And these seven were closely related to each other by ties of friendship or kinship. . . . Among such a tight-knit group, the risk of betrayal was minimal.

But by ensuring secrecy, Nat was forced to . . . give up the possibility of systematic recruitment and effective organization. He would have to recruit his forces in spontaneous fashion as the group moved on from one farm to another. Their numbers would increase as they went along, he argued. The places Nat planned to attack were all familiar to him. He had lived his entire life in the neighborhood, and his party of insurrectionists was well known to many of the slaves in the region. When these slaves saw their owners actually lying dead, and felt themselves masterless, they would surely join the liberating army. And since the slaves in Southampton County outnumbered the whites, the county would belong to *them.*

So Nat argued, as he and his six friends sat by the pond, watching afternoon turn to dusk, and dusk slip into darkness.

183

Finally, then, it was agreed: That very night they would begin. They would head to the house of Joseph Travis, the master of Nat and Hark. There they would stop and "kill all the white people." Then they would collect weapons and horses, recruit other male Travis slaves—slaves now without a master—to join them, and march on to other farms and plantations. There the scene would be repeated, and their army of recruits would swell to over-whelming proportions. At first, they would spare no white person in their path, whether man, woman, or child—that much was necessary in order to "strike terror and alarm" through the countryside and cause the remaining white people of the county to flee for their lives. Within a day, if all went well, the black army could march unopposed and triumphant into the county seat—a town whose biblical name, Jerusalem, could not have escaped Nat's notice.

The killings had to be brutal, to intensify the general terror. The heads of some victims were to be severed, and the bodies of others dismembered. But Nat also insisted on clear limits: There was to be no torture, no rape, and (except for necessary supplies) no looting. There was no room for indulging in simple revenge or personal gratification. Furthermore, the slaughter would not continue indefinitely. Nat later told a white questioner that "indiscriminate massacre was not their intention after they obtained a foothold. Women and children would afterward be spared, and men too who ceased to resist."

An Historian Explains
the Scarcity of Slave Revolts

The small number of slave revolts in North America as compared with the numerous large-scale uprisings that plagued other slave societies has long intrigued historians. The following selection identifies some of the factors that account for this striking disparity. Which of them best explains the failure of Nat Turner's revolt? Abridged from John B. Boles, Black Southerners, 1619–1869 *(Lexington, Kentucky, 1983), 172–76.*

Reprinted from *Black Southerners, 1619–1869*, by John B. Boles. Copyright © 1983 by The University Press of Kentucky. Reprinted by permission.

Many factors mitigated against successful armed insurrection by slaves in the Old South. Unlike the situation in Latin America, in the Old South as a whole whites far outnumbered slaves, and of course totally controlled the police power of the states. . . . [N]onslaveholding whites almost unanimously supported slavery as a method of controlling blacks even if slave ownership was not their personal goal. . . . In certain regions like the sea islands of South Carolina and Georgia and the sugar districts of Louisiana, blacks were in a significant majority, yet even there the distance between individual plantations and the maze of unbridged estuaries, rivers, bayous, sloughs, and swamps made communication and travel between plantations difficult. The geography of the Old South conspired with demography to complicate still further slave attempts at rebellion and escape. Slaves in Brazil and in the Guiana region of northeastern South America, for example, had the huge, unexplored jungle fastness of the Amazon River basin in which to escape; similarly, plantations were located on the perimeters of the West Indian islands, whose interiors offered sure havens for runaways. In both regions slaves escaped to the interior and in maroon settlements often managed to survive for years, occasionally fighting white authorities to a

This wood engraving shows escaping slaves. Although attempts were made, the geography of the Old South made successful slave escapes nearly impossible.

standstill and achieving treaty recognition of their status (often in exchange for returning newly escaped slaves).

This kind of escape from slavery was never possible for the overwhelming majority of bondsmen in the Old South. Except for those few who lived near the Dismal Swamp on the eastern Virginia-North Carolina boundary, and some in Florida and Georgia near the Okefenokee Swamp and the trackless Everglades, there was no safe hinterland where maroons could survive. Moreover, cold winters, particularly in the Upper South, made the prospect of hiding out in the woods uninviting. In the early decades of plantation development, the Indians in the backcountry quickly learned they would be rewarded for capturing and returning slave runaways. The Indians were replaced in later decades by yeoman farmers who either returned the runaways for the reward or kept them. For most slaves the freedom territory north of the Mason-Dixon line or the Ohio River was simply too far away, and while several thousand bondsmen in the last half-century of slavery did escape by way of the Underground Railroad, most of them came from the border states of Maryland and Kentucky.

In Latin America and the Caribbean Islands, where hundreds of slaves lived on huge plantations, the owners were absent, and the working conditions were far more harsh than those typical in the South, desperate slaves, often plagued with famine as well as overwork, occasionally struck out against their brutal oppression and escaped to preexisting maroon communities. The working conditions on the tropical sugar plantations drove slaves to rebellion, and the example of successful escape offered by the maroon settlements in the backcountry emboldened otherwise hesitant bondsmen to act. There was, in other words, a heritage of insurrection in the Caribbean and Latin America that offered slaves not only incentive to rebel but the expectation of success. No such vital spark of hope was possible in the Old South. The few insurrections were small, localized, and quickly and brutally suppressed, with many innocent slaves usually punished and the general restrictions against all slaves made temporarily more harsh. . . .

During the era of the cotton kingdom most slaves were American born, the sex ratio was practically equal (more so than the white ratio), and slaves typically lived in family groupings. As a result the slave family became the single most important bond holding members together[;] . . . naming practices and kinship systems evolved to cement relationships made fragile by the possibility of sale or removal. This demographic development also prevented slave insurrection.

While a population composed mostly of unattached young males can be very explosive (especially when faced with harsh conditions and the possibility of escape), a population where males and females are equally present, family relationships have been formed and there are small children to love and care for, is far more conservative. The possibility of an entire family escaping was practically nil, and parents were loath to forsake their children to save themselves. Likewise few men would leave their loved ones for an escape attempt with little chance of success. If family attachments lessened runaway efforts, so much more did the ties of family affection reduce the possibilities of insurrection. Few male slaves would risk almost sure death when to do so would leave their families fatherless. Moreover, the knowledge that family members and innocent bystanders would be pitilessly punished and their rights severely circumscribed in the aftermath of a rebellion attempt must have restrained many discontented slaves.

In the Old South, where family structures, leisure time, and fairly good living conditions prevented most slaves from being driven into utter desperation, slaves usually found less risky avenues of countering the dehumanization of chattel bondage. Because hunger and abject hopelessness were less common in the Old South, slaves calculated their options more carefully, waiting—sometimes all their lives—for good chances for successful rebellion. Thousands did not find the right moment to strike until the Civil War and the presence of Union troops profoundly changed the balance. Then no one was more shocked than complacent planters when droves of their seemingly most devoted, most responsible slaves "deserted" and chose freedom.

The realities of power and geography in the Old South also minimized the kind of slave rebellion that often occurred in the other New World plantation societies. In the antebellum South, slaves were very seldom driven to mindless, suicidal acts of outrage and rebellion. Fully aware of their situation, they learned, socialized, and passed on to their children a wide range of behavior—voice intonations, facial expressions, feigned illness, purposeful laziness and slowness of motion, dumb-like-a-fox incomprehension—that combined equal portions of insubordination and minor rebellion to produce a constant undercurrent of resistance to psychological bondage. Although never completely giving in to authority, most slaves were able, at least in the eyes of their master, to acquiesce in their state of servitude and thus survive with their essential humanity intact. In the most fundamental sense, racial slavery as it existed in the Old South was premised on the assumption by whites that blacks were inferior, either a subhuman or a permanently childlike race. Planters' everyday experience, of course, gave the lie to this assumption, and therein may have been the cause of the guilt that some historians believe troubled many whites, particularly those who constructed elaborate proslavery defenses. Had slaves in general accepted this racial subordination and aspired to be only what the white man prescribed, then blacks would have been total slaves, and all resistance—except occasional outbursts of violence—would have disappeared. But the rich panoply of Afro-American culture, their tales, music, art, and religion protected bondsmen from complete capitulation. Out of the inner reserves of their humanity slaves in measured ways resisted servitude and defended the limited rights that had become, through mutual accommodation, accepted by whites. The black community evolved a culture from which proceeded all forms of slave resistance other than rebellion.

Questions

1. *What effect do you think the presence of a hostile and potentially dangerous element in southern society had on southern life and culture?*
2. *Were resistance and revolt inevitable in a slaveholding society? Was there any way to avoid them?*
3. *Did the danger that slaves posed to the security of white southern society have any effect on the North, or was it solely a southern concern?*
4. *What do such events as Nat Turner's revolt tell us about the institution of slavery itself? Can you think of any way a successful slave revolt could have been organized in spite of obstacles?*
5. *Does Nat Turner appear to be a fanatic or a shrewd planner and leader? Could he have been both?*

SLAVE REVOLT AND SLAVE VIOLENCE: THEIR CAUSES AND CONSEQUENCE

Resistance to slavery, common throughout its existence, took various forms, each of them annoying and costly to the owners. Feigning illness, breaking or losing tools, slow or shoddy work, insolence, running away—these were only a few of the many unspectacular ways slaves exerted their independence and countered their owners' power.

Every slaveowner and every plantation experienced such resistance to some degree at one time or another. It apparently was inseparable from the institution itself. Rarer than any of these mundane forms of resistance, but more to be feared, was slave violence directed against whites. Most incidents of assault and murder resulted from identifiable grievances experienced by individual slaves; the motive appeared limited to personal revenge and retribution. In rare instances, however, slaves joined together in overt action calculated to damage, or even destroy, the institution of slavery itself and to free themselves from it. On those occasions when slaves organized revolts, they used violence to achieve a political rather than a personal end. North American slaves made only a few such attempts, and their success was nil, especially when compared with the more frequent, extensive, and long lasting revolts undertaken by slaves in the West Indies and in South America. The Stono Revolt in South Carolina (1739), the revolt in Louisiana (1811), and Nat Turner's revolt in Virginia (1831) practically exhaust the list. Each was limited in scope and readily put down. Nevertheless, each of them had important consequences for the slave community and for white southerners as well as for the future of slavery itself and of opposition to it. Of the three North American revolts, the one led by Nat Turner (sometimes called the Southampton revolt) is by far the best known and the most extensively documented. That revolt, like its predecessors, led to vicious reprisals

189

against black people and to intensified efforts by slaveholders to make slavery more secure. In the North it contributed to the growth of an antislavery movement.

A Virginia State Official Explains Nat Turner's Revolt

John Floyd, governor of Virginia, pondering the causes of Turner's revolt, concluded that it resulted from influences other than those inherent in slavery itself. Here Floyd tells James Hamilton, Jr., the governor of South Carolina, his explanation of the revolt and the plan he will propose to prevent its repetition. Excerpted from The Southampton Slave Revolt of 1831, *ed. Henry Irving Tragle (Amherst, 1971), 275–76.*

Richmond
November 19, 1831

Sir:

I received your letter yesterday and with great pleasure will give you my impressions freely—

I will notice this affair in my annual message, but here only give a very careless history of it, as it appeared to the public—

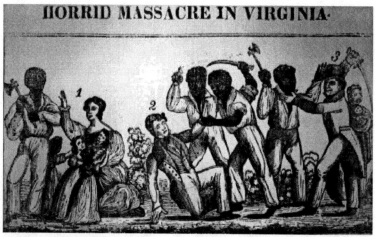

Nat Turner's revolt dramatized in a popular woodcut.

I am fully persuaded, the spirit of insubordination which has, and still manifests itself in Virginia, had its origin among, and eminated . . . from, the Yankee population, upon their *first* arrival amongst us, but mostly especially the Yankee pedlers and traders.

The course has been by no means a direct one—they began first, by making them religious—their conversations were of that character—telling the blacks God was no respecter of persons—the black man was as good as the white—that all men were born free and equal—that they cannot serve two masters—that the white people rebelled against England to obtain freedom, so have the blacks a right to do.

In the mean time, I am sure without any purpose of this kind, the preachers, principally Northern—were very assidious in operating upon our population, day and night, they were at work—and religion became, and is, the fashion of the time—finally our females and of the most respectable were persuaded that it was piety to teach negroes to read and write, to the end that they might read the Scriptures—many of them became tutoress in Sunday schools and, pious distributors of tracts, from the New York Tract Society.

At this point, more active operations commenced—our magistrates and laws became more inactive—large assemblages of negroes were suffered to take place for religious purposes—Then commenced the efforts of the black preachers, often from the pulpits these pamphlets and papers were read—followed by the incendiary publications of Walker, Garrison and Knapp of Boston, these too with songs and hymns of a similar character were circulated, read and commented upon—We resting in apathetic security until the Southampton affair.

From all that has come to my knowledge during and since this affair—I am fully convinced that every black preacher in the whole country east of the Blue Ridge was in [on] the secret, that the plans as published by those Northern presses were adopted and acted upon by them—that their congregations, as they were called knew nothing of this intended rebellion, except a few leading and intelligent men, who may have been head men in the

---

Reprinted from *The Southampton Slave Revolt of 1831*, Henry I. Tragle, Editor. Amherst: The University of Massachusetts Press, 1971. Copyright © 1971 by Henry I. Tragle.

Church—*the mass* were prepared by making them aspire to an equal station by such conversations as I have related as the first step.

I am informed that they had settled the form of government to be that of white people, whom they intended to cut off to a man— with the difference that the preachers were to be their Governors, Generals and Judges. I feel fully justified to myself, in believing the Northern incendiaries, tracts, Sunday Schools, religion and reading and writing has accomplished this end.

I shall in my annual message recommend that laws be passed—To confine the Slaves to the estates of their masters— prohibit negroes from preaching—absolutely to drive from this State all free negroes—and to substitute the surplus revenue in our Treasury annually for slaves, to work for a time upon our Rail Roads etc etc and these sent out of the country, preparatory, or rather as the first step to emancipation—This last point will of course be tenderly and cautiously managed and will be urged or delayed as your State and Georgia may be disposed to co-operate.

In relation to the extent of this insurrection I think it greater than will ever appear. . . .

I am Sir,
with consideration and respect
your obt Sevnt
[obedient servant,]
s/John Floyd/

Religion as a Bulwark of Slavery

As Governor Floyd suggests, slaveowners generally did not object to their slaves being exposed to religious teachings. In fact, some viewed such instruction as one of their responsibilities, but, like Governor Floyd, they believed that in the "wrong" hands (as in Turner's), religion could be a subversive or revolutionary force. The following excerpt was written in 1842 by Lunsford Lane, a North Carolina slave. This memoir illustrates the use of religion for conservative ends. Excerpted from Five Slave Narratives: A Compendium *(New York, 1968), 20–21, with some minor grammatical corrections.*

I had never been permitted to learn to read; but I used to attend church, and there I received instruction which I trust was of some benefit to me. . . .

I often heard select portions of the scriptures read. And on the Sabbath there was one sermon preached expressly for the colored people which it was generally my privilege to hear. I became quite familiar with the texts, "Servants be obedient to your masters."—"Not with eye service as men pleasers."—"He that knoweth his master's will and doeth it not, shall be beaten with many stripes," and others of this class: for they formed the basis of most of these public instructions to us. The first commandment impressed upon our minds was to obey our masters, and the second was like unto it, namely, to do as much work when they or the overseers were not watching us as when they were. But connected with these instructions there was more or less that was truly excellent; though mixed up with much that would sound strangely in the ears of freedom. There was one very kind hearted Episcopal minister whom I often used to hear; he was very popular with the colored people. But after he had preached a sermon to us in which he argued from the Bible that it was the will of heaven from all eternity we should be slaves, and our masters be our owners, most of us left him; for like some of the faint hearted disciples in early times we said,—"This is a hard saying, who can bear it?"

Popular Reaction to Nat Turner's Revolt

Following revolts, retribution against African Americans, slave or free, guilty or innocent, was severe and indiscriminate and may help to account for the rarity of such revolts. The following newspaper report describes the aftermath of Nat Turner's revolt and the part that armed forces played in halting the reprisals. From the Constitutional Whig, *Richmond, Virginia, 3 September 1831, reprinted in* The Southampton Slave Revolt of 1831, *ed. Henry Irving Tragle (Boston, 1971), 69–70.*

It is with pain we speak of another feature of the Southampton Rebellion; for we have been most unwilling to have our sympathies for the sufferers diminished or affected by their misconduct. We allude to the slaughter of many blacks, without trial, and under circumstances of great barbarity. How many have thus been put into death (generally by decapitation or shooting) reports vary; probably however some five and twenty and from that to 40; possibly a yet larger number. To the great honor of General Eppes, he used every precaution in his power, and we hope and believe with success, to put a stop to the disgraceful procedure.—We met with one individual of intelligence, who stated that he himself had killed between 10 and 15. He justified himself on the grounds of the barbarities committed on the whites; and that he thought himself right is certain from the fact that he narrowly escaped losing his own life in an attempt to save a negro woman whom he thought innocent but who was shot by the multitude in despite of his exertions. We (the Richmond Troop) witnessed with surprise the sanguinary temper of the population who evinced a strong disposition to inflict immediate death on every prisoner. Not having witnessed the horrors committed by the blacks, or seen the unburried and disfigured remains of their wives and children, we were unprepared to understand their feelings, and could not at first admit of their extenuation, which a closer observation of the atrocities of the insurgents suggested. Now, however, we feel individually compelled to offer an apology for the people of Southampton, while we deeply deplore that human nature urged them to such extremities. Let the fact not be doubted by those whom it most concerns, that another such insurrection will be the signal for the extirmination of the whole black population in the quarter of the state where it occurs. . . .

The presence of the troops from Norfolk and Richmond alone prevented retaliation from being carried much farther.

Popular Reaction to a Rumored Revolt in Louisiana

Solomon Northup, a slave in Louisiana during the 1840s, describes an abortive attempt by slaves to organize a mass escape to Mexico and the retaliation that followed. Note the apparent absence of a religious im-

pulse for the revolt and the similarities with the aftermath of Nat Turner's revolt. Note, too, that the violence against slaves came to an end in a similar way. Abridged from Solomon Northup, Twelve Years a Slave: Narrative of Solomon Northup . . . *(Auburn, 1853), 246–49.*

The year before my arrival in the country there was a concerted movement among a number of slaves on Bayou Boeuf, that terminated tragically indeed. It was, I presume, a matter of newspaper notoriety at the time, but all the knowledge I have of it, has been derived from the relation of those living at that period in the immediate vicinity of the excitement. It has become a subject of general and unfailing interest in every slave-hut on the bayou, and will doubtless go down to succeeding generations as their chief tradition. Lew Cheney, with whom I became acquainted—a shrewd, cunning negro, more intelligent than the generality of his race, but unscrupulous and full of treachery—conceived the project of organizing a company sufficiently strong to fight their way against all opposition, to the neighboring territory of Mexico.

A remote spot, far within the depths of the swamp back of Hawkins' plantation, was selected as the rallying point. Lew flitted from one plantation to another, in the dead of night, preaching a crusade to Mexico, and, like Peter the Hermit, creating a furor of excitement wherever he appeared. At length a large number of runaways were assembled; stolen mules, and corn gathered from the fields, and bacon filched from smoke-houses, had been conveyed into the woods. The expedition was about ready to proceed, when their hiding place was discovered. Lew Cheney, becoming convinced of the ultimate failure of his project, in order to curry favor with his master, and avoid the consequences which he foresaw would follow, deliberately determined to sacrifice all his companions. Departing secretly from the encampment, he proclaimed among the planters the number collected in the swamp, and, instead of stating truly the object they had in view, asserted their intention was to emerge from their seclusion the first favorable opportunity, and murder every white person along the bayou.

Such an announcement, exaggerated as it passed from mouth to mouth, filled the whole country with terror. The fugitives were surrounded and taken prisoners, carried in chains to Alexandria, and hung by the populace. Not only those, but many who were suspected, though entirely innocent, were taken from the field and from the cabin, and without the shadow of process or form of trial, hurried to the scaffold. The planters on Bayou Boeuf finally rebelled against such reckless destruction of property, but it was not until a regiment of soldiers had arrived from some fort on the Texan frontier, demolished the gallows, and opened the doors of the Alexandria prison, that the indiscriminate slaughter was stayed. Lew Cheney escaped, and was even rewarded for his treachery. He is still living, but his name is despised and execrated by all his race throughout the parishes of Rapides and Avoyelles.

Such an idea as insurrection, however, is not new among the enslaved population of Bayou Boeuf. More than once I have joined in serious consultation, when the subject has been discussed, and there have been times when a word from me would have placed hundreds of my fellow-bondsmen in an attitude of defiance. Without arms or ammunition, or even with them, I saw such a step would result in certain defeat, disaster and death, and always raised my voice against it.

During the Mexican war I well remember the extravagant hopes that were excited. The news of victory filled the great house with rejoicing, but produced only sorrow and disappointment in the cabin. In my opinion—and I have had opportunity to know something of the feeling of which I speak—there are not fifty slaves on the shores of Bayou Boeuf, but would hail with unmeasured delight the approach of an invading army.

A Northern Editor Reacts to Nat Turner's Revolt

Slave unrest obviously was primarily a southern problem, but Nat Turner's revolt led even northerners who were not abolitionists to worry about its probable effects on the nation at large. Here, a northern newspaper editor speculates on possible solutions to the "problem" of slave revolts. From the Ohio State Journal and Columbus Gazette, *October 20, 1831, 3.*

Since the suppression of the late Negro insurrection in Southampton county, Va. it appears that similar outrages have been attempted by the slaves and free colored people in different parts of North and South Carolina, Louisiana, Delaware, and the Eastern Shore of Maryland; and although the designs of the poor wretches concerned therein have been for the most part discovered and frustrated before much actual mischief had been done, yet the frequency of their late attempts has occasioned no little alarm in those parts of the union which have most to fear from a servile war. Whether these almost simultaneous movements in sections of the country so remote from each other be the result of accident, or of something like a preconcerted plan for a general insurrection among the slaves about this time does not fully appear. The latter supposition, however, is not altogether improbable; and although every man possessed of common sense will at once see that an attempt of this kind, however well matured, must ultimately result in the total extermination of at least all those engaged in it, if not of the entire colored population, yet, it is evident that it would inevitably occasion the loss of many valuable lives, and be productive of a vast amount of misery, before it could be suppressed.

A southern paper, speaking of these movements, and of the probability of their frequent recurrence so long as slavery shall be tolerated among us, suggests, whether it would not be right and expedient, after the National Debt shall have been paid, to apply the surplus revenue to the general emancipation of the slaves, and their removal beyond our territorial limits; and without intending to express an opinion, either as to the expediency or the feasibility of such a measure, we must say that it appears to us to be worthy of serious consideration. We believe that the people of these United States ought no longer to shut their eyes to the dreadful evils of slavery, and the consequences which, sooner or later, must inevitably result from it; and that the time has fully arrived when some plan should be devised for the removal of this curse from among us. We shall probably recur to the subject in a future number.

An Abolitionist Reacts to Nat Turner's Revolt

For many years before 1831, opponents of slavery had warned that slaves in the South would someday follow the example of the slaves in Saint-

Domingue who successfully rebelled in the 1790s. In this selection, William Lloyd Garrison, the best known of the abolitionists, interprets Nat Turner's revolt as a fulfillment of that prophecy, calling for immediate emancipation as the only means to prevent a catastrophic race war for liberation. Abridged from William Lloyd Garrison, "The Insurrection," Liberator, Boston, September 3, 1831, 143.

What we have so long predicted,—at the peril of being stigmatized as an alarmist and declaimer,—has commenced its fulfilment. The first step of the earthquake, which is ultimately to shake down the fabric of oppression, leaving not one stone upon another, has been made. The first drops of blood, which are but the prelude to a deluge from the gathering clouds, have fallen. The first flash of the lightning, which is to smite and consume, has been felt. The first wailings of a bereavement, which is to clothe the earth in sackcloth, have broken upon our ears. . . .

True, the rebellion is quelled. Those of the slaves who were not killed in combat, have been secured, and the prison is crowded with victims destined for the gallows!

'Yet laugh not in your carnival of crime
Too proudly, ye oppressors!'

You have seen, it is to be feared, but the beginning of sorrows. All the blood which has been shed will be required at your hands. At your hands alone? No—but at the hands of the people of New-England and of all the free states. The crime of oppression is national. The south is only the agent in this guilty traffic. But, remember! the same causes are at work which must inevitably produce the same effects; and when the contest shall have again begun, it must be again a war of extermination. In the present instance, no quarters have been asked or given.

[Garrison now attempts to voice the slaveholders' justification for revenge against Nat Turner's band:]

But we have killed and routed them [the slaves] now. . . We have the power to kill *all*—let us, therefore, continue to apply the whip and forge new fetters! . . . They were black—brutes, pretending to be men—legions of curses upon their memories! They were black—God made them to serve us! . . .

[Garrison, as an abolitionist, now addresses the slaveholders:]

Ye accuse the pacific friends of emancipation of instigating the slaves to revolt. Take back the charge as a foul slander. The slaves need no incentives at our hands. They will find them in their stripes—in their emaciated bodies—in their ceaseless toil—in their ignorant minds—in every field, in every valley, on every hill-top and mountain, wherever you and your fathers have fought for liberty—in your speeches, your conversations, your celebrations, your pamphlets, your newspapers—voices in the air, sounds from across the ocean, invitations to resistance above, below, around them! What more do they need? Surrounded by such influences, and smarting under their newly made wounds, is it wonderful that they should rise to contend—as other 'heroes' have contended—for their lost rights? It is *not* wonderful.

In all that we have written, is there aught to justify the excesses of the slaves? No. Nevertheless, they deserve no more censure than the Greeks in destroying the Turks, or the Poles in exterminating the Russians, or our fathers in slaughtering the British. Dreadful, indeed, is the standard erected by worldly patriotism!

For ourselves, we are horror-struck at the late tidings. We have exerted our utmost efforts to avert the calamity. We have warned our countrymen of the danger of persisting in their unrighteous conduct. We have preached to the slaves the pacific precepts of Jesus Christ. We have appealed to christians, philanthropists and patriots, for their assistance to accomplish the great work of national redemption through the agency of moral power—of public opinion—of individual duty. How have we been received? We have been threatened, proscribed, vilified and imprisoned—a laughing-stock and a reproach. Do we falter, in view of these things? Let time answer. If we have been hitherto urgent, and bold, and denunciatory in our efforts,—hereafter we shall grow vehement and active with the increase of danger. We shall cry, in trumpet tones, night and day,—Wo to this guilty land, unless she speedily repent of her evil doings! The blood of millions of her sons cries aloud for redress! IMMEDIATE EMANCIPATION can alone save her from the vengeance of Heaven, and cancel the debt of ages!

Slave Violence Directed against Individual Owners

Instances of slaves murdering their masters were frequent enough to cause concern even though slaveowners usually insisted that their own slaves could be trusted. Here, Mary Chesnut of South Carolina recounts the fate of two white women, one her acquaintance, the other her relative, who met their deaths at the hands of aggrieved slaves. Note that in each instance, the cause of the murders, as Mrs. Chesnut understands it, was not too much, but too little, discipline. How might the slaves' explanation for the murders differ from that given by Mrs. Chesnut? Excerpted from Mary Chesnut's Civil War, *ed. C. Vann Woodward (New Haven, 1981), 209–12.*

And now comes back on us that bloody story that haunts me night and day, Mrs. Witherspoon's murder.

The man William, who was the master spirit of the gang, once ran away and was brought back from somewhere west. And then his master and himself had a reconciliation, and the master henceforth made a pet of him.

The night preceding the murder, John Witherspoon went over to his mother's to tell her of some of William and Rhody's misdeeds. While their mistress was away from home, they had given a ball fifteen miles away from Society Hill. To that place they had taken their mistress's china, silver, house linen, &c&c. After his conversation with his mother, as he rode out of the gate, he shook his whip at William and said, "Tomorrow I mean to come here and give every one of you a thrashing."

That night Mrs. Witherspoon was talking it all over with her grandson, a half-grown boy who lived with her—slept, indeed, in a room opening into hers.

"I do not intend John to punish these negroes. It is too late to begin discipline now. It is all nonsense. I have indulged them past bearing, they all say. I ought to have tried to control them. It is all my fault. That's the end of it."

Mrs. Edwards, who was a sister of Mrs. Witherspoon, was found dead in her bed. It is thought this suggested their plan of action to the negroes. What more likely than she should die as her sister had done.

They were all in great trouble when John went off. William said, "Listen to me, and there will be no punishment here tomorrow." They made their plan, and then all of them *went to sleep*, William remaining awake to stir up the others at the proper hour.

What first attracted the attention of the family was the appearance of black and blue spots about the face and neck of the body of their mother. Then someone in moving the candle from the table at her bedside found blood upon their fingers. . . .

. . . [T]hey began to scent mischief and foul play in earnest, and they sent for the detective. Before he came they searched all houses and found bloody rags.

The detective dropped in from the skies quite unexpectedly. He saw that one of the young understrappers of the gang looked frightened and uncomfortable. This one he fastened upon and got up quite an intimacy with him. Finally he told this boy that he knew all about it. William had confessed privately to him to save himself and hang the others. But as the detective had taken a fancy to this boy, if he would confess everything, he would take him as state's evidence instead of William. The young man was utterly confounded at first but fell in the trap laid for him and told every particular from beginning to end.

Then they were all put in jail, the youth who had confessed among them, as he did not wish them to know of his *treachery* to them.

This was his story. "After John went away that night, Rhody and William made a great fuss—were furious at Mars John threatening them after all these years—to talk to them that away."

William said: "Mars John more than apt to do what he say he will do. You-all follow what I say and he'll have something else to think of beside stealing and breaking glass and china and tablecloths. If ole Marster was alive now, what would he say? Talk of whipping us at this time of day, &c&c."

Rhody kept the key of the house to let herself in every morning. So they arranged to go in at twelve. And then William watched, and they slept the sleep of the righteous.

Before that, however, they had a "rale fine supper and a heap of laughing at the way dey's all look tomorrow."

They smothered her with a counterpane [quilt] from a bed in the entry. He had no trouble the first time because they found her asleep and "done it all 'fore she waked." But after Rhody took her keys and went into the trunk and got a clean nightgown—for they had spoiled the one she had on—and fixed everything, candle, medicine, and all—she came to! Then she begged them hard for life. She asked them what she had ever done that they should want to kill her? She promised them before God never to tell on them. Nobody should ever know. But Rhody stopped her mouth by the counterpane. William held her head and hands down. And the other two sat on her legs. Rhody had a thrifty mind and wished to save the sheets and nightgown. She did not destroy them—they were found behind her mantelpiece. There the money was also, all in a hole made among the bricks behind the wooden mantelpiece.

A grandson of Rhody's slept in her house. Him she locked up in his room. She did not want him to know anything of this fearful night.

That innocent old lady and her gray hairs moved them not a jot.

Fancy how we feel. I am sure I will never sleep again without this nightmare of horror haunting me.

Mrs. Chesnut [Mary Chesnut's mother-in-law], who is their good angel, is and has always been afraid of negroes. In her youth the St. Domingo stories were indelibly printed on her mind.

She shows her dread now by treating everyone as if they were a black Prince Albert or Queen Victoria.

We were beginning to forget Mrs. Cunningham, the only other woman we ever heard of murdered by her negroes.

Poor Cousin Betsey was goodness itself. After years of freedom and indulgence and tender kindness, it was an awful mistake to threaten them like children. It was only threats. Everybody knew she would never do anything.

How about Mrs. Cunningham? He [Mr. Cunningham] was an old bachelor, and the negroes had it all their own way till he married. And then they hated her. They took her from her room, just over one in which her son-in-law and her daughter slept. They smothered her, dressed her, and carried her out—all without the slightest noise—and hung her by the neck to an apple tree, as if she had committed suicide. Waked nobody in the house by all this. If they want to kill us, they can do it when they please—they are noiseless as panthers.

They were discovered—first, because dressing her in the dark, her tippet [nightcap] was put on hind part before. And she was supposed to have walked out and hung herself in a pair of brand-new shoes whose soles evidently had never touched the ground.

We ought to be grateful that any one of us is alive. But nobody is afraid of their own negroes. These are horrid brutes—savages, monsters—but I find everyone like myself, ready to trust their own yard. I would go down on the plantation tomorrow and stay there, if there were no white person in twenty miles. My Molly and half a dozen others that *I know*—and all the rest I believe— would keep me as safe as I should be in the Tower of London.

Questions

1. *How do you account for the indiscriminate fury directed against African Americans in the wake of Nat Turner's revolt and the abortive revolt in Louisiana? Why do you think the armed forces quelled that fury instead of supporting it?*
2. *Both Governor John Floyd and William Lloyd Garrison agreed that outside influences were partly responsible for slave unrest, but their understanding of those influences varied greatly. Explain.*
3. *Religion is sometimes assumed to be a conservative force. Yet, it appears to have been a prime influence in the Nat Turner revolt. How do you account for this discrepancy? Can you think of other situations in which religion has been employed in support of radical causes?*

FURTHER READING

Nearly all the surviving sources for studying Nat Turner's revolt can be found in The Southampton Slave Revolt of 1831: A Compilation of Source Material Including the Full Text of the Confessions of Nat Turner, *ed. Henry Irving Tragle (Boston, 1971). For two good accounts of the revolt based on the documents in Tragle's book, see Stephen B. Oates,* The Fires of Jubilee: Nat Turner's Fierce Rebellion *(New York, 1975); and Herbert Aptheker,* Nat Turner's Slave Rebellion *(New York, 1966). Herbert Aptheker,* American Negro Slave Revolts *(New York, 1943), provides extensive information about various forms of African American resistance to slavery. For a discussion of the relation of slave discontent to American political and diplomatic history and to American wars see Merton L. Dillon,* Slavery Attacked: Southern Slaves and Their Allies, 1619–1865 *(Baton Rouge, 1990).*

The First Women's Rights Movement

Susan M. Hartmann

INTRODUCTION

Examining women's history in the 1830s and 1840s demonstrates the inaccuracy of the term "Jacksonian Democracy" to characterize that era. At a time when white men achieved full rights of citizenship, women were just beginning their own movement to secure equality. As early as 1642, the New England poet Anne Bradstreet chafed at being denied the full use of her talents, writing, "I am obnoxious to each carping tongue, who sayes, my hand a needle better fits." During the next two centuries, other women expressed their dissatisfaction at being deemed inferior to men, legally subordinated to their fathers and husbands, and barred from intellectual and public pursuits. In the 1840s, these isolated protests swelled into a concerted movement for women's rights.

Feminist activism grew out of women's increasing participation in church-related benevolent societies and in social reform, which claimed substantial numbers of white and free black women in the North. Susan B. Anthony's feminist consciousness originated with her work in the temperance movement, but most women's rights leaders, including Sarah and Angelina Grimké, Elizabeth Cady Stanton, Lucretia Mott, and Lucy Stone, came to women's rights through abolitionism. Although white women dominated the women's rights movement, prominent black abolitionists, such as Frederick Douglass and Sojourner Truth, also championed the cause. Women inaugurated their bold and radical movement in 1848 at Seneca Falls, New York, where three hundred women and men approved a sweeping list of grievances and demands. Ministers, journalists, and other spokesmen viewed these demands as a radical challenge to the social order and dismissed their advocates as "old maids, whose personal charms were never very attractive," "women who have been badly married," and "hen-pecked husbands." In the face of intense opposition and hostility, the women's rights movement gained converts slowly. Women made piecemeal progress in the North, winning state laws expanding the rights of married women and gaining access to some colleges. But it took seventy-two years to achieve their most controversial demand, the right to vote. Although succeeding waves of feminism have introduced new issues, the women's rights movement of the nineteenth century established goals and arguments that continue to shape the debate over gender roles today.

ABOLITIONISM AND THE EARLY YEARS OF FEMINIST ACTIVISM

Scholars have noted the connections between agitation for women's rights and other reform movements, especially in the antebellum period and in the 1960s. Ellen Carol DuBois shows how the antislavery movement helped women to overcome the barriers to organization for their own rights and points out the limitations of this relationship. This excerpt is from Ellen Carol DuBois, Feminism and Suffrage: The Emergence of an Independent Women's Movement in America, 1848–1869 *(Ithaca, New York, 1978), 21–25, 27–38, 40–42, 44–52.*

For many years before 1848, American women had manifested considerable discontent with their lot. They wrote and read domestic novels in which a thin veneer of sentiment overlaid a great deal of anger about women's dependence on undependable men. They attended female academies and formed ladies' benevolent societies, in which they pursued the widest range of interests and activities they could imagine without calling into question the whole notion of "woman's sphere." In such settings, they probed the experiences that united and restrained them—what one historian has called "the bonds of womanhood." Yet women's discontent remained unexamined, implicit, and above all, disorganized. Although increasing numbers of women were questioning what it meant to be a woman and were ready to challenge their traditional position, they did not yet know each other.

"Women's Rights Before the Civil War," reprinted from *Feminism and Suffrage: The Emergence of an Independent Women's Movement in America 1848–1869* by Ellen Carol DuBois, published by Cornell University Press, 1978. Copyright © 1978 by Cornell University.

The women's rights movement crystallized these sentiments into a feminist politics. Although preceded by individual theorists like Margaret Fuller, and by particular demands on behalf of women for property rights, education, and admission to the professions, the women's rights movement began a new phase in the history of feminism. It introduced the possibility of social change into a situation in which many women had already become dissatisfied. It posed women, not merely as beneficiaries of change in the relation of the sexes, but as agents of change as well. As Elizabeth Cady Stanton said at the meeting that inaugurated the movement, "Woman herself must do the work." . . .

The women's rights movement developed in the dozen years before the Civil War. It had two sources. On the one hand, it emerged from women's growing awareness of their common conditions and grievances. Simultaneously, it was an aspect of antebellum reform politics, particularly of the antislavery movement. The women who built and led the women's rights movement combined these two historical experiences. They shared in and understood the lives of white, native-born American women of the working and middle classes: the limited domestic sphere prescribed for them, their increasing isolation from the major economic and political developments of their society, and above all their mounting discontent with their situation. Women's rights leaders raised this discontent to a self-conscious level and channeled it into activities intended to transform women's position. They were able to do this because of their experience in the antislavery movement, to which they were led, in part, by that very dissatisfaction with exclusively domestic life. . . . Borrowing from antislavery ideology, they articulated a vision of equality and independence for women, and borrowing from antislavery method, they spread their radical ideas widely to challenge other people to imagine a new set of sexual relations. Their most radical demand was enfranchisement. More than any other element in the women's rights program of legal reform, woman suffrage embodied the movement's feminism, the challenge it posed to women's dependence upon and subservience to men.

The first episode of the women's rights movement was the 1848 Seneca Falls Convention, organized by Elizabeth Cady Stanton, Lucretia Mott, and several other women. As befitted an enterprise handicapped by the very injustices it was designed to protest, the proceedings were a mixture of womanly modesty and feminist militancy. When faced with the task of composing a manifesto for the convention, the organizers, in Stanton's words, felt "as helpless and hopeless as if they had been suddenly asked to construct a steam engine." Nor was any woman willing to chair the meeting, and the office fell to Lucretia Mott's husband. Yet the list of grievances which the organizers presented was comprehensive. In retrospect, we can see that their Declaration of Sentiments and Resolutions anticipated every demand of nineteenth-century feminism. To express their ideas about women's rights and wrongs, they chose to rewrite the Preamble of the Declaration of Independence around "the repeated injuries and usurpations on the part of man towards woman." On the one hand, this decision reflected their need to borrow political legitimacy from the American Revolution. On the other, it permitted them to state in the clearest possible fashion that they identified the tyranny of men as the cause of women's grievances.

The Seneca Falls Convention was consciously intended to initiate a broader movement for the emancipation of women. For the women who organized the convention, and others like them, the first and greatest task was acquiring the skills and knowledge necessary to lead such an enterprise. In Elizabeth Cady Stanton's words, they had to transform themselves into a "race of women worthy to assert the humanity of women." Their development as feminists, as women able to bring politics to bear on the condition of their sex, had as its starting point the experience they shared with other women. While many accounts of this first generation of feminist activists stress what distinguished them from other women—their bravery and open rebellion—it is equally important to recognize what they had in common with nonfeminists: lack of public skills; lives marked by excessive domesticity; husbands and fathers hostile to their efforts; the material pressures of housekeeping and child-rearing; and the deep psychological insecurity bred by all these factors. A movement is a process by which rebellion generates more rebellion. The women's rights pioneers did not begin their political activities already "emancipated," freed from the limitations that other women suffered. Many of the personal and political resources they drew on to challenge the oppression of women were developed in the course of mounting the challenge itself.

213

"The Infancy of Our Movement"

Even the most committed and militant of the first-generation women's rights activists hesitated on the brink of the public activity necessary to build a feminist movement. Although a successful writer, Frances Dana Gage was as homebound as other women, when she was asked to preside over a women's rights convention in Akron in 1851. She was reluctant, but accepted the responsibility. "I have never in my life attended a regular business meeting," she told her audience, whose vistas were even more circumscribed than hers. . . . Abigail Bush spoke for an entire generation of feminists committed to acquiring political skills in service to their sex. When the audience at a convention in Rochester in 1848 called down the women speakers with cries of "louder, louder!" Bush responded: "Friends, we present ourselves here before you, as an oppressed class, with trembling frames and faltering tongues, and we do not expect to be able to speak as to be heard by all at first, but we trust we shall have the sympathy of the audience, and that you will bear with our weakness now in the infancy of our movement. . . ."

. . . The opposition of men, particularly the fathers and husbands on whom they were dependent, reinforced women's lack of public experience to restrain their feminist activism. . . . Elizabeth Cady Stanton, who was singularly unafflicted with psychological insecurity, faced her greatest obstacles in her husband and her father. . . .

Unlike Stanton, Lucy Stone and Antoinette Brown assumed domestic responsibilities after they had become prominent women's rights advocates. Stone married Henry Blackwell in 1855, and Brown married his brother Samuel a year later. Brown had seven children; Stone had one, which kept her out of political work for over a decade. "I wish I felt the old impulse and power to lecture . . . , but I am afraid and dare not trust Lucy Stone," Stone wrote to Brown, when her daughter was a year and a half old. . . . Brown experienced this same dilemma. Unable even to keep up a political correspondence because of the press of household obligations, she wrote to Anthony, "This, Susan, is 'woman's sphere.'" Anthony was unsympathetic to her comrade's preference for what she called "the ineffable joys of Maternity," and resentful of the political responsibilities that devolved on her. She wrote to Brown in frustration over Stone's preparations for an important debate: "A woman who *is* and *must* of necessity continue for the

214

present at least the representative woman has no right to *disqualify* herself for such a *representative occasion*. I do feel that it is so foolish for her to put herself in the position of *maid of all work* and *baby tender*. What man would dream of going before the public on such an occasion as this one night-tired and worn from such a multitude of engrossing cares." Indeed, even though Brown and Stone had foresworn marriage while young girls, Anthony was the only first-generation national women's rights leader who remained single. "Where are you Susan and what are you doing?" Stanton wrote when she hadn't heard from Anthony for some time. "Are you dead or married?"

In the face of such obstacles, the major resource on which women's rights activists drew to support themselves and advance their cause was one another. Like many nineteenth-century women, they formed intense and lasting friendships with other women. Frequently these were the most passionate and emotionally supportive relationships that they had. While feminists' mutual relationships were similar to other female friendships in emotional texture, they were different in their focus on the public and political concerns that made their lives as women unique. The most enduring and productive of these friendships was undoubtedly that of Elizabeth Cady Stanton and Susan B. Anthony, which began in 1851. The initial basis of their interdependency was that Anthony gave Stanton psychological and material support in domestic matters, while Stanton provided Anthony with a political education. . . .

Antoinette Brown and Lucy Stone were also bound by an intense friendship, formed when they were both students at Oberlin. They turned to each other to fortify their common feminism against the assaults of friends and teachers. . . . Their relationship continued to sustain them after they left Oberlin and became abolitionists and women's rights agitators. When Stone was subject to particularly intense harassment for wearing bloomers, Brown offered her support. "Tonight I could nestle closer to your heart than on the night when I went through the dark and the rain and Tappan Hall and school rules—all to feel your arm around me," she wrote, "and to know that in all this wide world I was not alone."

An important aspect of these relationships was overtly political. Given the strength of men's commitment to maintaining their political monopoly, the few women who were fortunate enough to have acquired a political education had to share their skills and knowledge with others. Stanton's contribution to Anthony's political development has already been noted. When Brown and Stone first met, they organized six other women students into "an informal debating and speaking society" to provide the oratorical experience they were denied in Oberlin's "ladies" course. They were so afraid of official intervention that they met in a black woman's home "on the outskirts of town," and occasionally in the woods, with a guard posted "against possible intruders." . . .

There were limits, however, to the support women's rights pioneers could offer one another. One such constraint was physical distance. As reformers they traveled to a degree unheard of among pre-Civil War women and, when unmarried, could scarcely be said to have a home. They were usually alone. In addition, the attacks on them for stepping outside women's sphere were constant, severe, and beyond the power of friends to halt or counteract. . . . Surrounded on all sides by hostility, women's rights agitators had to work most of the time without the companionship and sisterhood they so prized. . . .

Abolitionist Politics

The abolitionist movement provided the particular framework within which the politics of women's rights developed. From the 1837 clerical attack on the Grimké sisters, through the 1840 meeting of Lucretia Mott and Elizabeth Cady Stanton at the World's Anti-Slavery Convention, to the Civil War and Reconstruction, the development of American feminism was inseparable from the unfolding of the antislavery drama. . . . What American women

Lucretia Mott, a Quaker, abolitionist, and founder of the first women's rights movement. (Courtesy of The National Archives.)

learned from abolitionism was less that they were oppressed than what to do with that perception, how to turn it into a political movement. Abolitionism provided them with a way to escape clerical authority, an egalitarian ideology, and a theory of social change, all of which permitted the leaders to transform the insights into the oppression of women which they shared with many of their contemporaries into the beginnings of the women's rights movement.

Women's involvement in abolitionism developed out of traditions of pietistic female benevolence that were an accepted aspect of women's sphere in the early nineteenth century. . . . For the movement's first half-decade, the role women had in it was consistent with that in other benevolent religious efforts such as urban missionary activities and moral reform. Women organized separate antislavery auxiliaries, in which they worked to support men's organizations and gave particular attention to the female victims and domestic casualties of slavery. . . . As the movement became secularized, so did the activities of benevolent women in it. "Those who urged women to become missionaries and form tract societies . . . have changed the household utensil to a living, energetic being," wrote domestic author and abolitionist Lydia Maria Child, "and they have no spell to turn it into a broom again."

The emergence of the Garrisonian wing of the abolitionist movement embodied and accelerated these secularizing processes. In 1837 William Lloyd Garrison was converted by utopian John Humphrey Noyes to the doctrine of perfectionism, which identified the sanctified individual conscience as the supreme moral standard, and corrupt institutions, not people, as the source of sin. In particular, Garrisonians turned on their churchly origins and attacked the Protestant clergy for its perversion of true Christianity and its support of slavery. Garrisonians' ability to distinguish religious institutions from their own deeply-felt religious impulses was an impressive achievement for evangelicals in an evangelical age. . . .

The clergy was the major force that controlled women's moral energies and kept pietistic activism from becoming political activism. Garrisonian anticlericalism was therefore critical to the emergence of abolitionist feminism and its subsequent development into the women's rights movement. This was clear in the 1837

217

confrontation between the Grimké sisters and the Congregational clergy of Massachusetts. . . .

Women in the Garrisonian abolitionist movement not only absorbed its anticlericalism, but also drew on its principle of the absolute moral equality of all human beings. Because the Garrisonian abolitionists' target was Northern racial prejudice and their goal the development of white empathy for the suffering slave, they focused their arguments on convincing white people of their basic identity with black people. . . .

Abolitionist feminists appropriated this belief and applied it to women. The philosophical tenet that women were essentially human and only incidentally female liberated them from the necessity of justifying their own actions in terms of what was appropriate to women's sphere. In other words, Garrisonianism provided an ideology of equality for women to use in fighting their way out of a society built around sexual difference and inequality. . . . "Too much has already been said and written about woman's sphere," Lucy Stone said in 1854. "Leave women, then, to find their sphere." The 1851 women's rights convention resolved that: "We deny the right of any portion of the species to decide for another portion . . . what is and what is not their 'proper sphere'; that the proper sphere for all human beings is the largest and highest to which they are able to attain." . . .

Along with a philosophical basis, Garrisonian abolitionism provided the women's rights movement with a theory and practice of social change, a strategy that gave direction to its efforts for female emancipation. The core of Garrisonian strategy was the belief that a revolution in people's ideas must precede and underlie institutional and legal reform, in order to effect true social change. . . . While Garrisonian agitation did not develop political mechanisms for ending slavery, it was well suited to the early years of the antislavery movement when the primary problem was overcoming public apathy.

Faced with an equally stubborn and widespread indifference to the oppression of women, women's rights leaders drew on this abolitionist precedent and formulated their task as the agitation of public sentiment. "Disappointment is the lot of woman," Lucy Stone wrote in 1855. "It shall be the business of my life to deepen this disappointment in every woman's heart until she bows down to it no longer." . . .

The Demand for Woman Suffrage

From the beginning, gaining the franchise was part of the program of the women's rights movement. It was one of a series of reforms that looked toward the elimination of women's dependent and inferior position before the law. The women's rights movement demanded for married women control over their own wages, the right to contract for their own property, joint guardianship over their children, and improved inheritance rights when widowed. For all women, the movement demanded the elective franchise and the rights of citizenship. Compared to legal reforms in women's status articulated before 1848, for instance equal right to inherit real property, the women's rights program was very broadly based, and intentionally so. In particular, the right to control one's earnings and the right to vote were demands that affected large numbers of women—farm women, wives of urban artisans and laborers, millgirls and needlewomen.

While part of this general reform in women's legal status, the demand for woman suffrage was always treated differently from other women's rights. In the first place, it initially met with greater opposition within the movement than other demands did. At the Seneca Falls Convention, Elizabeth Cady Stanton submitted a resolution on "the duty of the women of this country to secure to themselves the sacred right to the elective franchise." . . . Although the convention passed all other motions unanimously, it was seriously divided over the suffrage. Frederick Douglass, who, himself disfranchised [because he was black], appreciated the importance of membership in the political community, was Stanton's staunchest supporter at Seneca Falls. The woman suffrage resolution barely passed.

Soon, however, woman suffrage was distinguished from other reforms by being elevated to a preeminent position in the women's rights movement. . . .

. . . [T]he demand for woman suffrage also generated much more opposition outside the movement. Public opinion and politicians were more sympathetic to feminists' economic demands than to their political ones. In the mid-1850's, state legislatures began to respond favorably to women's lobbying and petition efforts for reforms in property law. By 1860, fourteen states had passed some form of women's property rights legislation. Encouraged by these victories, the movement escalated its demands and shifted its emphasis from property rights to the suffrage. . . .

To both opponents and advocates of women's rights, therefore, the demand for woman suffrage was significantly more controversial than other demands for equality with men. Why was this the case? Like the overwhelming majority of their contemporaries, nineteenth-century feminists believed that the vote was the ultimate repository of social and economic power in a democratic society. They wanted that power for women and relied on well-developed natural rights arguments and the rhetorical traditions of the American Revolution and the Declaration of Independence to make their demand. "In demanding the political rights of woman," the 1853 national convention resolved, "we simply assert the fundamental principle of democracy—that taxation and representation should go together, and that, if the principle is denied, all our institutions must fall with it." . . .

. . . The ideas of democratic political theory were not systematically applied to women until feminist leaders, anxious to challenge the subservient position of women, appropriated those ideas and demanded the vote. Like black men, women were excluded from the actual expansion of the suffrage in the late eighteenth and early nineteenth centuries, but the exclusion of women from political life went even further. Women were so far outside the boundaries of the antebellum political community that the fact of their disfranchisement, unlike that of black men, was barely noticed. . . .

On what basis were women excluded from any consideration in the distribution of political power, even when that power was organized on democratic principles? At least part of the answer seems to lie in the concept of "independence," which was the major criterion for enfranchisement in classical democratic political theory, and which acted to exclude women from the political community. Even the radical Tom Paine thought that servants should not have the vote because they were economically and socially dependent on their masters, and "freedom is destroyed by dependence." . . . Women's traditional relationships to men within their families constituted the essence of dependence. When John Adams considered the question, "Whence arises the right of men to govern the women without their consent?" he found the answer in men's power to feed, clothe, and employ women and therefore to make political decisions on their behalf. Not only were eighteenth- and early nineteenth-century women prohibited from owning real property or controlling wealth; they could not be said even to hold property in themselves. Law and custom granted the husband ownership, not only of his wife's labor power and the wages she earned by it, but of her physical person as well, in the sexual rights of the marriage relation. No people, with the exception of chattel slaves, had less proprietary rights over themselves in eighteenth- and early nineteenth-century America than married women. Until the emergence of feminism, the dependent status that women held was considered natural, and if not right, then inescapable.

Thus, the demand that women be included in the electorate was not simply a stage in the expansion and democratization of the franchise. It was a particularly feminist demand, because it exposed and challenged the assumption of male authority over women. To women fighting to extend their sphere beyond its traditional domestic limitations, political rights involved a radical change in women's status, their emergence into public life. The right to vote raised the prospect of female autonomy in a way that other claims to equal rights could not. Petitions to state legislatures for equal rights to property and children were memorials for the redress of grievances, which could be tolerated within the traditional chivalrous framework that accorded women the "right" to protection. In 1859 the *New York Times* supported the passage of the New York Married Women's Property Act by distinguishing the "legal protection and fair play to which women are justly entitled" from "the claims to a share of political power which the extreme advocates of Women's Rights are fond of advancing." By contrast, the suffrage demand challenged the idea that women's interests were identical or even compatible with men's. As such, it embodied a vision of female self-determination that placed it at the center of the feminist movement. "While we would not undervalue other methods," the 1851 national women's rights convention resolved, "the Right of Suffrage for Women is, in our opinion, the corner-stone of this enterprise, since we do not seek to protect woman, but rather to place her in a position to protect herself."

The feminist implications of the suffrage demand are further evident in the reverberations it sent through the ideology of sexual spheres, the nineteenth-century formulation of the sexual division of labor. Most obviously, woman suffrage constituted a serious challenge to the masculine monopoly of the public sphere. Although the growing numbers of women in schools, trades,

221

professions, and wage-labor were weakening the sexual barriers around life outside the family, most adult women remained at home, defined politically, economically, and socially by their family position. In this context, the prospect of enfranchisement was uniquely able to touch all women, offering them a public role and a relation to the community unmediated by husband or children. While the suffrage demand did not address the domestic side of the nineteenth-century sexual order directly, the connections between public and private spheres carried its implications into the family as well. In particular, the public honor of citizenship promised to elevate women's status in the home and raised the specter of sexual equality there. Women's rights leaders were relatively modest about the implications of the franchise for women's position in the family. . . . Their opponents, however, predicted that woman suffrage would have a revolutionary impact on the family. "It is well known that the object of these unsexed women is to overthrow the most sacred of our institutions . . . ," a New York legislator responded to women's rights petitions. "Are we to put the stamp of truth upon the libel here set forth, that men and women, in the matrimonial relation, are to be equal?" . . .

Obstacles to Growth

The process by which women's rights ideas were spread was a highly informal one. As the first activists reached the small towns of New York, Massachusetts, Ohio, and Indiana, their example drew local women out of their isolation. A speech by Lucy Stone impelled two Rockland, Maine, women to become printers. Olympia Brown was brought into the movement when, still a student at Antioch College, she heard author and abolitionist Frances Gage. "It was the first time I had heard a woman preach," she recalled, "and the sense of victory lifted me up." Frances Ellen Burr, who went on to lead suffrage forces in Connecticut, attended a women's rights convention in Cleveland when she was twenty-two. She was surprised at how attracted she was to the militance of the speakers and noted in her diary, "Never saw anything of the kind before." . . .

Nonetheless, the movement grew slowly. As Stone rationalized after a particularly disappointing lecture tour, "I sell a great many of the tracts, so seed is being scattered that will grow *sometime.*" In the wake of their lectures and conventions, Stone,

Anthony, and others left a trail of strong-minded women behind them. Sarah Burger attended a women's rights convention in 1853, when she was sixteen. What she heard there convinced her that the University of Michigan should be opened to women and "that women themselves should move in the matter." She located twelve other girls to join with her and in 1858 petitioned the university for admission. She continued her campaign for several years, and, although she had to attend a normal school, the University of Michigan finally admitted women in 1869. Two Ellsworth, Maine, women organized a lecture series on women's rights. Despite threats to the livelihood of one of them, they persisted and the lectures were held. Other local activists, more than we may ever know, launched their own protests, but often the women's rights movement was too small and weak to sustain them. In 1859, Mary Harrington of Claremont, New Hampshire, refused to pay her taxes because she was disfranchised. The tax collector seized her furniture and the local newspaper editor attacked her in print. She was too isolated to do anything more, and her rebellion went underground for the time being. "Such unjust treatment seemed so cruel that I sometimes felt I could willingly lay down my life," she wrote later, "if it would deliver my sex from such degrading oppression. I have, every year since, submissively paid my taxes, humbly hoping and praying that I may live to see the day that women will not be compelled to pay taxes without representation." . . .

Ironically, the Garrisonian politics and abolitionist alliance that had enabled the women's rights movement to develop in the first place were beginning to restrain its continued growth. Like the abolitionists before them, women's rights activists saw themselves as agitators, stirring up discontent. However, they had no way to consolidate the feminist sentiment that their agitation was beginning to create. Once the level of their discontent was raised, there was nothing for most women to do with it. Women's rights activities were organized around a small group who were politically skilled, willing to shoulder the opprobrium of "strong-mindedness," and able to commit a great deal of their energies to the movement. Women who were just beginning to develop political skills and sensibilities could not normally find an active role to play. The limitations to growth inherent in the agitational focus of prewar women's rights were embodied in the movement's organizational underdevelopment. There were no national or state organizations. Annual conventions were planned by an informal and constantly changing coordinating committee. Speaking tours and legislative campaigns were highly individualistic matters, which put a premium on personal initiative and bravery. The movement's close political relationship with abolitionism further restrained its organizational growth, in that its ability to rely on the organizational resources of the American Anti-Slavery Society meant that it did not develop its own. Women's rights articles were published in antislavery newspapers, and its tracts were printed with antislavery funds. . . .

Above all, the prewar women's rights movement depended on abolitionism for its constituency. It is impossible to estimate how many women were touched by women's rights, and how many of these were abolitionists. Still, the movement's strongest, most reliable, and most visible support came from abolitionist ranks, particularly from the women. This dependence on an organized constituency borrowed from abolitionism was particularly marked on the national level. The call for the first national women's rights convention was timed to coincide with the annual meeting of the American Anti-Slavery Society. Abolitionist women provided women's rights with an audience well suited to its first, highly controversial years. Their antislavery activity had already put them outside the pale of respectable womanhood, where they were less likely to be frightened by public hostility. However, the availability of an audience among antislavery women kept feminist leaders from a systematic effort to reach the many women who were not reformers. . . .

Although primarily a source of strength, the relation of women's rights to abolitionism was thus a potential liability as well. The partnership was unequal, with women's rights dependent on abolitionism for essential resources and support. The basic precepts, strategic methods, and organizational forms of Garrisonian abolitionism had sustained the women's rights movement through its first dozen years. On this basis, feminist leaders were able to transform insights into the oppression of women that they shared with many other women into a social movement strong enough to have a future. This achievement raised other political problems—the extent of the movement's reforming ambitions, the nature of its constituency, the organizational form it would take, and above all, its relation to abolitionism. The resolution of these matters was interrupted by the outbreak of the Civil War. Women's rights activists subordinated all other interests to the fate of slavery, and suspended feminist activity for the length of the war. When they returned, four years later, to consider the future of women's rights, the political context within which they did so had been completely altered.

Questions

1. *What personal and public barriers did women have to overcome in order to mobilize a women's rights movement?*
2. *What role did religion play in the origins and growth of feminism?*
3. *How did abolitionism contribute to the development of the women's rights movement?*
4. *Why was the demand for women's suffrage so controversial?*

WOMEN MAKE THE CASE FOR WOMEN'S RIGHTS

In the 1830s women increasingly wrote and spoke about their condition as women and called on Americans to work against the ideas, laws, and practices that made them second-class citizens. The following documents provide a sampling of the issues that engaged activist women and the arguments they used in their efforts to transform society.

Maria Stewart Claims the Right of Women to Speak in Public

Maria W. Stewart was born in Connecticut in 1803 and orphaned at the age of five. Although, like most free blacks, she had little opportunity for formal education, she became an eloquent champion of the rights of blacks and women. In fact, she was the first American-born woman to address public audiences. In this selection, an address given in 1833, she challenges the nearly universal opposition to women speaking in public. Taken from "Mrs. Stewart's Farewell Address to Her Friends In the City of Boston," in Black Women in Nineteenth-Century American Life: Their Words, Their Thoughts, Their Feelings, *ed. Bert James Loewenberg and Ruth Bogin (University Park, Pennsylvania, 1976), 198–200.*

I felt that I had a great work to perform; and was in haste to make a profession of my faith in Christ, that I might be about my Father's business. Soon after I made this profession, the Spirit of God came before me, and I spake before many. When going home,

227

reflecting on what I had said, I felt ashamed, and knew not where I should hide myself. A something said within my breast, "press forward, I will be with thee." And my heart made this reply, Lord, if thou wilt be with me, then will I speak for thee so long as I live. And thus far I have every reason to believe that it is the divine influence of the Holy Spirit operating upon my heart. . . .

What if I am a woman; is not the God of ancient times the God of these modern days? Did he not raise up Deborah, to be a mother, and a judge in Israel? Did not queen Esther save the lives of the Jews? And Mary Magdalene first declare the resurrection of Christ from the dead? . . . St. Paul declared that it was a shame for a woman to speak in public, yet our great High Priest and Advocate did not condemn the woman for a more notorious offence than this; neither will he condemn this worthless worm. . . . Did St. Paul but know of our wrongs and deprivations, I presume he would make no objections to our pleading in public for our rights. Again; holy women ministered unto Christ and the apostles; and women of refinement in all ages, more or less, have had a voice in moral, religious and political subjects. . . .

. . . Among the Greeks, women delivered the Oracles; the respect the Romans paid to the Sybils, is well known. The Jews had their prophetesses. The prediction of the Egyptian women obtained much credit at Rome, even under the Emperors. And in the most barbarous nations, all things that have the appearance of being supernatural, the mysteries of religion, the secrets of physic, and the rites of magic, were in the possession of women.

If such women as are here described have once existed, be no longer astonished then, my brethren and friends, that God at this eventful period should raise up your own females to strive, by their example both in public and private, to assist those who are endeavoring to stop the strong current of prejudice that flows so profusely against us at present. No longer ridicule their efforts, it will be counted for sin. For God makes use of feeble means sometimes, to bring about his most exalted purposes. . . .

What if such women as are here described should rise among our sable race? And it is not impossible. For it is not the color of the skin that makes the man or the woman, but the principle formed in the soul. Brilliant wit will shine, come from whence it will; and genius and talent will not hide the brightness of its lustre.

Black Women's Activism

Although Northern black and white women sometimes cooperated in abolitionist activities, they had different priorities. Whereas white women focused singularly on abolition, black women activists pursued a much broader agenda for the elimination of racial injustice. Maria Stewart calls for women to work for the development of the black community in this selection from her pamphlet, "Religion and the Pure Principles of Morality . . . " issued in 1831 and reprinted in Black Women in Nineteenth-Century American Life: Their Words, Their Thoughts, Their Feelings, *ed. Bert James Loewenberg and Ruth Bogin (University Park, Pennsylvania, 1976), 189–90.*

Shall it any longer be said of the daughters of Africa, they have no ambition, they have no force? By no means. Let every female heart become united, and let us raise a fund ourselves; and at the end of one year and a half, we might be able to lay the corner-stone for the building of a High School, that the higher branches of knowledge might be enjoyed by us; and God would raise us up, and enough to aid us in our laudable designs. Let each one strive to excel in good house-wifery, knowing that prudence and economy are the road to wealth. Let us not say, we know this, or, we know that, and practise nothing; but let us practise what we do know.

How long shall the fair daughters of Africa be compelled to bury their minds and talents beneath a load of iron pots and kettles? Until union, knowledge and love begin to flow among us. How long shall a mean set of men flatter us with their smiles, and enrich themselves with our hard earnings; their wives' fingers sparkling with rings, and they themselves laughing at our folly? Until we begin to promote and patronize each other. . . . Do you ask, what can we do? Unite and build a store of your own, if you cannot procure a license. Fill one side with dry goods, and the other with groceries. . . . We have never had an opportunity of displaying our talents; therefore the world thinks we know nothing. . . . Do you ask the disposition I would have you possess? Possess the spirit of independence. The Americans do, and why should not you? Possess the spirit of men, bold and enterprising, fearless and undaunted. Sue for your rights and privileges. Know the reason that you cannot attain them. Weary them with your importunities. You can but die, if you make the attempt; and we shall certainly die if you do not. The Americans have practised nothing but head-work these 200 years, and we have done their drudgery. And is it not high time for us to imitate their examples, and practise head-work too, and keep what we have got, and get what we can? We need never to think that any body is going to feel interested for us, if we do not feel interested for ourselves.

Sarah Grimké Challenges the Clergy

Sarah Grimké and her sister Angelina, daughters of a prominent Charleston, South Carolina slaveholder, were the first American-born white women to give public speeches. Their hatred of slavery had driven them from the South to Philadelphia, where they became Quakers and leading abolitionists. In this selection, Sarah Grimké responds with sarcasm and wit to the "Pastoral Letter," a denunciation of women's public speaking promulgated by a group of clergymen in the Congregational General Association. Taken from The Liberator, *6 October 1837.*

DEAR FRIEND,— . . . [T]he Pastoral Letter of the General Association . . . is . . . so extraordinary a document, that when the minds of men and women become emancipated from the thraldom of superstition, and 'traditions of men,' it will be recurred to with as much astonishment as the opinions of Cotton Mather and other distinguished men of his day, on the subject of witchcraft; nor will it be deemed less wonderful, that a body of divines should gravely assemble and endeavor to prove that woman has no right to 'open her mouth for the dumb,' than it now is that judges should have sat on the trials of witches, and solemnly condemned nineteen persons and one dog to death for witchcraft.

But to the letter: it says, 'we invite your attention to the dangers which at present seem to threaten the FEMALE CHARACTER with wide-spread and permanent injury.' I rejoice that they have called the attention of my sex to this subject, because I believe if woman investigates it, she will soon discover that danger is impending, though from a totally different source from that which the Association apprehends,—danger from those who, having long held the reins of *usurped* authority, are unwilling to permit us to fill that sphere which God created us to move in, and who have entered into league to crush the immortal mind of woman. I rejoice, because I am persuaded that the rights of woman, like the rights of slaves, need only be examined, to be understood and asserted, even by some of those who are now endeavoring to smother the irrepressible desire for mental and spiritual freedom which glows in the breast of many who hardly dare to speak their sentiments. . . .

No one can desire more earnestly than I do, that woman may move exactly in the sphere which her Creator has assigned her; and I believe her having been displaced from that sphere, has introduced confusion into the world. It is therefore of vast importance to herself, and to all the rational creation, that she should ascertain what are her duties and her privileges as a responsible and immortal being. The New Testament has been referred to, and I am willing to abide by its decisions, and must enter my protest against the false translations of some passages by the MEN who did that work, and against the perverted interpretation by the MEN who undertook to write commentaries thereon. I am inclined to think, when we are admitted to the honor of studying Greek and Hebrew, we shall produce some various readings of the Bible, a little different from those we now have.

I find the Lord Jesus defining the duties of his followers in his sermon on the Mount. . . . giving the same directions to women as to men, never even referring to the distinction now so strenuously insisted upon between masculine and feminine virtues: this is one of the anti-christian 'traditions of men' which are taught instead of the 'commandments of God.' Men and women were CREATED EQUAL: they are both moral and accountable beings, and whatever is right for man to do, is right for woman to do.

But the influence of woman, says the Association, is to be private and unobtrusive; her light is not to shine before man like that of her brethren; but she is passively to let the lords of the creation, as they call themselves, put the bushel over it . . . 'Her influence is the source of mighty power.' This has ever been the language of man since he laid aside the whip as a means to keep woman in subjection. He spares her body, but the war he has waged against her mind, her heart, and her soul, has been no less destructive to her as a moral being. How monstrous is the doctrine that woman is to be dependent on man! Where in all the sacred scriptures is this taught? But, alas, she has too well learned the lesson which he has labored to teach her. She has surrendered her dearest RIGHTS, and been satisfied with the privileges which man has assumed to grant her; whilst he has amused her with the show of power, and absorbed all the reality into himself. He has adorned the creature, whom God gave him as a companion, with baubles and gewgaws, turned her attention to personal attractions, offered incense to her vanity, and made her the instrument of his selfish gratification, a plaything to please his eye, and amuse his hours of leisure. . . . This doctrine of dependence upon man is utterly at variance with the doctrine of the Bible. In that book I find nothing like the softness of woman, nor the sternness of man; both are equally commanded to bring forth the fruits of the Spirit—Love, meekness, gentleness.

. . . [O]ur powers of mind have been crushed, as far as man could do it, our sense of morality has been impaired by his interpretation of our duties, but no where does God say that he made any distinction between us as moral and intelligent beings. . . .

The General Association say that 'when woman assumes the place and tone of man as a public reformer, our care and protection of her seem unnecessary; we put ourselves in self-defence against her, and her character becomes unnatural.' . . . The motto of woman, when she is engaged in the great work of public reformation, should be.—'The Lord is my light and my salvation; whom shall I fear? The Lord is the strength of my life; of whom shall I be afraid?' She must feel, if she feels rightly, that she is fulfilling one of the important duties laid upon her as an accountable being, and that her character, instead of being 'unnatural,' is in exact accordance with the will of Him to whom and to no other, she is responsible for the talents and the gifts confided to her. . . .

232

And my sex now feel in the dominion so unrighteously exercised over them, under the gentle appellation of protection, that what they have leaned upon has proved a broken reed at best, and oft a spear.

Birth of the Women's Rights Movement: The Seneca Falls Convention

The conflict over women's public participation in the abolitionist movement simmered for a decade and helped to split the antislavery movement itself. In 1848, two women who still felt the humiliation of their exclusion from the World Antislavery Convention in 1840, Lucretia Mott and Elizabeth Cady Stanton, called a meeting to discuss women's rights. Some three hundred people, including about forty men, gathered in Seneca Falls, New York, on 19 and 20 July 1848. The assembly issued a broad declaration of grievances and list of demands, drafted primarily by Stanton and modeled after the Declaration of Independence. The "Declaration of Sentiments" is abridged from History of Woman Suffrage, *ed. Elizabeth Cady Stanton, Susan B. Anthony, and Matilda Joslyn Gage (Rochester, New York, 1889), 1:70–73.*

When, in the course of human events, it becomes necessary for one portion of the family of man to assume among the people of the earth a position different from that which they have hitherto occupied, but one to which the laws of nature and of nature's God entitle them, a decent respect to the opinions of mankind requires that they should declare the causes that impel them to such a course.

We hold these truths to be self-evident: that all men and women are created equal. . . . [The rest of this paragraph follows almost exactly the second paragraph of the Declaration of Independence, up to the final sentence.] Such has been the patient sufferance of the women under this government, and such is now the necessity which constrains them to demand the equal station to which they are entitled.

The history of mankind is a history of repeated injuries and usurpations on the part of man toward woman, having in direct

233

object the establishment of an absolute tyranny over her. To prove this, let facts be submitted to a candid world.

He has never permitted her to exercise her inalienable right to the elective franchise.

He has compelled her to submit to laws, in the formation of which she had no voice.

He has withheld from her rights which are given to the most ignorant and degraded men—both natives and foreigners.

Having deprived her of this first right of a citizen, the elective franchise, thereby leaving her without representation in the halls of legislation, he has oppressed her on all sides.

He has made her, if married, in the eye of the law, civilly dead.

He has taken from her all right in property, even to the wages she earns.

He has made her, morally, an irresponsible being, as she can commit many crimes with impunity, provided they be done in the presence of her husband. In the covenant of marriage, she is compelled to promise obedience to her husband, he becoming, to all intents and purposes, her master—the law giving him power to deprive her of her liberty, and to administer chastisement.

He has so framed the laws of divorce, as to what shall be the proper causes, and in case of separation, to whom the guardianship of the children shall be given, as to be wholly regardless of the happiness of women—the law, in all cases, going upon a false supposition of the supremacy of man, and giving all power into his hands.

After depriving her of all rights as a married woman, if single, and the owner of property, he has taxed her to support a government which recognizes her only when her property can be made profitable to it.

He has monopolized nearly all the profitable employments, and from those she is permitted to follow, she receives but a scanty remuneration. He closes against her all the avenues to wealth and distinction which he considers most honorable to himself. As a teacher of theology, medicine, or law, she is not known.

He has denied her the facilities for obtaining a thorough education, all colleges being closed against her.

He allows her in Church, as well as State, but a subordinate position, claiming Apostolic authority for her exclusion from the ministry, and, with some exceptions, from any public participation in the affairs of the Church.

He has created a false public sentiment by giving to the world a different code of morals for men and women, by which moral delinquencies which exclude women from society, are not only tolerated, but deemed of little account in man.

He has usurped the prerogative of Jehovah himself, claiming it as his right to assign for her a sphere of action, when that belongs to her conscience and to her God.

He has endeavored, in every way that he could, to destroy her confidence in her own powers, to lessen her self-respect, and to make her willing to lead a dependent and abject life.

Now, in view of this entire disfranchisement of one-half the people of this country, their social and religious degradation—in view of the unjust laws above mentioned, and because women do feel themselves aggrieved, oppressed, and fraudulently deprived of their most sacred rights, we insist that they have immediate admission to all the rights and privileges which belong to them as citizens of the United States.

In entering upon the great work before us, we anticipate no small amount of misconception, misrepresentation, and ridicule; but we shall use every instrumentality within our power to effect our object. We shall employ agents, circulate tracts, petition the State and National legislatures, and endeavor to enlist the pulpit and the press in our behalf. We hope this Convention will be followed by a series of Conventions embracing every part of the country.

The following resolutions were . . . adopted:

WHEREAS, The great precept of nature is conceded to be, that "man shall pursue his own true and substantial happiness." Blackstone in his Commentaries remarks, that this law of Nature being coeval with mankind, and dictated by God himself, is of course superior in obligation to any other. It is binding over all the globe, in all countries and at all times; no human laws are of any validity if contrary to this, and such of them as are valid, derive all their force, and all their validity, and all their authority, mediately and immediately, from this original; therefore,

Resolved, That such laws as conflict, in any way, with the true and substantial happiness of woman, are contrary to the great precept of nature and of no validity. . . .

Resolved, That all laws which prevent woman from occupying such a station in society as her conscience shall dictate, or which

235

place her in a position inferior to that of man, are contrary to the great precept of nature, and therefore of no force or authority.

Resolved, That woman is man's equal—was intended to be so by the Creator, and the highest good of the race demands that she should be recognized as such.

Resolved, That the women of this country ought to be enlightened in regard to the laws under which they live, that they may no longer publish their degradation by declaring themselves satisfied with their present position, nor their ignorance, by asserting that they have all the rights they want.

Resolved, That inasmuch as man, while claiming for himself intellectual superiority, does accord to woman moral superiority, it is pre-eminently his duty to encourage her to speak and teach, as she has an opportunity, in all religious assemblies.

Resolved, That the same amount of virtue, delicacy, and refinement of behavior that is required of woman in the social state, should also be required of man, and the same transgressions should be visited with equal severity on both man and woman.

Resolved, That the objection of indelicacy and impropriety, which is so often brought against woman when she addresses a public audience, comes with a very ill-grace from those who encourage, by their attendance, her appearance on the stage, in the concert, or in feats of the circus.

Resolved, That woman has too long rested satisfied in the circumscribed limits which corrupt customs and a perverted application of the Scriptures have marked out for her, and that it is time she should move in the enlarged sphere which her great Creator has assigned her.

Resolved, That it is the duty of the women of this country to secure to themselves their sacred right to the elective franchise.

Resolved, That the equality of human rights results necessarily from the fact of the identity of the race in capabilities and responsibilities.

Resolved, therefore, That, being invested by the Creator with the same capabilities, and the same consciousness of responsibility for their exercise, it is demonstrably the right and duty of woman, equally with man, to promote every righteous cause by every righteous means; and especially in regard to the great subjects of morals and religion, it is self-evidently her right to participate with her brother in teaching them, both in private and in public, by writing and by speaking, by any instrumentalities proper to be used, and in any assemblies proper to be held; and this being a self-evident truth growing out of the divinely implanted principles of human nature, any custom or authority adverse to it, whether modern or wearing the hoary sanction of antiquity, is to be regarded as a self-evident falsehood, and at war with mankind. . . .

Resolved, That the speedy success of our cause depends upon the zealous and untiring efforts of both men and women, for the overthrow of the monopoly of the pulpit, and for the securing to woman an equal participation with men in the various trades, professions, and commerce.

The Stanton-Anthony Partnership

Elizabeth Cady Stanton and Susan B. Anthony became the most prominent women's rights leaders in the nineteenth century. Married and the mother of seven children, Stanton grew discontented with women's status through her abolitionist work, where she was deeply influenced by the Quaker, Lucretia Mott. Anthony, who never married, was first active in the temperance movement. After the two met in 1851, they forged a personal friendship and public partnership that gave direction to women's rights ideology and agitation throughout the nineteenth century. The following correspondence reflects the nature of their relationship and the burden that women's traditional domestic responsibilities placed on their public work. Taken from Elizabeth Cady Stanton As Revealed in Her Letters, Diary and Reminiscences, *ed. Theodore Stanton and Harriot Stanton Blatch (New York, 1922), 2:41–42, 54–55, 59–60, 64–67, 70–71.*

Stanton to Anthony, April 2, 1852

Men and angels give me patience! I am at the boiling point! If I do not find some day the use of my tongue on this question, I

"Correspondence Between Elizabeth Cady Stanton and Susan B. Anthony," reprinted from *Elizabeth Cady Stanton as Revealed in Her Letters, Diary and Reminiscences* edited by Theodore Stanton and Harriet Stanton Blatch. Published by Harper and Brothers, 1922. Copyright © 1922 by Harper & Brothers.

shall die of an intellectual repression, a woman's rights convulsion! Oh, Susan! Susan! Susan! You must manage to spend a week with me before the Rochester convention, for I am afraid that I cannot attend it; I have so much care with all these boys on my hands. But I will write a letter. How much I do long to be free from housekeeping and children, so as to have some time to read, and think, and write. But it may be well for me to understand all the trials of woman's lot, that I may more eloquently proclaim them when the time comes.

Stanton to Anthony, Dec. 1, 1853

Can you get any acute lawyer . . . sufficiently interested in our movement to look up just eight laws concerning us—the very worst in all the code? I can generalize and philosophize easily enough of myself; but the details of the particular laws I need, I have not time to look up. You see, while I am about the house, surrounded by my children, washing dishes, baking, sewing, etc., I can think up many points, but I cannot search books, for my hands as well as my brains would be necessary for that work. . . . I seldom have one hour undisturbed in which to sit down and write. Men who can, when they wish to write a document, shut themselves up for days with their thoughts and their books, know little of

The great suffrage team, Susan B. Anthony and Elizabeth Cady Stanton, pose together in 1870, the year they founded the National Woman Suffrage Association (Courtesy of The Schlesinger Library.)

what difficulties a woman must surmount to get off a tolerable production.

Stanton to Anthony, September 10, 1855

I wish that I were as free as you and I would stump the state in a twinkling. But I am not, and what is more, I passed through a terrible scourging when last at my father's. I cannot tell you how deep the iron entered my soul. I never felt more keenly the degradation of my sex. To think that all in me of which my father would have felt a proper pride had I been a man, is deeply mortifying to him because I am a woman. That thought has stung me to a fierce decision—to speak as soon as I can do myself credit. But the pressure on me just now is too great. Henry sides with my friends, who oppose me in all that is dearest to my heart. They are not willing that I should write even on the woman question. But I will both write and speak.

Anthony to Stanton, June 5, 1856

And, Mrs. Stanton, not a word on that Address for the Teachers' Convention. This week was to be leisure to me, and the Mercy only knows when I can get a moment; and what is worse, as the Lord knows full well, if I get all the time the world has, I can't get up a decent document. Oh, dear, dear! There is so much to say and I am so without constructive power to put in symmetrical order. So, for the love of me and for the saving of the reputation of womanhood, I beg you, with one baby on your knee and another at your feet, and four boys whistling, buzzing, hallooing "Ma, Ma," set yourself about the work. It is of but small moment who writes the Address, but of vast moment that it be well done. Ah! Mrs. Stanton, don't say No, nor don't delay it a moment; for I must have it all done and almost commit to memory. . . . Don't delay one mail to tell me what you will do, for I must not and will not allow these schoolmasters to say: "See, these women can't or won't do anything when we do give them a chance." . . . Now do, I pray you, give heed to my prayer. Those of you who have the talent to do honor to poor—oh! how poor—womanhood, have all given yourself over to baby-making; and left poor brainless me to do battle alone. It is a shame. Such a body as I might be spared to rock cradles. But it is a crime for you and Lucy Stone and

239

Antoinette Brown to be doing it. I have just engaged to attend a progressive meeting in Erie County, the first of September, just because there is no other woman to be had, but not because I feel in the least competent.

Stanton to Anthony, June 10, 1856

Your servant is not dead but liveth. Imagine me, day in and day out, watching, bathing, dressing, nursing, and promenading the precious contents of a little crib in the corner of the room. I pace up and down these two chambers of mine like a caged lioness, longing to bring to a close nursing and housekeeping cares.... Is your speech to be exclusively on the point of educating the sexes together, or as to the best manner of educating women? I will do what I can to help you with your lecture. Let Lucy and Antoinette rest awhile in peace and quietness and think great thoughts for the future. It is not well to be in the excitement of public life all the time; do not keep stirring them up or mourning over their repose. You need rest too, Susan. Let the world alone awhile. We cannot bring about a moral revolution in a day or year. Now that I have two daughters, I feel fresh strength to work. It is not in vain that in myself I have experienced all the wearisome cares to which woman in her best estate is subject.

Stanton to Anthony, July 20, 1857

A man in marrying gives up no right; but a woman, every right, even the most sacred of all—the right to her own person. There will be no response among women to our demands until we have first aroused in them a sense of personal dignity and independence; and so long as our present false marriage relation continues, which in most cases is nothing more nor less than legalized prostitution, woman can have no self-respect, and of course man will have none for her; for the world estimates us according to the value we put upon ourselves. Personal freedom is the first right to be proclaimed, and that does not and cannot now belong to the relation of wife, to the mistress of the isolated home, to the financial dependent.

Stanton to Anthony, August 20, 1857

DEAR SUSAN,—I did indeed see by the papers that you had once more stirred that part of intellectual stagnation, the educational convention. The *Times* was really quite complimentary. Henry brought me every item he could see about you. "Well," he would say, "another notice about Susan. You stir up Susan, and she stirs the world." What a set of fools those schoolmarms must be! Well, if in order to please men they wish to live on air, let them. I was glad you went to torment them. I will do anything to help you on. If I do nothing else this fall I am bound to aid you to get up an antislavery address. You must come here for a week or two and we will accomplish wonders. You and I have a prospect of a good long life. We shall not be in our prime before fifty, and after that we shall be good for twenty years at least.

Questions

1. *Why did women use religious arguments to claim their rights? What arguments did they use? What claims did they make based on republican ideas?*

2. *Did women's rights advocates emphasize sex differences or did they stress what men and women had in common? What differences and commonalities did they acknowledge?*

3. *How might the Seneca Falls Declaration of Sentiments have differed if Maria Stewart or other black women had helped write it?*

4. *If Elizabeth Cady Stanton were alive today, how might she assess the results of the movement she helped found? Have all the grievances been redressed and all the demands been achieved? What ideas or arguments of the nineteenth-century women's rights movement are still relevant today?*

FURTHER READING

The classic history of women's activism remains Eleanor Flexner, Century of Struggle: The Woman's Movement in the United States *(1959; rev. ed., Cambridge, Massachusetts, 1975). Shirley Yee,* Black Women Abolitionists: A Study in Activism, 1828–1860 *(Knoxville, 1992), tells the story of African American women's work for their race and their sex. Gerda Lerner,* The Grimké Sisters from South Carolina: Pioneers for Woman's Rights and Abolition *(New York, 1971), places these two women in the context of antebellum reform. Details of the lives and work of Anthony and Stanton can be found in* The Elizabeth Cady Stanton-Susan B. Anthony Reader: Correspondence, Writings, Speeches, *ed. Ellen Carol DuBois, rev. ed. (Boston, 1992).*

The Mexican-American War: America's First Foreign War

James M. McCaffrey

INTRODUCTION

Spanish explorers arrived in what is now Mexico in 1519 and for the next three hundred years worked hard to establish and maintain it as a viable colony. Spain grew very wealthy on the vast mineral riches it extracted therefrom, and Spanish missionaries brought Christianity to the native peoples. By the early years of the nineteenth century colonists in most of Spain's colonies had grown restive to the point of rebellion. In Mexico, that rebellion began in 1810 and finally succeeded eleven years later in achieving an independent Mexico.

Concurrent with independence, settlers from the United States began moving to the sparsely settled Mexican province of Texas in the 1820s. Mexican officials welcomed them, expecting their presence to provide a buffer zone with the neighboring United States and to serve as a lure for Mexican settlers. In 1835, however, the Americans, dissatisfied with Mexican rule, rose up in a successful revolution. From 1836 to 1845 Texas existed as a sovereign, independent nation, although Mexico never officially acknowledged this status. Not only did Mexico refuse to recognize the loss of Texas, but it resented Texan claims to lands between the Rio Grande and Nueces rivers that had traditionally been part of the Mexican state of Tamaulipas. In 1845, the United States annexed Texas into the Union, something Mexico regarded as an act of war, and actual hostilities commenced on the lower Rio Grande River in April 1846.

Militarily, the war was an almost unbroken string of American victories. Brigadier General Zachary Taylor ("Old Rough and Ready" to his men) twice led his force to victory over Mexican troops near Matamoros in May, forcing them to retreat toward

246

Monterrey. *In the meantime, a second American force occupied Santa Fe, New Mexico, without a struggle and continued on to Mexican California.*

When peace still seemed elusive following Taylor's victory at Monterrey in September, a third force was organized under the command of Major General Winfield Scott. Scott landed his men at Veracruz in early March 1847, and proceeded to fight his way all the way to Mexico City. Scott occupied the Mexican capital in September, and peace soon followed.

To arrive at a good understanding of any conflict such as that between the United States and Mexico one must study it from a myriad of perspectives—diplomatic, political, military, and social. The selections that follow seek to introduce some of these important viewpoints.

CONTEMPORARIES DISCUSS THE MEXICAN-AMERICAN WAR

Primary sources, documents created by participants in historic events, are often excellent windows into the minds of the writers. Even among primary sources, however, there are gradations. The following section, for example, presents documents created by President James K. Polk and Congressman Abraham Lincoln. These men undoubtedly spent considerable time preparing these writings. They may have added some passages, deleted others, and rewritten still others before reaching the final version. The results of these efforts reflect the considered opinions of their writers, men who likely were aware that these documents would be scrutinized not only by their contemporaries but by later readers all the way down to the present.

This section also contains excerpts from the letters of two volunteer soldiers. Letters and diaries leave us a more immediate record of events. These men were writing home to family members not for posterity. They had little reason to believe that anyone outside of their families would ever read them. Unlike government officials they can give vent to their feelings about commanding officers, for example, without worrying about how their comments could affect their careers. Documents such as these are especially valuable for understanding how the common soldiers perceived the war.

Whose Land Is It Anyway?

In President James K. Polk's message to Congress on May 11, 1846, asking it to declare war on Mexico, he emphasizes that Mexican forces brought on the war by their invasion of American territory—the area north of the Rio Grande. Excerpted from House Executive Document, 29th Congress, 1st session, No. 196, contained in Origins of the Mexican War: A Documentary Source Book, *ed. Ward McAfee and J. Cordell Robinson (Salisbury, North Carolina, 1982), 2:146-49.*

In my message at the commencement of the present session, I informed you that, upon the earnest appeal both of the Congress and convention of Texas, I had ordered an efficient military force to take a position "between the Nueces and the Del Norte [Rio Grande]." This had become necessary to meet a threatened invasion of Texas by the Mexican forces, for which extensive military preparations had been made. The invasion was threatened solely because Texas had determined, in accordance with a solemn resolution of the Congress of the United States, to annex herself to our Union; and, under these circumstances, it was plainly our duty to extend our protection over her citizens and soil. . . .

Meantime, Texas, by the final action of our Congress, had become an integral part of our Union. The Congress of Texas, by its act of December 19, 1836, had declared the Rio del Norte [Rio Grande] to be the boundary of that republic. Its jurisdiction had been extended and exercised beyond the Nueces. The country between that river and the Del Norte had been represented in the [Texas] Congress and in the convention of Texas [and] had thus taken part in the act of annexation itself; and is now included within one of our Congressional districts. . . . It became, therefore, of urgent necessity to provide for the defense of that portion of our country. Accordingly, on the 13th of January last instructions were issued to the general in command of these troops to occupy the left bank of the Del Norte. This river, which is the southwestern boundary of the State of Texas, is an exposed frontier; from

Excerpts reprinted from *Origins of the Mexican War: A Documentary Source Book*, by Ward McAfee and J. Cordell Robinson, 1982, Documentary Publications.

this quarter invasion was threatened; upon it, and in its immediate vicinity, in the judgement of high military experience, are the proper stations for the protecting forces of the government. . . .

The Mexican forces at Matamoros assumed a belligerent attitude, and, on the 12th of April [1846] General [Pedro de] Ampudia, then in command, notified General [Zachary] Taylor to break up his camp within twenty-four hours and to retire beyond the Nueces River, and in the event of his failure to comply with these demands, announced that arms, and arms alone, must decide the question. But no open act of hostility was committed until the 24th of April. On that day, General [Mariano] Arista, who had succeeded to the command of the Mexican forces, communicated to General Taylor that "he considered hostilities commenced, and should prosecute them." A party of dragoons, of 63 men and officers, were on the same day dispatched from the American camp up the Rio del Norte, on its left bank, to ascertain whether the Mexican troops had crossed, or were preparing to cross, the river; [it] "became engaged with a large body of these troops, and, after a short affair, in which some 16 were killed and wounded, appear to have been surrounded and compelled to surrender.". . .

[W]e have been exerting our best efforts to propitiate her [Mexico's] good will. Upon the pretext that Texas, a nation as independent as herself, thought proper to unite its destinies with our own, she has affected to believe that we have severed her rightful territory, and in official proclamations and manifestoes has repeatedly threatened to make war upon us for the purpose of reconquering Texas. In the meantime, we have tried every effort at reconciliation. The cup of forbearance had been exhausted, even before the recent information from the frontier of the Del Norte. But now, after reiterated menaces, Mexico has passed the boundary of the United States, has invaded our territory, and shed American blood upon the American soil. She has proclaimed that hostilities have commenced and that the two nations are now at war.

As war exists, and, notwithstanding all our efforts to avoid it, exists by the act of Mexico herself, we are called upon by every consideration of duty and patriotism to vindicate with decision the honor, the rights, and the interests of our country. . . .

Lincoln Questions Polk

Freshman Whig Congressman Abraham Lincoln, from Illinois, disagreed with the president's characterization of "American soil" when he offered the following resolution on December 22, 1847. Excerpted from Journal of the House of Representatives of the United States: Being the First Session of the Thirtieth Congress; Begun and Held at the City of Washington, December 6, 1847, in the Seventy-Second Year of the Independence of the United States *(Washington, 1847-48), 149-51.*

Whereas the President of the United States, in his message of May 11, 1846, has declared that "the Mexican government not only refused to receive him" (the envoy of the United States) "or listen to his propositions, but, after a long continued series of menaces, have at last invaded *our territory*, and shed the blood of our fellow *citizens* on *our own soil:*"

And again, in his message of December 8, 1846, that "we had ample cause of war against Mexico, long before the breaking out of hostilities; but even then we forbore to take redress into our own hands, until Mexico herself became the aggressor, by invading *our soil* in hostile array, and shedding the blood of our *citizens*:["]

And yet again, in his message of December 7, 1847, that "the Mexican government refused even to hear the terms of adjustment which he" (our minister of peace) "was authorized to propose; and finally, under wholly unjustifiable pretexts, involved the two countries in war, by invading the territory of the State of Texas, striking the first blow, and shedding the blood of our *citizens* on *our own soil*."

And whereas this House desires to obtain a full knowledge of all the facts which go to establish whether the particular spot of soil on which the blood of our *citizens* was so shed was, or was not, *our own soil*, at that time: therefore,

Resolved, by the House of Representatives, That the President of the United States be respectfully requested to inform this House,

First. Whether the spot of soil on which the blood of our *citizens* was shed, as in his messages declared, was, or was not, within the territories of Spain, at least from the treaty of 1819 until the Mexican revolution.

Second. Whether that spot is, or is not, within the territory which was wrested from Spain by the Mexican revolution.

Third. Whether that spot is, or is not, within a settlement of people, which settlement had existed ever since long before the Texas revolution, until its inhabitants fled from the approach of the United States army.

Fourth. Whether that settlement is, or is not, isolated from any and all other settlements, by the Gulf of Mexico and the Rio Grande on the south and west, and by wide uninhabited regions on the north and east.

Fifth. Whether the *people* of that settlement, or a *majority* of them, or *any* of them, had ever, previous to the bloodshed mentioned in his message, submitted themselves to the government or laws of Texas, or of the United States, by *consent*, or by *compulsion*, either by accepting office, or voting at elections, or paying taxes, or serving on juries, or having process served upon them, or in *any other way.*

Sixth. Whether the people of that settlement did, or did not, flee from the approach of the United States army, leaving unprotected their homes and their growing crops, *before* the blood was shed, as in message stated; and whether the first blood so shed was, or was not, shed within the *inclosure* of the people, or some of them, who had thus fled from it.

Seventh. Whether our *citizens*, whose blood was shed, as in his messages declared, were, or were not, at that time, *armed* officers and *soldiers*, sent into that settlement by the military order of the President, through the Secretary of War; and,

Eighth. Whether the military force of the United States, including those *citizens*, was, or was not, so sent into that settlement after General Taylor had, more than once, intimated to the War Department that, in his opinion, no such movement was necessary to the defence or protection of Texas.

Soldiers' Letters Home

Excerpt from a letter from Lieutenant Will Wallace (near Monclova, Mexico), to his father, November 6, 1846, Wallace-Dickey Collection, Illinois State Historical Library, Springfield, Illinois.

My dear Father

I believe I wrote to you while on the march from San Antonio but in the hurry & bustle of recent events I have no distinct recollection of what I wrote or from what precise point. These letters seem to me like firing at the moon, the distance is so great & the means of communication so uncertain. Yet I cannot resist the inclination I feel to write whenever I have time or anything like an opportunity of sending. We are now lying in camp on the edge of the town of Monclova, a place of some 8000 inhabitants, situated at the foot of a lofty & barren chain of Mountains, a spur of the Bolson Massimi Range. In whatever direction you look from our camp the bold or indistinct outlines of these mountains as they are near or more remote, rise like mighty barriers to oppose our progress or our retreat. A stream some larger than Pine Creek comes down from the Mountains & rushes past the town, supplying innumerable ducts & hydrants that water every part of the town. A broad valley of fine land borders this stream & is dotted here and there with Ranchos & Hasiendas (cattle & grain farms) in some of them in a fine state of cultivation, covered with luxurious crops of corn, cotton & sugar cane. All the cultivated lands here require to be irrigated, & for this purpose their fields & farms are intersected with numerous ditches running in every direction. For the same reason lands are never cultivated except near some running stream that can afford sufficient water for irrigation. The farms or Ranchos are generally miserable affairs, with little or no fencing & mud Huts; though occasionally we passed one of superior order. Two days before we reached here we encamped at the Hot Springs where was the finest Hasienda I have seen. The main building & out houses, including a sugar house, & stables were enclosed by a heavy stone wall 12 feet high, the whole covering a space of about 7 acres. The place is owned by two brothers Sanchez, one of whom lives in Saltillo & the other in the city of Mexico. They own all the country from San Fernando to this place

& on to near Saltillo, a scope of country some 250 miles in extent. The Hasienda is now occupied by Senor Miguel Blanco, a nephew of Sanchez. He works 160 servants. I visited every part of the establishment in company with a Texan who speaks Spanish. The quarters of the working people were far inferior to those of the slaves on the Mississippi, but they appeared neat & clean as far as could be. A system of slavery exists here which is a vast improvement on the Slavery in our southern states. Whenever a man is in debt, his creditor sues him, gets a judgement, & if the debtor has not the means to satisfy it, the creditor may take him as his servant, & compel him to work out the debt at the rate of $3.00 per month, finding his own clothing. I am told that hunderds of men here enter this Kind of service to avoid being drafted into the Army. Before they can discharge the original debt they have necessarily contracted others, & thus they continue for years in slavery, until old age & hard labor have rendered them unfit for farther service, & then they are released to the wretched liberty of a penniless old age. The differences in the classes are as distinctly marked here as in the slave states. The *peans* [peons] or servants are generally a dark swarthy shaggy haired race—evidently a mixture of Indian & Negro with occasionally a touch of the Spanish blood. The leading men & men of wealth are much whiter & more intelligent in appearance, & some of the women of the upper class are decidedly beautiful. It is difficult to tell their true feelings towards us—some of them profess to be greatly dissatisfied with the rapacity & imbecility of the Central [Mexican] Government, & are very willing to sell us corn & other commodities at about three prices. On the other hand, I have concluded from what I have seen in Monclova that there is a deep feeling of hostility toward us; & I know that Senor Blanco at the Hot Springs had assembled a considerable force at his Hasienda to oppose our progress, & only disbanded it a few days before our arrival. I am also informed by a young Spaniard, a resident of Monclova, who speaks English, that the priests exerted their utmost influence to raise the people against us, representing us as a plundering band, with whom their property & families would be ruined. Thus far they have nothing to complain of, & indeed they say themselves that we are not half so great a terror to them as their own armies. From the policy that Gen. [John] Wool has adopted I think we will not give them any reason to complain for we pay them their own price for every thing we get from them—the war thus far is more injury to us than to Mexico. Gen. Shield[s] thinks all these northern provinces are ripe for a revolution. He came up from Matamoros & Camargo to Presidio, & was very kindly received by the authorities of all the frontier towns, & the feeling he found there is what he bases his presumption upon. But I've no doubt he overestimates the extent of this feeling, & if we should meet with any reverses these very fellows who are now so kind & so full of professions of friendship would be the first to cut our throats. Treachery is a characteristic of the Race, & after getting all our money I've no doubt they would shoot us for the sake of our clothes. I don't think they will ever fight us with anything like equal numbers. Taylors victory at Monterey over a superior force & that force entrenched has frightened them. It is said that Santa Anna is now fortifying San Luis Potosi, & if peace is not concluded before the expiration of the armistice, Gen. Taylor will push on to that point, & our greatest hope is to join him. Wool is very unpopular with his command—he has quarrelled with every field officer in it. . . . Gen. Wool is a very old & a very vain man; I do not blame, tho I pity him. The Management of our army in the field is "above his hair" & the Government & the Department is culpably & criminally foolish for putting him in command of a division. I have a matter to settle after the war is over—he cussed me— charges will be preferred against him & I hope to see him relieved from his command. . . .

Excerpt from a letter from Henry Smith Lane (Matamoros) to his brother, November 5, 1846, Henry Smith Lane Collection, Filson Club, Louisville, Kentucky.

My dear Brother:

Since I last wrote to you I have seen & suffered much. You are no doubt apprized of my position in the Army. I am at present stationed with a part of our Regiment at Palo Altotucks, miles below this city. On the 22d of July we arrived upon the Rio Grande, since which time our Regiment has been stationed at the mouth of the River in a very sickly & unpleasant location. We have suffered a vast deal from fevers, there have been over sixty deaths in the regiment & about two hundred discharged on account of ill health, but we hope that this sickly season has passed by. My own health is now good but I have had fever & a constant bow[e]l complaint a great part of the time since I landed. We are now daily expecting orders to march into the interior of the country towards Tampico. Our position did not enable us to participate in the glory of the fight at Monterey but we are confident that we shall have a chance at Saltillo or Tampico to show what we are made of; the boys are exceedingly anxious for a free fight & I think the Mexicans will gratify them for we shall have no peace with the copper skinned rascals until they are soundly thrashed and that will be whenever they stand long enough before Old Rough & Ready & his boys to take it. . . . The country so far as I have seen of it along the Rio Grande is very fertile but miserably cultivated; the people are lazy, ignorant & perfidious with no patriotism, no public spirit, no enterprise and it would be a great mercy to them to take their country & give them a settled form of free government & Americanize their Republic; it is known to you that I have always been opposed to the Annexation of Texas & that I said that a war with Mexico would grow out of it, but the deed is done. Texas is a part of the United States & I feel as much bound to fight for her as I would for Indiana, or even old Kentucky.

The people here are ignorant & bigotted Roman Catholics & are more than One Hundred years behind the improvement & the spirit of the age & it requires no gift of prophecy to foretell their doom, they are destined soon to fall before the all grasping & all conquering genius of genuine Americanism. We have a singular climate here at least it seems to a Northern man, there is now in market here green corn, peas, beans, water melons, musk melons, onions, radishes & every variety of vegetables which we have in the Spring at the North, besides a great many more which are peculiar to this climate. In a word God has done as much to bless & man to curse this country as any region on earth.

I shall be home about next July, if I live until that time. I got a letter a short time since from my dear Joan. She was well but rather gloomy on account of my absence. I sometimes reproach myself for leaving her, for she is all the time anxious & uneasy about me, but if she will forgive me I promise to do so no more. . . . Brother Higgins wrote to me in Sept. He & his family were all well then, he was very anxious to come out with me to Mexico but I persuaded him not to think of it & he very reluctantly yielded. Major Hazelrigg wrote to me about the same time, they are all well.

My pay as Major is $130 per month & I like the service very well if we could get into a battle & have some chance for distinction. I am on excellent terms so far as I know or believe with every officer & private in our Brigade & shall take pains to remain so.

Give my love to Father & Mother & to Sister Sally & the dear children & to all the relatives & friends & tell them that tho far removed from them I still think of them very often & very kindly & that I love them as much as ever.

Farewell, may God bless & preserve you and yours, I am

Your affectionate brother,
Henry S. Lane

Questions

1. *Compare Polk's and Lincoln's characterizations of the land and inhabitants between the Nueces and the Rio Grande. Who do you think makes the stronger case?*

2. *Lincoln suggests that the residents of the area between the Nueces and the Rio Grande were not truly governed by Texas, but he does not assert that they were governed by Mexico. Why not?*

3. *Why does Lincoln appear to differentiate between the deaths of our citizens and the deaths of our soldiers?*

4. *Lane's descriptions of Mexican civilization reveals a lot about himself. What can we surmise about the background—religion, occupation, etc.—of Henry Lane from these descriptions?*

5. *Having been unable to experience "the glory" of the battle at Monterey, what possible reasons might Lane have for discouraging his brother from joining him?*

FURTHER READING

The standard treatment of this conflict from the American viewpoint is still The Mexican War, 1846-1848 *by K. Jack Bauer (New York, 1974), although John S. D. Eisenhower's very readable* So Far From God: The U.S. War With Mexico, 1846-1848 *(New York, 1989) is also good. An early Mexican account is Ramon Alcaraz et al.,* The Other Side; or, Notes for the History of the War Between Mexico and the United States, *trans. and ed. by Albert C. Ramsey (New York, 1850). Robert W. Johannsen's* To the Halls of the Montezumas: The Mexican War in the American Imagination *(New York, 1985) examines the impact the war had on American culture. The two best studies of the American army during the war are Richard Bruce Winder's* Mr. Polk's Army: The American Military Experience in the Mexican War *(College Station, Texas, 1997) and James M. McCaffrey's* Army of Manifest Destiny: The American Soldier in the Mexican War, 1846-1848 *(New York, 1992), while the Mexican Army is examined by Pedro Santoni in* Mexicans at Arms: Pyro Federalists and the Politics of War, 1845-1848 *(Fort Worth, Texas, 1996) and William A. DePalo, Jr. in* The Mexican National Army, 1822-1852 *(College Station, Texas, 1997). For a video treatment of the war see Public Broadcasting's* The U.S.-Mexican War *(Dallas, 1998).*

The Decision for Emancipation

Mark Grimsley and Allan R. Millett

INTRODUCTION

If the Civil War was the single most important episode in American history—and numerous historians have argued that it was—then the pivotal event of that conflict was President Abraham Lincoln's decision to free the 4.5 million enslaved African Americans living in the Confederate South. As many recognized at the time, the decision for emancipation had sweeping implications, not only for the Union war effort but also for the future development of the entire nation. It changed a limited war to quell rebellion into an all-out struggle to shatter the political, economic and social foundation of the South. It overthrew the fundamental basis on which American race relations had rested since colonial times. And it was an unprecedented extension of federal power—magnificent to some, alarming to others—that deeply undermined the American republic's original, sharply limited conception of national government.

THE SLAVES FREED: LINCOLN, THE ADVANCED REPUBLICANS, AND EMANCIPATION

"Lincoln's [Emancipation] proclamation," notes historian Stephen B. Oates, "was the most revolutionary measure ever to come from an American President up to that time." In the article below, Oates eloquently describes how this unprecedented step came about. He highlights the role played by what he calls the "advanced Republicans," a group more familiarly known as the Radical Republicans. Rejecting a traditional view of Lincoln and the Radicals as sharp antagonists, Oates argues that their disagreements had mainly to do with questions of timing, not principle. Abridged from Stephen B. Oates, "The Slaves Freed," American Heritage *32 (December 1980): 74–81, 83.*

[In the winter of 1861,] as Lincoln's inauguration approached and more Southern congressmen resigned to join the Confederacy, Republicans gained control of both houses and voted to expel the secessionists as traitors. Senator Lyman Trumbull of Illinois pronounced them all mad, and Charles Sumner of Massachusetts exhorted the free states to stand firm in the crisis. Michigan's Zachariah Chandler vowed to whip the South back into the Union and preserve the integrity of the government. And Ben Wade of Ohio predicted that secession would bring about the destruction of slavery, the very thing Southerners dreaded most. "The first blast of civil war," he had thundered at them, "is the death warrant of your institution."

"The Slaves Freed," by Stephen B. Oates, reprinted by permission of *American Heritage Magazine*, a division of Forbes, Inc., Vol. 32, No. 1, December 1980. Copyright © 1994 by Forbes, Inc.

After the events at Fort Sumter, Wade, Chandler, and Sumner called repeatedly at the White House and spoke with Lincoln about slavery and the rebellion. Sumner was a tall, elegant bachelor, with rich brown hair, a massive forehead, blue eyes, and a rather sad smile. He had traveled widely in England, where his friends included some of the most eminent political and literary figures. A humorless, erudite Bostonian . . . [h]e was so conscious of manners "that he never allowed himself, even in the privacy of his own chamber, to fall into a position which he would not take in his chair in the Senate. "Habit," he said, "is everything." Sumner spoke out with great courage against racial injustice and was one of the few Republicans who advocated complete Negro equality. Back in 1856 Representative Preston Brooks of South Carolina had beaten him almost to death in the Senate Chamber for his "Crime Against Kansas" speech, and Sumner still carried physical and psychological scars from that attack. The senator now served as Lincoln's chief foreign policy adviser, often accompanied him on his carriage rides, and became the President's warm personal friend.

Zachariah Chandler was a Detroit businessman who had amassed a fortune in real estate and dry goods. Profane, hard-drinking, and eternally grim, Chandler had been one of the founders of the national Republican party and had served on the Republican National Committee in 1856 and 1860. Elected to the Senate in 1857, he had plunged into the acrimonious debates over slavery in the West, exhorting his colleagues not to surrender another inch of territory to slaveholders. When Southerners threatened to

Senator Charles Sumner of Massachusetts. (Courtesy of The Library of Congress.)

murder Republicans, brandishing pistols and bowie knives in the Senate itself, Chandler took up calisthenics and improved his marksmanship in case he had to fight. Once civil war commenced, he demanded that the government suppress the "armed traitors" of the South with all-out warfare.

Now serving his second term in the Senate, Benjamin Franklin Wade was short and thick chested, with iron-gray hair, sunken black eyes, and a square and beardless face. He was blunt and irascible, known as "Bluff Ben" for his readiness to duel with slaveowners. . . . Once the war began, he was determined that Congress should have an equal voice with Lincoln in shaping Union war policies. [Wade was] described by observers as "perhaps the most energetic personality in the entire Congress . . . "and as one who" doesn't care a pinch of snuff whether people like what he says or not." Wade hated slavery as Sumner and Chandler did. But like most whites of his generation, he was prejudiced against blacks: he complained about their "odor," growled about all the "Nigger" cooks in Washington, and insisted that he had eaten food "cooked by Niggers until I can smell and taste the Nigger . . . all over." Like many Republicans, he thought the best solution to America's race problem was to ship all Negroes back to Africa.

As far as the Republican party was concerned, the three senators belonged to a loose faction inaccurately categorized as "radicals," a misnomer that has persisted through the years. These "more advanced Republicans," as the Detroit *Post* and *Tribune* referred to them, were really progressive, nineteenth-century liberals who felt a powerful kinship with English liberals like John Bright and Richard Cobden. What advanced Republicans wanted was to reform the American system—to bring their nation into line with the Declaration's premise—by ridding it of slavery and the South's ruling planter class. But while the advanced Republicans supported other social reforms, spoke out forthrightly against the crime and anachronism of slavery, and refused to compromise with the "Slave Power," they desired no radical break from basic American ideals and liberal institutions. Moreover, they were often at odds with one another on such issues as currency, the tariff, and precisely what rights black people should exercise in American white society.

Before secession, the advanced Republicans had endorsed the party's hands-off policy about slavery in the South: they all agreed that Congress had no constitutional authority to menace slavery as a state institution; all agreed, too, that the federal government could only abolish slavery in the national capital and outlaw it in the national territories, thus containing the institution in the South where they hoped it would ultimately perish. But civil war had removed their constitutional scruples about slavery in the Southern states, thereby bringing about the first significant difference between them and the more "moderate" and "conservative" members of the party. While the latter insisted that the Union must be restored with slavery intact, the advanced Republicans argued that the national government could now remove the peculiar institution by the war powers, and they wanted the President to do it in his capacity as Commander-in-Chief. This was what Sumner, Wade, and Chandler came to talk about with Lincoln. They respected the President, had applauded his nomination, campaigned indefatigably in his behalf, and cheered his firm stand at Fort Sumter. Now they urged him to destroy slavery as a war measure, pointing out that this would maim and cripple the Confederacy and hasten an end to the rebellion. Sumner flatly asserted that slavery and the rebellion were "mated" and would stand or fall together.

Lincoln seemed sympathetic. He detested human bondage as much as they did, and he wanted to stay on good terms with advanced Republicans on Capitol Hill, for he needed their support in prosecuting the war. Moreover, he respected the senators and referred to men like Sumner as the conscience of the party.

Yet to the senators' dismay, he would not free the slaves, could not free them. For one thing, he had no intention of alienating moderate and conservative Republicans—the majority of the party—by issuing an emancipation decree. For another, emancipation would almost surely send the loyal slave states—Delaware, Maryland, Kentucky, and Missouri—spiraling into the Confederacy, something that would be calamitous to the Union. Then, too, Lincoln was waging a bipartisan war with Northern Democrats and Republicans alike enlisting in his armies. An abolition policy, Lincoln feared, would splinter that coalition, perhaps even cause a new civil war behind Union lines.

Though deeply disappointed, the three senators at first acquiesced in Lincoln's policy because they wanted to maintain Republican unity in combating the rebellion. Sumner told himself that at bottom Lincoln was "a deeply convinced and faithful anti-slavery man" and that the sheer pressure of war would force him to strike at Negro bondage eventually.

On July 4, 1861, the Thirty-seventh Congress convened with a rebel army entrenched less than thirty miles away. Republicans controlled both houses, and the advanced Republicans quickly gained positions of leadership out of proportion to their numbers. Many had been in Congress for years, and their uncompromising stand against slavery expansion and concessions to secessionists had won them accolades from all manner of Republicans. Like Chandler, several advanced Republicans had helped establish the national party; all were prominent in their state parties. Their prestige, skill, and energy—Chandler, for example, routinely put in eighteen-hour workdays—had helped bring them to positions of power on Capitol Hill.

Advanced Republicans were equally prominent in the House. There was James Ashley of Ohio, an emotional, dramatic man with a curly brown mane, who chaired the committee on territories. There was George Washington Julian from Indiana, protégé of Joshua "Old War Horse" Giddings and a contentious, frowning individual who proved himself a formidable antislavery legislator. There was portly, unkempt Owen Lovejoy of Illinois, brother of Elijah, the abolitionist martyr; and eloquent antislavery orator, he headed the committee on agriculture. Like Sumner, Lovejoy was a close friend of Lincoln's—"the *best* friend I had in Congress," the President once remarked—and strove to sustain administration policies while simultaneously pushing the main cause of emancipation.

Finally there was sixty-nine-year-old Thaddeus Stevens of Pennsylvania, who controlled the nation's purse strings as chairman of the powerful committee on ways and means. Afflicted with a clubfoot, Stevens was a grim, sardonic bachelor with a cutting wit ("I now yield to Mr.

Representative Thaddeus Stevens of Pennsylvania. (Courtesy of the United States Signal Corp.)

267

B.," he once said, "who will make a few feeble remarks") and a fondness for gambling that took him almost nightly to Washington's casinos. To the delight of his colleagues, he indulged in witticisms so off color that they had to be deleted from the *Congressional Globe*. A wealthy ironmaster with a Jekyll-and-Hyde personality, he had contributed generously to charities and causes, crusaded for public schools in Pennsylvania, and defended fugitive slaves there. Crippled, as Fawn Brodie has noted, Stevens spoke of bondage "in terms of shackled limbs and a longing for freedom to dance." He lived with his mulatto housekeeper, Lydia Smith, and there is strong evidence that they were lovers. Antimiscegenation laws made marriage impossible, and their liaison not only generated malicious gossip but probably kept Stevens from becoming what he most wanted to be—a United States senator. He liked to quote the Bible that "He hath made of one blood all nations of men," yet he never championed complete equality for blacks—"not equality in all things," he once asserted, "simply before the laws, nothing else." Serving a fourth term as congressman, this bitter, intimidating, high-minded man was to rule the Civil War House and become "the master-spirit," said Alexander McClure, "of every aggressive movement in Congress to overthrow the rebellion and slavery."

As the session progressed that summer, congressional Republicans demonstrated remarkable harmony. They all wanted to preserve the Union and help the President fight the war through to a swift and successful conclusion. In agreement with Lincoln's slave policy, congressional Republicans also voted for the so-called Crittenden-Johnson resolutions, which declared that the sole purpose of the war was to restore the Union. For the sake of party unity, most advanced Republicans reluctantly supported the resolutions, too. But they agreed with Congressman Albert Riddle of Ohio that slavery ought to be destroyed. "You all believe that it is to go out, when it does, through convulsion, fire and blood," Riddle stormed on the House floor. "That convulsion is upon us. The man is a delirious ass who does not see it and realize this. For me, I mean to make a conquest of it; to beat it to extinction under the iron hoofs of our war horses."

For the advanced Republicans, the first chance to strike at slavery came late in July, after the Union rout at Bull Run. Observing that rebel forces used slaves to carry weapons and perform other military tasks, the advanced Republicans vigorously championed a confiscation bill, which authorized the seizure of any slave employed in the Confederate war effort, and they mustered almost unanimous Republican support in pushing the measure through Congress. Border-state Democrats like John J. Crittenden of Kentucky complained that the bill was unconstitutional, but most Republicans agreed with Henry Wilson that "if traitors use bondmen to destroy this country, my doctrine is that the Government shall at once convert those bondmen into men that cannot be used to destroy our country." In war, Republicans contended, the government had every right to confiscate enemy property—including slave property—as legitimate contraband. Though the bill was hardly a general emancipation act, advanced Republicans hailed its passage as an important first step. They were glad indeed when Lincoln signed the bill into law and commanded his armies to enforce it. At last the President appeared to be coming around to their views.

But they had misunderstood him. When John General Charles Frémont, commander of the Western Department, ordered that the slaves of all rebels in Missouri be "declared freemen," Lincoln pronounced this a dangerous and unauthorized political act that would alienate the loyal border [states] and commanded Frémont to modify his order so that it accorded strictly with the congressional confiscation act. Though border Unionists applauded Lincoln, advanced Republicans were dismayed that he had overruled Frémont's emancipation decree. Sumner declared that Lincoln "is now a dictator." Wade charged that Lincoln's opinions on slavery "could only come of one, born of 'poor white trash' and educated in a slave State." And Fessenden denounced the President for his "weak and unjustifiable concession to the Union men of the border States."

Still, the Frémont episode did not cause an irreparable split between Lincoln and the advanced Republicans, as some writers have claimed. In fact, when Lincoln subsequently removed the general from command, Trumbull, Chandler, and Lovejoy sustained the President, conceding that the celebrated Pathfinder and first standard-bearer of their party was a maladroit administrator. But in the fall and winter of 1861, advanced Republicans did mount an all-out campaign to make the obliteration of slavery a Union war objective. One after another they came to the White House—Wade, Chandler, and Trumbull, Sumner, Julian, and Lovejoy—and implored and badgered the President to issue an emancipation proclamation on military grounds. With the war dragging on, they insisted that slavery must be attacked in order to weaken the Confederate ability to fight.

Moreover, they argued, slavery had caused the conflict and was now the cornerstone of the Confederacy. It was absurd to fight a war without removing the thing that had brought it about. Should Lincoln restore the Union with slavery preserved, Southerners would just start another war whenever they thought the institution threatened, so that the present struggle would have been in vain. If Lincoln really wanted to salvage the Union, he must hurl his armies at the heart of the rebellion. He must tear slavery out root and branch and smash the South's arrogant planters—those mischievous men the advanced Republicans believed had masterminded secession and fomented war. The annihilation of slavery, Julian asserted, was "not a debatable and distant alternative, but a pressing and absolute necessity." So what if most of the country opposed emancipation lest it result in an exodus of Southern blacks into the North? "It was the duty of the President," he said "to lead, not follow public opinion."

Sumner, as Lincoln's foreign policy adviser, also linked emancipation to opinion overseas. There was a strong possibility that Britain would recognize the Confederacy as an independent nation—potentially disastrous for the Union since the Confederacy could then form alliances and seek mediation, perhaps even armed intervention. But, Sumner argued, if Lincoln made the destruction of slavery a Union war aim, Britain would balk at recognition and intervention because of her own anti-slavery tradition. And whatever powerful Britain did, the rest of Europe was sure to follow.

Also, as Sumner kept saying, emancipation would break the chains of several million oppressed human beings and right America at last with her own ideals. Lincoln and the Republican party could no longer wait to remove slavery. The President must do it by the war powers. The rebellion, monstrous and terrible though it was, had given him the opportunity.

But Lincoln still did not agree. "I think Sumner and the rest of you would upset our applecart altogether if you had your way," he told some advanced Republicans one day. "We didn't go into the war to put down slavery, but to put the flag back; and to act differently at this moment would, I have no doubt, not only weaken our cause, but smack of bad faith. . . . This thunderbolt will keep." And in his message to Congress in December of 1861, the President declared that he did not want the war degenerating into "a violent and remorseless revolutionary struggle." He was striving, he said, "to keep the integrity of the Union prominent as the primary object of the contest."

Advanced Republicans were deeply aggrieved. Fessenden thought the President had lost all hold on Congress, and Wade complained that not even a galvanic battery could inspire Lincoln to "courage, decision and enterprise." "He means well," wrote Trumbull, "and in ordinary times would have made one of the best of Presidents, but he lacks confidence in himself and the *will* necessary in this great emergency."

By year's end, though, Lincoln's mind had begun to change. He spoke with Sumner about emancipation and assured the senator that "the only difference between you and me on this subject is a difference of a month or six weeks in time." And he now felt, he said, that the war "was a great movement by God to end Slavery and that the man would be a fool who should stand in the way." But out of deference to the loyal border states, Lincoln still shied away from a sweeping executive decree and searched about for an alternative. On March 6, 1862, he proposed a plan to Congress he thought would make federal emancipation unnecessary—a gradual, compensated abolition program to begin along the loyal border and then be extended into the rebel states as they were conquered. According to Lincoln's plan, the border states would gradually remove slavery over the next thirty years, and the national government would compensate slaveholders for their loss. The whole program was to be voluntary; the states would adopt their own emancipation laws without federal coercion. At the same time (as he had earlier told Congress), Lincoln favored a voluntary colonization program, to be sponsored by the federal government, that would resettle liberated blacks outside the country.

On Capitol Hill Stevens derided Lincoln's scheme as "diluted milk-and-water-gruel." But other advanced Republicans, noting that Lincoln's was the first emancipation proposal ever offered by an American President, acclaimed it as an excellent step. On April 10 the Republican-controlled Congress endorsed Lincoln's emancipation plan. But the border-state representatives, for whom it was intended, rejected the scheme emphatically. "I utterly spit at it and despise it," said one Kentucky congressman. "Emancipation in the cotton States is simply an absurdity. . . . There is not enough power in the world to compel it to be done."

As Lincoln promoted his gradual, compensated scheme, advanced Republicans on Capitol Hill launched a furious antislavery attack of their own. They sponsored a tough new confiscation bill, championed legislation that weakened the fugitive-slave law and assailed human bondage in the national capital as well as the territories. What was more, they won over many Republican moderates to forge a new congressional majority so far as slavery was concerned. As the war ground into its second year, moderate Republicans came to agree with their advanced colleagues that it was senseless to pretend the Union could be restored without removing the cause of the rebellion.

So, over strong Democratic opposition, the Republican Congress approved a bill that forbade the return of fugitive slaves to the rebels, and on March 13, 1862, Lincoln signed it into law. Congress also adopted legislation which abolished slavery in Washington, D.C., compensated owners for their loss, and set aside funds for the voluntary colonization of blacks in Haiti and Liberia, and Lincoln signed this as well. Democrats howled. One castigated the bill as an entering wedge for wholesale abolition, another predicted that liberated Negroes would crowd white ladies out of congressional galleries. Washingtonians accused the "abolitionists" in Congress of converting the capital into "a hell on earth for the white man." Republicans brushed aside all such criticism. "If there be a place upon the face of the earth," asserted a Minnesota Republican, "where human slavery should be prohibited, and where every man should be protected in the rights which God and Nature have given him, that place is the capital of this great Republic."

In June the Republican Congress lashed at slavery again: it passed a bill that outlawed human bondage in all federal territories, thus overriding the Dred Scott decision, and Lincoln signed the measure into law. Congress and the President also joined together in recognizing the black republics of Haiti and Liberia, a move that would facilitate colonization efforts in those lands. Meanwhile, a fierce debate raged over the second confiscation bill, which authorized the seizure and liberation of all slaves held by those in rebellion. Advanced Republicans not only pushed the bill with uninhibited zeal but also advocated that emancipated blacks be enlisted in the army. But even some Republicans thought full-scale confiscation too drastic, and "conservatives" like Jacob Collamer of Vermont, Orville Browning of Illinois, and Edgar Cowan of Pennsylvania sided with the Democrats in denouncing the bill as uncivilized and unconstitutional. "Pass these acts," cried one opponent, "confiscate under the bills the property of these men, emancipate their negroes, place arms in the hands of these human gorillas to murder their masters and violate their wives and daughters, and you will have a war such as was never witnessed in the worst days of the French Revolution and horrors never exceeded in San Domingo."

On July 4, in the midst of the debate, Sumner hurried back to the White House and admonished Lincoln to attack slavery himself. Sumner was extremely disappointed in the President, for he did not seem a month or six weeks behind the senator at all. In fact, Lincoln recently had overruled another general, David Hunter, who liberated the slaves inside his lines, and again the advanced Republicans had groaned in despair. Now, on July 4, Sumner urged "the reconsecration of the day by a decree of emancipation." The senator pointed out that the Union was suffering from troop shortages on every front and that the slaves were an untapped reservoir of manpower. "You need more men," Sumner argued, "not only at the North, but at the South, in the rear of the Rebels; you need the slaves." But Lincoln insisted that an emancipation edict was still "too big a lick." And, in a White House interview, he warned border-state legislators that his gradual, state-guided plan was the only alternative to federal emancipation and that they must commend it to their people. Once again they refused.

On July 17, five days after Lincoln spoke with the border men, Congress finally passed the second confiscation bill. If the rebellion did not end in sixty days, the measure warned, the executive branch would seize the property of all those who supported, aided, or participated in the rebellion. Federal courts were to determine guilt. Those convicted would forfeit their estates and their slaves to the federal government, and their slaves would be set free. Section nine liberated other categories of slaves without court action: slaves of rebels who escaped to Union lines, who were captured by federal forces or were abandoned by their owners, "shall be deemed captives of war, and shall be forever free." On the other hand, the bill exempted loyal Unionists in the rebel South, allowing them to retain their slaves and other property.

Another section empowered Lincoln to enlist Negroes in the military. Still another, aimed at easing Northern racial fears and keeping Republican unity, provided for the voluntary resettlement of confiscated blacks in "some tropical country." A few days later Congress appropriated $500,000 for colonization.

Controversial though it was, the second confiscation act still fell far short of genuine emancipation. Most slaves were to be freed only after protracted case-by-case litigation in the courts. And of course, the slaves of loyal masters were not affected. Yet the bill was about as far as Congress could go in attacking slavery, for most Republicans still acknowledged that Congress had no constitutional authority to eradicate bondage as a state institution. Only the President with his war powers—or a constitutional amendment—could do that. Nevertheless, the measure seemed a clear invitation for the President to exercise his constitutional powers and annihilate slavery in the rebellious states. And Stevens, Sumner, and Wilson repeatedly told him that most congressional Republicans now favored this. On the other hand, conservatives like Orville Browning beseeched Lincoln to veto the confiscation bill and restore the old Union as it was. "I said to him that he had reached the culminating point in his administration," Browning recorded in his diary, "and his course upon this bill was to determine whether he was to control the abolitionists and radicals, or whether they were to control him."

For several days, Lincoln gave few hints as to what he would do, and Congress awaited his response in a state of high tension. Finally, on July 17, he informed Capitol Hill that he agreed entirely with the spirit of the confiscation bill remarking that "the traitor against the general government" deserved to have his slaves and other property forfeited as just punishment for rebellion. While he thought some of the wording unfortunately vague, he nevertheless raised no objection to the sections on slave liberation. He did, however, disagree with other portions on technical grounds, especially those which permanently divested a rebel of title to his land, and Lincoln hinted that he would veto the bill as a consequence. To avoid that, congressional Republicans attached an explanatory resolution removing most of Lincoln's complaints. Satisfied, the President signed the bill and commanded the army to start enforcing it after sixty days.

Even so, several advanced Republicans were angered by Lincoln's threatened veto and peeved by what they perceived as his legalistic quibbling when the Union was struggling for its life against a mutinous aristocracy founded on slavery. Julian, for his part, thought Lincoln's behavior "inexpressibly provoking," and when Congress adjourned, he called at the White House to find out once and for all where the President stood on emancipation and all-out war against the rebels. Julian said he was going home to Indiana and wanted to assure his constituents that the President would "co-operate with Congress in vigorously carrying out the measures we had inaugurated for the purpose of crushing the rebellion, and that now the quickest and hardest blows were to be dealt." Complaining that advanced Republicans had unfairly criticized him, Lincoln said he had no objection at all to what Julian wished to tell his constituents. In Indiana that summer, Julian announced that Lincoln had now decided on a radical change in his policy toward slavery.

In August Sumner learned that Lincoln had at last decided to issue an emancipation proclamation. Convinced that the peculiar institution could be destroyed only through executive action, Lincoln actually had drawn up a draft of the proclamation and read it to his Cabinet. But couldn't Sumner have predicted it? Lincoln had let Secretary of State William H. Seward dissuade him from issuing the edict until after a Union victory. At the White House, Sumner demanded that the decree "be put forth—the sooner the better—without any reference to our military condition." But the President refused, and Sumner stalked out, dismayed again at what he once called Lincoln's "immense *vis inertiae.*" The senator feared that only the confiscation act would ever free any slaves.

But in September Lincoln came through. After the Confederate reversal at Antietam, he issued his preliminary emancipation proclamation, a clear warning that if the rebellion did not cease in one hundred days, the executive branch would use the military to free *all* the slaves in rebel states—those belonging to secessionists and loyalists alike. Thus the President would go beyond the second confiscation act—he would handle emancipation himself, avoid tangled litigation over slavery in the courts, and vanquish it as an institution in the South. He believed he could do this by the war powers, and he deemed it "a fit and necessary military measure" to preserve the Union.

The advanced Republicans, of course, were delighted. "Hurrah for Old Abe and the proclamation," Wade exulted. Stevens extolled Lincoln for his patriotism and said his proclamation

A depiction of President Lincoln presenting the Emancipation Proclamation to his Cabinet. (Courtesy of The Library of Congress.)

"contained precisely the principles which I had advocated." "Thank God that I live to enjoy this day!" Sumner exclaimed in Boston. "Freedom is practically secured to all who find shelter within our lines, and the glorious flag of the Union, wherever it floats, becomes the flag of Freedom." A few days later, Sumner announced that "the Emancipation Proclamation . . . is now the corner-stone of our national policy."

As it turned out, though, the preliminary proclamation helped lead to a Republican disaster in the fall by-elections of 1862. Northern Democrats already were angered by Lincoln's harsh war measures, especially his use of martial law and military arrests. Now, Negro emancipation was more than they could bear, and they stumped the Northern states beating the drums of Negrophobia and warning of massive influxes of Southern blacks into the North once emancipation came. Sullen, war-weary, and racially antagonistic, Northern voters dealt the Republicans a smashing blow as the North's five most populous states—all of which had gone for Lincoln in 1860—now returned Democratic majorities to Capitol Hill. Republicans narrowly retained control of Congress, but they were steeped in gloom as it convened that December.

Though most Republicans stood resolutely behind emancipation, Browning and other conservatives now begged Lincoln to abandon his "reckless" abolition policy lest he shatter his party and wreck what remained of his country. At the same time, Sumner and Wade admonished Lincoln to stand firm, and he promised that he would. On January 1, 1863, the President officially signed the final proclamation in the White House. In it Lincoln temporarily exempted all of Tennessee and certain occupied places in Louisiana and Virginia (later, in reconstructing those states, he would withdraw the exemptions and make emancipation mandatory). He also excluded the loyal slave states because they were not in rebellion and he lacked the legal authority to uproot slavery there. With these exceptions, the final proclamation declared that all slaves in the rebellious states "from henceforth shall be free." The document also asserted that black men—Southern and Northern alike—might now be enlisted in Union military forces.

All in all, the advanced Republicans were pleased. Perhaps the President should not have exempted Tennessee and southern Louisiana, Horace Greeley said, "but let us not cavil." Lincoln had now "played his grand part" in the abolition of slavery, Julian declared, and "brought relief to multitudes of anxious people." "On that day," Sumner wrote of January 1, 1863, "an angel appeared upon the earth."

In truth, Lincoln's proclamation was the most revolutionary measure ever to come from an American President up to that time, and the advanced Republicans took a lot of credit for goading him at last to act. Slavery would now die by degrees with every Union advance, every Northern victory.

Now that Lincoln had adopted emancipation, advanced Republicans watched him with a critical eye, making sure that he enforced his edict and exhorting him to place only those firmly opposed to slavery in command of Union armies. In February rumor had it that if Lincoln wavered even once in his promise of freedom to the slaves, Wade would move for a vote of "no confidence" and try to cut off appropriations. But Lincoln did not waiver. Even though a storm of anti-Negro, anti-Lincoln protest broke over the land, the President refused to retract a single word of his decree. "He is stubborn as a mule when he gets his back up," Chandler said, "& *it is up* now on the Proclamation." "His mind acts slowly," Lovejoy observed, "but when he moves, it is *forward.*"

In the last two years of the war, Lincoln and the advanced Republicans had their differences, but they were scarcely locked in the kind of blood feud depicted in Civil War histories and biographies of an earlier day. Several advanced Republicans did oppose Lincoln's renomination in 1864 because the war was going badly and they thought him an inept administrator. In addition, Sumner, Stevens, and Wade clashed bitterly with Lincoln over whether Congress or the President should oversee reconstruction. Sumner, Julian, Chandler, and a handful of other legislators also insisted that Southern black men be enfranchised. But Lincoln, sympathetic to Negro voting rights, hesitated to force them on the states he reconstructed. Nevertheless, in April, 1865, he publicly endorsed limited Negro suffrage and conceded that the black man deserved the right to vote.

In truth, despite their differences, Lincoln and the advanced Republicans worked together closely. And they stood together on several crucial issues: they all wanted to abolish slavery entirely in the South and to muzzle the rebellious white majority there so that it could not overwhelm Southern Unionists and return the old Southern ruling class to power. They also came to see that colonization was probably an unworkable solution to the problem of racial adjustment. . . . In place of colonization, the Lincoln administration devised a refugee system for blacks in the South, a program that put them to work in military and civilian pursuits there and prepared them for life in a free society. And in 1864 the Republican Congress canceled all funds it had set aside for colonization efforts.

Most important of all, advanced Republicans cooperated closely with Lincoln in pushing a constitutional amendment through Congress that would guarantee the permanent freedom of all slaves, those in the loyal border as well as in the rebel South. Since he had issued the proclamation, Lincoln and his congressional associates had worried that it might be nullified in the courts or thrown out by a later Congress or a subsequent administration. As a consequence, they wanted a constitutional amendment that would safeguard the proclamation and prevent emancipation from ever being overturned. Accordingly, in December, 1863, Iowa senator James F. Wilson introduced an emancipation amendment in the Senate, and the following February Trumbull reported it from the judiciary committee, reminding his colleagues that nobody could deny that all the death and destruction of the war stemmed from slavery and that it was their duty to support this amendment. In April the Senate adopted it by a vote of thirty-eight to six, but it failed to muster the required two-thirds majority in the House.

After Lincoln's re-election in 1864, advanced Republicans joined forces with the President to get the amendment passed.... Republicans who sponsored the amendment plotted with Lincoln to pressure conservative Republicans and recalcitrant Democrats for their support. On January 6, 1865, a heated debate began over the amendment, with James Ashley quoting Lincoln himself that *"if slavery is not wrong, nothing is wrong."* A week later, Thaddeus Stevens, still tall and imposing at seventy-two, limped down the aisle of the House and closed the debate with a spare and eloquent address, declaring that he had never hesitated, even when threatened with violence, "to stand here and denounce this infamous institution." With the outcome much in doubt, Lincoln and congressional Republicans participated in secret negotiations never made public—negotiations that allegedly involved patronage, a New Jersey railroad monopoly, and the release of rebels kin to congressional Democrats—to bring wavering opponents into line. "The greatest measure of the nineteenth century," Stevens claimed, "was passed by corruption, aided and abetted by the purest man in America." When the amendment did pass, by just three votes, a storm of cheers broke over House Republicans, who danced, embraced one another, waved their hats and canes.... When ratified by the states, the amendment would end human bondage in America.

See, Julian rejoiced, "the world *does* move." He could have added that he and his advanced Republican colleagues, in collaboration with their President, had made it move, had done all they could in the smoke and steel of civil war to right their troubled land with its own noblest ideals.

279

Questions

1. *Two decades ago, most Civil War historians thought that Lincoln and what Oates calls the "advanced" Republicans—"Radical Republicans" was the older, somewhat sinister label for them— were practically mortal antagonists. Oates rejects this view. Why?*

2. *What difficulties stood in the way of adopting a policy of emancipation when the war began in 1861? In particular, why was the constitutionality of the policy open to question? Why did some advanced Republicans nevertheless insist that emancipation be implemented anyway?*

3. *Lincoln opposed emancipation when the war began in 1861. What developments led him to reverse his opposition by the summer of 1862?*

4. *When Lincoln issued the Emancipation Proclamation, he defended its constitutionality by arguing that it was a legitimate exercise of his war powers as commander-in-chief. Military necessity, he claimed, justified the policy. Many Democrats objected that this rationale was specious—that it was a mere constitutional "fig leaf" for a decision made primarily on other grounds. Judging by Oates's article, were the Democrats correct? Why or why not?*

5. *What exactly did the Emancipation Proclamation accomplish? Why was it necessary to pass a constitutional amendment abolishing slavery?*

"SLAVERY HAS FORFEITED ITS RIGHT TO THE LIFE OF ANY MAN": THE JOURNEY TO EMANCIPATION

It is common, but quite mistaken, to imagine that the Civil War began as a contest for human freedom. In fact the North began the war with a political commitment to defeat the South without touching slavery and maintained that commitment for well over a year. Most Northerners did not wish to vindicate Southern fears about an "Abolitionist" Republican administration and thus legitimize their decision to secede. They also wanted to hold the border states and hoped to tap latent Unionist sentiment in the South. An anti-slavery course would jeopardize all these aims.

Other considerations reinforced this basic contention. While Lincoln personally believed that slavery formed the heart of the rebellion and a substantial minority of other Northerners agreed, the majority did not. Most believed that the free and slave states might have coexisted indefinitely but for abolitionist agitation; others feared that emancipation would lead at once to an influx into the North of African Americans who would compete for jobs.

For all these reasons, the Lincoln administration began the war scrupulously avoiding the slave issue whenever possible. As time went on, however, Lincoln began to reconsider this basic policy. The documents that follow, drawn from Lincoln's private and official correspondence, reflect the president's evolving thoughts on the subject as he wrestled with this issue from the autumn of 1861 through the summer of 1862. Also included is a letter from a Union officer to his wife, reflecting the growing sentiment in favor of emancipation even from Northern soldiers who initially enlisted only to save the Union.

281

Lincoln's Views on Emancipation, September 1861

Late in August 1861, Major General John C. Frémont, Lincoln's military commander in Missouri, responded to guerrilla warfare in his department by issuing a proclamation that freed the slaves in much of that state. Although well known for his fervent opposition to slavery, Frémont claimed that military necessity, not politics, lay behind his decision. Lincoln, however, rejected this argument and forced Frémont to rescind the order. In a private letter to a friend, Senator Orville Browning of Illinois, he explained his reasons. Taken from The Collected Works of Abraham Lincoln, *ed. Roy P. Basler (New Brunswick, New Jersey, 1953), 4:531–32.*

Genl. Fremont's proclamation . . . is *purely political,* and not within the range of *military* law, or necessity. If a commanding General finds a necessity to seize the farm of a private owner, for a pasture, an encampment, or a fortification, he has the right to do so, and to so hold it, as long as the necessity lasts; and this is within military law, because within military necessity. But to say the farm shall no longer belong to the owner, or his heirs forever; and this as well when the farm is not needed for military purposes as when it is, is purely political, without the savor of military law about it. And the same is true of slaves. . . . The proclamation in the point in question, is simply "dictatorship.". . .

So much as to principle. Now as to policy. . . . The Kentucky legislature [Kentucky was a slave-holding border state] would not budge till that proclamation was modified; and [upon hearing news of Frémont's proclamation] . . . a whole company of our [Kentucky] Volunteers threw down their arms and disbanded. I was so assured, as to think it probable, that the very arms we had furnished Kentucky would be turned against us. I think to lose Kentucky is nearly the same as to lose the whole game. Kentucky gone, we can not hold Missouri, nor, as I think, Maryland. These all against us, and the job on our hands is too large for us. We would as well consent to separation at once, including the surrender of this capitol.

Reprinted from *Collected Works of Abraham Lincoln,* Roy P. Basler, editor, published by Rutgers University Press, 1953.

Lincoln Urges Congress to Accept Compensated Emancipation, March 1862

Troubled by both the constitutional obstacles to immediate emancipation and the opposition of the border states, Lincoln at first tried to float a program of compensated emancipation, whereby the U.S. government would reimburse slaveowners for the slaves they voluntarily freed. He explained his program to Congress in March 1862. Note how his proposal tried to deal with the constitutional issues; note too why he thought this proposal might help bring the war to an early end. From Basler, ed., The Collected Works of Abraham Lincoln, *5:144–46.*

Fellow-citizens of the Senate, and House of Representatives,

I recommend the adoption of a Joint Resolution by your honorable bodies which shall be substantially as follows:

"Resolved that the United States ought to co-operate with any state which may adopt gradual abolishment of slavery, giving to such state pecuniary aid, to be used by such state in it's [its] discretion, to compensate for the inconveniences public and private, produced by such change of system[.]"

If the proposition contained in the resolution does not meet the approval of Congress and the country, there is the end; but if it does command such approval, I deem it of importance that the states and people immediately interested, should be at once distinctly notified of the fact, so that they may begin to consider whether to accept or reject it. The federal government would find it's [its] highest interest in such a measure, as one of the most efficient means of self-preservation. The leaders of the existing insurrection entertain the hope that this government will ultimately be forced to acknowledge the independence of some part of the disaffected region, and that all the slave states North of such part will then say "the Union, for which we have struggled, being already gone, we now choose to go with the Southern section." To deprive them of this hope, substantially ends the rebellion; and the initiation of emancipation completely deprives them of it, as to all the states initiating it. . . . I say "initiation" because, in my judgment, gradual, and not sudden emancipation, is better for all. In the mere financial, or pecuniary view, any member of Congress, with the census-tables and Treasury-reports before him, can readily see for himself how very soon the current expenditures of this war would purchase, at fair valuation, all the slaves in any named State. Such a proposition, on the part of the general government, sets up no claim of a right, by federal authority, to interfere with slavery within state limits, referring, as it does, the absolute control of the subject, in each case, to the state and it's [its] people, immediately interested. It is proposed as a matter of perfectly free choice with them.

In the annual message last December, I thought fit to say "The Union must be preserved; and hence all indispensable means must be employed." I said this, not hastily, but deliberately. War has been made, and continues to be, an indispensable means to this end. A practical re-acknowledgement of the national authority would render the war unnecessary, and it would at once cease. If, however, resistance continues, the war must also continue; and it is impossible to foresee all the incidents, which may attend and all the ruin which may follow it. Such as may seem indispensable, or may obviously promise great efficiency towards ending the struggle, must and will come.

Lincoln Urges the Border State Congressmen to Support Compensated Emancipation, 12 July 1862

In the months that followed his compensated emancipation proposal, Lincoln and Congress worked amicably for the overthrow of slavery wherever the federal government had clear authority to act. In mid-April the president signed into law a bill for the compensated emancipation of slaves in the District of Columbia. Subsequent legislation ended slavery in the territories—without compensation, provided for a more vigorous suppression of the African slave trade, and made provision for the education of black children in the District of Columbia.

In the meantime, Lincoln eagerly waited for the border states to take up his call for compensated emancipation. Their failure to do so profoundly disappointed him. In May 1862 another of Lincoln's generals, David Hunter, independently proclaimed emancipation within his military department. Lincoln revoked this order just as he had Frémont's, but this time warned the border states to act on his moderate proposition while they still could. Two months later he made a final appeal to the congressmen from the border states. The following excerpt is from Basler, ed., The Collected Works of Abraham Lincoln, *5:318–19.*

"Can you, for your states, do better than to take the course I urge?"... You prefer that the constitutional relation of the states to the nation shall be practically restored, without disturbance of the institution [of slavery]; and if this were done, my whole duty, in this respect, under the constitution, and my oath of office, would be performed. But it is not done, and we are trying to accomplish it by war. The incidents of the war can not be avoided. If the war continue long, as it must, if the object be not sooner attained, the institution in your states will be extinguished by mere friction and abrasion—by the mere incidents of the war. It will be gone, and you will have nothing valuable in lieu of it. Much of it's [its] value is gone already. How much better for you, and for your people, to take the step which, at once, shortens the war, and secures substantial compensation for that which is sure to be wholly lost in any other event. How much better to thus save the money which else we sink forever in the war. How much better to do it while we can, lest the war ere long render us pecuniarily unable to do it. How much better for you, as seller, and the nation as buyer, to sell out, and buy out, that without which the war could never have been, than to sink both the thing to be sold, and the price of it, in cutting one another's throats.

I do not speak of emancipation *at once*, but of a *decision* at once to emancipate *gradually*. Room in South America for colonization, can be obtained cheaply, and in abundance; and when numbers shall be large enough to be company and encouragement for one another, the freed people will not be so reluctant to go.

I am pressed with a difficulty not yet mentioned—one which threatens division among those who, united are none too strong. An instance of it is known to you. Gen. Hunter is an honest man. He was, and I hope, still is, my friend. I valued him none the less for his agreeing with me in the general wish that all men everywhere, could be free. He proclaimed all men free within certain states, and I repudiated the proclamation. He expected more good, and less harm from the measure, than I could believe would follow. Yet in repudiating it, I gave dissatisfaction, if not offence, to many whose support the country can not afford to lose. And this is not the end of it. The pressure, in this direction, is still upon me, and is increasing. By conceding what I now ask, you can relieve me, and much more, can relieve the country, in this important point. Upon these considerations I have again begged your attention to the message of March last. Before leaving the Capital, consider and discuss it among yourselves. You are patriots and statesmen; and, as such, I pray you, consider this proposition; and, at the least, commend it to the consideration of your states and people.

Lincoln Betrays
Growing Impatience, 28 July 1862

The border-state Congressmen continued their steadfast opposition to emancipation in any form. Meanwhile other Southern Unionists voiced concern with some of the military measures taken by the Lincoln administration. Reading one such complaint from a Louisiana Unionist, Lincoln penned this exasperated response. Abridged from Basler, ed., The Collected Works of Abraham Lincoln, *5:344–46.*

Sir: The copy of a letter addressed to yourself by Mr. Thomas J. Durant, has been shown to me. The writer appears to be an able, a dispassionate, and an entirely sincere man. The first part of the letter is devoted to an effort to show that the Secession Ordinance of Louisiana was adopted against the will of a majority of the people. This is probably true; and in that fact may be found some instruction. Why did they allow the Ordinance to go into effect? Why did they not assert themselves? Why stand passive and allow themselves to be trodden down by a minority? Why not hold popular meetings, and have a convention of their own, to express and enforce the true sentiment of the state? If preorganization was against them *then*, why not do this *now*, that the United States Army is present to protect them? The paralysis—the dead palsy—of the government in this whole struggle is, that this class of men will do nothing for the government, nothing for themselves, except demanding that the government shall not strike its open enemies, lest they be struck by accident!

Mr. Durant complains that in various ways the relation of master and slave is disturbed by the presence of our Army; and he considers it particularly vexatious that this, in part, is done under cover of an act of Congress, while constitutional guaranties are suspended on the plea of military necessity. The truth is, that what is done, and omitted, about slaves, is done and omitted on the same military necessity. It is a military necessity to have men and money; and we can get neither, in sufficient numbers, or amounts, if we keep from, or drive from, our lines, slaves coming to them. Mr. Durant cannot be ignorant of the pressure in this direction; nor of my efforts to hold it within bounds till he, and such as he shall have time to help themselves.

. . . [Mr. Durant] speaks of no duty—apparently thinks of none—resting upon Union men. He even thinks it injurious to the Union cause that they should be restrained in trade and passage without taking sides. They are to touch neither a sail nor a pump, but to be merely passengers,—dead-heads at that—to be carried snug and dry, throughout the storm, and safely landed right side up. Nay, more; even a mutineer is to go untouched lest these sacred passengers receive an accidental wound.

Of course the rebellion will never be suppressed in Louisiana, if the professed Union men there will neither help to do it, nor permit the government to do it without their help.

Now, I think the true remedy is very different from what is suggested by Mr. Durant. It does not lie in rounding the rough angles of the war, but in removing the necessity for war. The people of Louisiana who wish protection to person and property, have but to reach forth their hands and take it. Let them, in good faith, reinaugurate the national authority, and set up a State government conforming thereto under the constitution. They know how to do it, and can have the protection of the Army while doing it. The Army will be withdrawn so soon as such State government can dispense with its presence; and the people of the State can then upon the old Constitutional terms, govern themselves to their own liking. This is very simple and easy.

If they will not do this, if they prefer to hazard all for the sake of destroying the government, it is for them to consider whether it is probable I will surrender the government to save them from losing all. If they decline what I suggest, you scarcely need to ask what I will do. What would you do in my position? Would you drop the war where it is? Or, would you prosecute it in future, with elder-stalk squirts, charged with rose water? Would you deal lighter blows rather than heavier ones? Would you give up the contest, leaving any available means unapplied? . . .

I am in no boastful mood. I shall not do *more* than I can, and I shall do *all* I can to save the government, which is my sworn duty as well as my personal inclination. I shall do nothing in malice. What I deal with is too vast for malicious dealing.

A Soldier's Views on Emancipation, 10 August 1862

Meanwhile, a growing number of Union soldiers stationed in the South were becoming convinced that slavery lay at the bottom of the entire Southern rebellion. In early August 1862, Hugh B. Ewing, an Ohio colonel stationed in the mountains of western Virginia, received a letter from his wife in which she criticized the emerging sentiment in favor of making emancipation a Union war aim. His response is from the Hugh B. Ewing Papers, Ohio Historical Society, Columbus.

My Darling—

. . . I know that in society husbands & wives differ on religion and other vital questions and "get on" after a manner. I believe there is no true marriage, without a union of the mind & soul— and this belief was all that kept me from marrying a protestant, as they form our chief society & I was thrown chiefly among them— but believing this, I felt that no true *union* could exist between two who differed so essentially in thought and principle—and I early resolved never to marry a protestant: and steeled my heart against the attractions of protestant ladies, who otherwise pleased me.

Was I right?—

When we married, my opinions on slavery, were these—

I had been taught, by Church history, that the Catholic religion was anti-slavery; that it tolerated it as it did mixed marriages, when it could not help it: that it found slavery in existence in every country on earth; that as soon as it began Evangelizing a country it began its efforts at abolition, and never ceased until it attained its object. It thus abolished Slavery from every country where it had power on Earth. It abolished it in England, Ireland, Scotland,

Norway, Sweden, Denmark, France, Spain, Portugal, Italy, Greece, Austria, Prussia, Poland, & all the German States, in parts of Asia & Africa, in Mexico, & all South America save Brazil, in all the Islands of Ocean save Cuba. Protestant historians, with a candor not common to them, learned me "That but for the heroic & untiring efforts of the Popes through the Middle Ages, one tenth of the human race in England Europe & America would be at this moment holding the other nine tenths in abject and unchristian bondage.["] Catholic historians all say the same, and point to it with exultation.

All history told me, that every country, without exception, that failed in due time to emancipate their slaves was through them brought to utter ruin by insurrections or external war—that the system was a disease—a social, moral, & political evil, and when no steps were taken for its case, it inevitably ended in terrible convulsions.

Knowing all this, I held the opinion, that the abolitionists, who wished to end it in a day, were wrong; as that would convulse—but that it should be left to the people who were affected by it, to effect the cure gradually. I never dreamed that they, with the light of the past before them, would hurry on the awful Judgment which had overtaken the persistant Slave holders of the past.

The time had come when the Southern people should have laid the foundation for gradual & future emancipation. They said—No, We will lay the foundation for its perpetuity & future extension—And we will lay it on the smoking ruins of the U S Government—that great gift of God to oppressed humanity, which Catholic Arch Bishops tell us is better for the progress & freedom of the Church than that of any other Country on the face of the earth. They have begun to clear away the ground for their new edifice. They have convulsed the entire Nation. The only reason why slavery was even allowed a days life by the Church, was to avoid convulsion. But Slavery has brought on a Convulsion & is shaking the whole Continant in its horrible Struggles. Now I say, in the name of Almighty God who abhors it, let it die; & disturb the world no more.

This convulsion, the child of Slavery, threatens, every day it lasts, to make you a widow and our children orphans. If emancipation would end it, would I be true to my wife & children to spare it? I think not. They are more dear to me than the System of

289

Slavery, and if in my judgment, the choice is between abolition, & a widowed wife & orphaned children, I will choose Abolition. Who can ask me to offer up my life on the Altar of Slavery? No one. Slavery has forfeited its right, if it even had any, to the life of any man—especially to mine which it is laboring day & night to destroy—It has already spilt rivers of blood—it has spent enough.

I am willing to shed my blood, to preserve our Government to our children & grand children, but not to preserve the Slave System to them, nor make them orphans; to preserve that system for anybody else's children.

If any man is willing to die to perpetuate Slavery, let him do so. It is an ignoble cause to cast life away in. I am willing to die in the Cause of Freedom—but will risk life in no meaner cause.

We ought to communicate our thoughts & feelings. The master thought with me is how to end the war & return to my wife & children. I believe the only way to do it is to strike with vigor at the root of the Evil. It will otherwise linger for years. If we cannot communicate on this subject, it will be because we are not united in thought and feeling: because we have no unity of hope & purpose. Until recently I hoped we were as one person—hence the shock your letters caused me. I know well I cannot force your thoughts nor do I desire to. I would rather we differed on religion, than on that on which my life is staked; & which threatens to orphan our children & widow you. Still if we differ on the policy threatening & affecting my life, there is no help for it. One who carries his life in his hands, is apt to think more correctly on the best means of saving it, than a Lady safe at home in her parlor. The hourly presence of danger makes men keen sighted—and I believe the chances are great, that you will not at the end of the war see preserved both the Slave system & your husband. If Slavery is not broken, the war will last long supported & fed by it, and the loss of life on both sides will be frightful.

Lincoln Responds to Horace Greeley's "Prayer of Twenty Millions," 22 August 1862

On 20 August 1862, the New York Tribune printed an open letter to Lincoln from its publisher, Horace Greeley, one of the North's most influential opinionmakers. Greeley expressed disappointment with "the policy you seem to be pursuing with regard to the slaves of Rebels." Congress had recently passed the Second Confiscation Act, which provided for the emancipation of slaves belonging to known secessionists. Greeley chided Lincoln for not enforcing this provision as vigorously as possible. In effect, he was urging Lincoln to pursue a full-blooded emancipation policy as a way to defeat the rebellion. Any other course, Greeley maintained, was "preposterous and futile."

Lincoln, in fact, had already decided by this time to issue an Emancipation Proclamation but was not yet ready to do so. His response to Greeley, although it disappointed the publisher, was really an attempt to prepare the groundwork for the coming proclamation. From Basler, ed., The Collected Works of Abraham Lincoln, 5:388–89.

Dear Sir:

I have just read your [open letter]. . . . As to the policy I "seem to be pursuing" as you say, I have not meant to leave any one in doubt.

I would save the Union. I would save it the shortest way under the Constitution. The sooner the national authority can be restored; the nearer the Union will be "the Union as it was." If there be those who would not save the Union, unless they could at the same time *save* slavery, I do not agree with them. If there be those who would not save the Union unless they could at the same time *destroy* slavery, I do not agree with them. My paramount object in this struggle *is* to save the Union, and is *not* either to save or to destroy slavery. If I could save the Union without freeing *any* slave I would do it, and if I could save it by freeing *all* the slaves I would do it; and if I could save it by freeing some and leaving others alone I would also do that. What I do about slavery, and the colored race, I do because I believe it helps to save the Union; and what I forbear, I forbear because I do *not* believe it would help to save the Union. I shall do *less* whenever I shall believe what I am doing hurts the cause, and I shall do *more* whenever I shall believe doing more will help the cause. . . .

I have here stated my purpose according to my view of *official* duty and I intend no modification of my oft-expressed *personal* wish that all men every where could be free.

Lincoln Replies to a Petition Urging Him to Adopt Emancipation, 13 September 1862

Early in September 1862, Lincoln received a group of clergymen who handed him a petition imploring him to free the slaves. Although the president spoke to them cordially, he chose to play the devil's advocate and pointed out the ways in which an emancipation proclamation might do more harm than good. From Basler, ed., The Collected Works of Abraham Lincoln, *5:420–21, 423–25.*

What *good* would a proclamation of emancipation from me do, especially as we are now situated? I do not want to issue a document that the whole world will see must necessarily be inoperative, like the Pope's bull against the comet! Would *my word* free the slaves, when I cannot even enforce the Constitution in the rebel States? Is there a single court, or magistrate, or individual that would be influenced by it there? And what reason is there to think it would have any greater effect upon the slaves than the late law of Congress, which I approved, and which offers protection and freedom to the slaves of rebel masters who come within our lines? [Lincoln here refers to the Second Confiscation Act, passed in July 1862.] Yet I cannot learn that that law has caused a single slave to come over to us. And suppose they could be induced by a proclamation of freedom from me to throw themselves upon us, *what should we do with them?* How can we feed and care for such a multitude? Gen. [Benjamin F.] Butler wrote me a few days since that he was issuing more rations to the slaves who have rushed to him than to all the white troops under his command. They *eat*, and that is all, though it is true Gen. Butler is feeding the whites also by the thousand; for it nearly amounts to a famine there. If, now, the pressure of the war should call off our forces from New Orleans to defend some other point, what is to prevent the masters from reducing the blacks to slavery again; for I am told that whenever the rebels take any black prisoners, free or slave, they immediately auction them off! They did so with those they took from a boat that was aground in the Tennessee river a few days ago. And then *I am very ungenerously attacked for it!* . . .

Now, then, tell me, if you please, what possible result of good would follow the issuing of such a proclamation as you desire? Understand, I raise no objections against it on legal or constitutional grounds; for, as commander-in-chief of the army and navy, in time of war, I suppose I have a right to take any measure which may best subdue the enemy. Nor do I urge objections of a moral nature, in view of possible consequences of insurrection and massacre at the South. I view the matter as a practical war measure, to be decided upon according to the advantages or disadvantages it may offer to the suppression of the rebellion. . . .

[The ministers then offered a number of pro-emancipation arguments, to which Lincoln replied:]

I admit that slavery is the root of the rebellion, or at least its *sine qua non.* The ambition of politicians may have instigated them to act, but they would have been impotent without slavery as their instrument. I will also concede that emancipation would help us in Europe, and convince them that we are incited by something more than ambition. I grant further that it would help *somewhat* at the North, though not so much, I fear, as you and those you represent imagine. Still, some additional strength would be added in that way to the war. And then unquestionably it would weaken the rebels by drawing off their laborers, which is of great importance. But I am not so sure we could do much with the blacks. If we were to arm them, I fear that in a few weeks the arms would be in the hands of the rebels; and indeed thus far we have not had arms enough to equip our white troops. I will mention another thing, though it meet only your scorn and contempt: There are fifty thousand bayonets in the Union armies from the Border Slave States. It would be a serious matter if, in consequence of a proclamation such as you desire, they should go over to the rebels. I do not think they all would—not so many indeed as a year ago, or as six months ago—not so many to-day as yesterday. Every day increases their Union feeling. They are also getting their pride enlisted, and want to beat the rebels. Let me say one thing more: I think you should admit that we already have an important principle to rally and unite the people in the fact that constitutional government is at stake. This is a fundamental idea, going down about as deep as anything. . . .

. . . Do not misunderstand me, because I have mentioned these objections. They indicate the difficulties that have thus far prevented my action in some such way as you desire. I have not decided against a proclamation of liberty to the slaves, but hold the matter under advisement. And I can assure you that the subject is on my mind, by day and night, more than any other. Whatever shall appear to be God's will I will do.

The Preliminary Emancipation Proclamation

Lincoln had informed his cabinet that he intended to issue an emancipation proclamation as far back as 22 July 1862. But William Seward, his secretary of state, had pointed out that the federal armies had recently suffered several defeats, and that if the president issued an emancipation proclamation it would seem an act of sheer desperation. Better, thought Seward, to wait until a Union victory. Lincoln saw the logic of this and put away his proclamation for the time being. Finally, the Union success at the Battle of Antietam (17 September 1862), furnished the needed victory. Five days later, Lincoln issued his preliminary Emancipation Proclamation. From Basler, ed., The Collected Works of Abraham Lincoln *5:433–36.*

September 22, 1862

I, Abraham Lincoln, President of the United States of America, and Commander-in-chief of the Army and Navy thereof, do hereby proclaim and declare that hereafter, as heretofore, the war will be prossecuted for the object of practically restoring the constitutional relation between the United States, and each of the states, and the people thereof, in which states that relation is, or may be suspended, or disturbed.

That it is my purpose, upon the next meeting of Congress to again recommend the adoption of a practical measure tendering pecuniary aid to the free acceptance or rejection of all slave-states, so called, the people whereof may not then be in rebellion against the United States, and which states, may then have voluntarily adopted, or thereafter may voluntarily adopt, immediate, or gradual abolishment of slavery within their respective limits; and that the effort to colonize persons of African descent, with their consent, upon this continent, or elsewhere, with the previously obtained consent of the Governments existing there, will be continued.

That on the first day of January in the year of our Lord, one thousand eight hundred and sixty-three, all persons held as slaves within any state, or designated part of a state, the people whereof shall then be in rebellion against the United States shall be then, thenceforward, and forever free; and the executive government of the United States, including the military and naval authority thereof, will recognize and maintain the freedom of such persons, and will do no act or acts to repress such persons, or any of them, in any efforts they may make for their actual freedom.

That the executive will, on the first day of January aforesaid, by proclamation, designate the States, and parts of states, if any, in which the people thereof respectively, shall then be in rebellion against the United States; and the fact that any state, or the people thereof shall, on that day be, in good faith represented in the Congress of the United States, by members chosen thereto, at elections wherein a majority of the qualified voters of such state shall have participated, shall, in the absence of strong countervailing testimony, be deemed conclusive evidence that such state and the people thereof, are not then in rebellion against the United States.

That attention is hereby called to an act of Congress entitled "An act to make an additional Article of War" approved March 13, 1862, and which act is in the words and figure following:

Be it enacted by the Senate and House of Representatives of the United States of America in Congress assembled, That hereafter the following shall be promulgated as an additional article of war for the government of the army of the United States, and shall be obeyed and observed as such:

Article—All officers or persons in the military or naval service of the United States are prohibited from employing any of the forces under their respective commands for the purpose of returning fugitives from service or labor, who may have escaped from any persons to whom such service or labor is claimed to be due, and any officer who shall be found guilty by a court-martial of violating this article shall be dismissed from the service.

SEC. 2. *And be it further enacted*, That this act shall take effect from and after its passage.

Also to the ninth and tenth sections of an act entitled "An Act to suppress Insurrection, to punish Treason and Rebellion, to seize and confiscate property of rebels, and for other purposes," approved July 17, 1862, and which sections are in the words and figures following:

SEC. 9. *And be it further enacted*, That all slaves of persons who shall hereafter be engaged in rebellion against the government of the United States, or who shall in any way give aid or comfort thereto, escaping from such persons and taking refuge within the lines of the army; and all slaves captured from such persons or deserted by them and coming under the control of the government of the United States; and all slaves of such persons found *on* (or) being within any place occupied by rebel forces and afterwards occupied by the forces of the United States, shall be deemed captives of war, and shall be forever free of their servitude and not again held as slaves.

SEC. 10. *And be it further enacted*, That no slave escaping into any State, Territory, or the District of Columbia, from any other State, shall be delivered up, or in any way impeded or hindered of his liberty, except for crime, or some offence against the laws, unless the person claiming said fugitive shall first make oath that the person to whom the labor or service of such fugitive is alleged to be due is his lawful owner, and has not borne arms against the United States in the present rebellion, nor in any way given aid and comfort thereto; and no person engaged in the military or naval service of the United States shall, under any pretence whatever, assume to decide on the validity of the claim of any person to the service or labor of any other person, or surrender up any such person to the claimant, on pain of being dismissed from the service.

And I do hereby enjoin upon and order all persons engaged in the military and naval service of the United States to observe, obey, and enforce, within their respective spheres of service, the act, and sections above recited.

And the executive will in due time recommend that all citizens of the United States who shall have remained loyal thereto throughout the rebellion, shall (upon the restoration of the constitutional relation between the United States, and their respective states, and people, if that relation shall have been suspended or disturbed) be compensated for all losses by acts of the United States, including the loss of slaves.

In witness whereof, I have hereunto set my hand, and caused the seal of the United States to be affixed.

Done at the City of Washington, this twenty second day of September, in the year of our Lord, one thousand eight hundred and sixty two, and of the Independence of the United States, the eighty seventh.

By the President: ABRAHAM LINCOLN
WILLIAM H. SEWARD, Secretary of State

Questions

1. *Many Northerners—even some who disliked slavery—were deeply troubled by the Emancipation Proclamation. For better or worse, slaves were a species of property, and under the Constitution no government could take property from an individual without due process of law. Thus they considered Lincoln's action a usurpation of his legitimate powers. Lincoln, on the other hand, argued that his war powers as commander-in-chief gave him the necessary authority. Who had the better case? In what specific ways would an emancipation policy help to defeat the South?*

2. *Lincoln clearly understood the constitutional difficulties of an emancipation policy. His compensated emancipation proposal was designed to avoid these. How?*

3. *During the war's first year, Lincoln was very solicitous of the border states and was anxious not to alienate them. Yet by July 1862 he adopted a policy that he knew would antagonize them. How would you account for his change of heart?*

4. *Lincoln often played his cards very close to his chest. Thus, in September 1862, even after he had privately decided to issue the Emancipation Proclamation, he suggested to a committee of clergymen that such a proclamation might be pointless. How serious were the potential drawbacks he mentioned?*

5. *Although its issuance was one of the most dramatic moments in American history, the preliminary Emancipation Proclamation is disappointingly dull—almost tedious—to read. Yet few state papers have ever been more carefully calculated to achieve a certain effect: namely, to assure the American public that the proclamation was both constitutional and prudent. How did the document's construction and wording help to achieve this effect?*

FURTHER READING

The Negro in the Civil War *(Boston, 1953), by Benjamin Quarles, remains the best introduction to the subject. A good survey of the background to the emancipation decision is John H. Franklin,* The Emancipation Proclamation *(Garden City, New York, 1963). For the abolitionist contribution see James M. McPherson,* The Struggle for Equality: Abolitionists and the Negro in the Civil War and Reconstruction *(Princeton, 1964). The most influential modern work on the "advanced" Republicans is Hans L. Trefousse,* The Radical Republicans: Lincoln's Vanguard for Racial Justice *(New York, 1969). Louis S. Gerteis traces the sometimes tortured evolution of Union policy toward enslaved African Americans in* From Contraband to Freedman: Federal Policy Toward Southern Blacks, 1861–1865 *(Contributions in American History, No. 29, Westport, Connecticut, 1973).*

Black Glory:
The African-American Role in Union Victory

Joseph T. Glatthaar

During the final year of the war, Lt. Gen. Ulysses S. Grant employed his overwhelming superiority in manpower to defeat the Confederacy. Simply stated, Grant's plan was to mobilize every available man, apply pressure on all fronts, and stretch the Confederacy to enable forces under Maj. Gen. William Tecumseh Sherman to break up one of the two primary Confederate commands, the Army of Tennessee. Then, with all other forces maintaining the same stranglehold, Sherman's army was to devastate the Confederate military infrastructure—its railroads, its factories, its agriculture, and its labor supply—thus bringing the Confederacy to its knees.[1]

There were, however, numerous drawbacks to this strategy of 1864. Grant's scheme required that regiments remained filled, that states achieve their manpower quotas, and that commanders position the maximum number of soldiers at the front. This compelled states to raise more troops, an unpopular and even dangerous policy, particularly in the wake of draft riots the previous summer. As Federal armies launched campaigns in all theaters, losses surpassed those of earlier years. Such a strategy exacerbated existing hardships for soldiers and their families and created an entirely new class of war widows, orphans, and mourners. Finally, to work, Grant's strategy needed time, one of the few commodities in very short supply for the Lincoln administration. After nearly three years of bloody fighting, and hundreds of thousands of casualties, the last thing the northern population had was patience. The Union was war-weary.

In retrospect, it seems that Grant adopted an appropriate strategy for the situation, one that, if he and his subordinates saw through to its conclusion, was most likely to result in a Federal victory. But at the time the outcome was far from certain. The Union party, an amalgamation of Republicans and War Democrats, could claim little more than limited progress after three years of combat; and 1864 was a presidential election year. Some Unionists plotted to dump Lincoln from the head of the ticket, and for a time that spring and summer Lincoln seriously doubted he would win re-election. The highly touted offensives of Grant in the East and Sherman in the West soon bogged down. Grant

"Black Glory: The African-American Role in Union Victory," by Joseph T. Glatthaar, reprinted from *Why the Confederacy Lost*, Oxford University Press.

locked into a siege at Petersburg, while Confederates apparently stalemated Sherman's forces outside Atlanta. Meanwhile, Union losses were staggering, some 60,000 in barely a month in Grant's campaign alone. To the northern public, a successful conclusion to the war appeared dim. Indeed, these were dark days for Lincoln and the advocates of reunion.

The president wisely stuck with Grant and his strategy and when Sherman cracked the tough Confederate nut called the Army of Tennessee and seized Atlanta, Lincoln's re-election was virtually assured. But suppose in the spring of 1864 his administration had to muster out of service one of its two primary commands, the Army of the Potomac or Sherman's Army of the West. How would that have effected the outcome of the war? Could Grant have even adopted this strategy without those 100,000 men? How would the campaigns of 1864–65 have transpired?

Such conjecture helps to elucidate, in just one area, the critical contributions of blacks to the defeat of the Confederacy. During those key months in the late spring and summer, when the picture for the Lincoln administration looked bleakest and the Union desperately struggled to maintain its uniformed strength, more than 100,000 blacks were serving in the Union army and thousands more were in the Federal navy. In fact, there were more blacks in Union blue than either Grant commanded outside Petersburg or Sherman directed around Atlanta. Their absence would have foiled Grant's strategy and quite possibly doomed efforts at reunion; their presence enabled Grant to embark on a course that promised the greatest hope of Federal victory.

At the outbreak of the war, leadership on neither side envisioned the varied and dramatic contributions that blacks would make to Confederate defeat. Nearly 180,000 served in the Union uniform with muskets in hand. As newfound laborers for the Federal war effort, blacks grew cotton and foodstuffs and aided in all sorts of construction and logistical endeavors, and as lost laborers for a fledgling wartime nation that so depended on its slaves for food production and other essentials, blacks caused shortages, hardships, and disillusionment among soldiers and civilians alike. Slaves who could not run away to northern lines supported the Union war effort through work sabotage, general unruliness that created insecurity among white southerners, and assistance to Federal troops who escaped from Confederate prison camps. Blacks alone did not win the war, but timely and extensive support from them contributed significantly and may have made the difference between a Union victory and stalemate or defeat. Lincoln himself admitted this in late 1864, when he wrote:

> Any different policy in regard to the colored man, deprives us of his help, and this is more than we can ear. We can not spare the hundred and forty or fifty thousand now serving us as soldiers, seamen, and laborers. This is not a question of sentiment or taste, by one of physical force which may be measured and estimated as horse-power and Steam-power are measured and estimated. Keep it and you can save the Union. Throw it away, and the Union goes with it.[2]

Free and slave, they tipped the delicate balance of power squarely in favor of the North.

Blacks were at the very heart of the Civil War. Although most southerners seceded and went to war first to preserve their "rights" and then to protect their homes, the issue of slavery was always central. Secessionists sought protection of individual and state rights from Federal interference, specifically, the right to own property (read slaves) and take that property anywhere without fear of loss or seizure; the right to retrieve stolen or runaway property anywhere; and the right to live peaceably, without attempts by outsiders to subvert the existing state of order, an order with slavery as its cornerstone. The ferocious aspersions that the Rebels cast toward "Black" Republicans and abolitionists suggested the central role of slavery. In the minds of most Confederate soldiers, these northerners were the arch-villains, the group that provoked this wholly unnecessary crisis and shattered the greatest government in the world through its anti-slavery activities.

Even more obscure but no less essential among northerners was the role of slavery. While there was considerable disapproval of the institution, racial prejudices were widely held, and few of the early enlistees sought the destruction of the slave system. Instead, in most cases, Federals marched off to war for the restoration of the Union. It took Lincoln's keen mind, with his uncanny ability to cut to the root of problems, to recognize that the status of blacks was the core issue of the war, something which few outside the black race grasped. Lincoln realized that had northerners not found slavery morally reprehensible, and the institution incom-

304

patible with the new economic, political, and social directions of the country, war never would have happened.

Nevertheless, whites on both sides wanted to keep blacks on the periphery. The Lincoln administration resisted pleas from blacks "to allow us the poor privilege of fighting and (if need be dieing) to support those in office who are our own choise."[3] There were more white volunteers than the government could accept into uniform, and black military service was highly controversial, especially in the border states where Lincoln had to struggle to maintain Unionist ascendancy.

In the Confederacy, several states permitted free blacks to join the militia, but President Jefferson Davis had no intention of opening the Confederate ranks to blacks, either free or slave. The entire premise of such service was incongruous with the concept of slavery, as Georgia governor Joseph E. Brown argued: "Whenever we establish the fact that they are a military race, we destroy our whole theory that they are unfit to be free."[4]

Instead, the Confederacy employed blacks as southerners had done for two hundred years, as laborers. Slaves continued to plow the earth, hoe the fields, and harvest the crops, producing foodstuffs to feed the huge Confederate armies and the civilian population, and cotton with which to purchase the tools of war. They also dug trenches, erected fortifications, maintained railroads, mined essential minerals, manufactured war matériel, and performed sundry tasks that benefited Confederate troops. No doubt, in the early stages of the war, and to a lesser degree to the end, black labor was an important asset to the Confederacy.

Since whites refused to thrust slavery into the forefront, blacks forced the issue. It all began on a quiet May night in 1861 near Fort Monroe in Virginia. Three slaves, hired out as laborers on a Confederate fortifications project, slipped away from quarters, commandeered a canoe, and paddled into Union lines. The following morning, a Confederate officer approached the fort under a flag of truce. He came, he stated, to claim the runaways based on the fugitive slave law. The Federal commander Brig. Gen. Benjamin Butler refused to hand over the slaves. A shrewd courtroom lawyer and prominent politician before the war, Butler insisted that since Virginia had seceded from the Union, the fugitive slave law was inapplicable. Furthermore, since the Confederates had used these men for strictly military purposes, they were contraband of a war and therefore subject to confiscation. Then, without much thought, Butler hired them for pay to construct a bakery for Federal soldiers. In one eventful day, Butler had, in effect, freed three slaves and then employed them to work for the Union army. The secretary of war promptly endorsed Butler's rationale, and two months later Congress passed the First Confiscation Act, which converted policy into law.

Together these three slaves and Benjamin Butler had struck a monstrous blow for freedom and the Federal war effort. They carved out the first path for wartime emancipation and set a precedent for military employment. Once the Federal government granted tacit freedom to runaways hired to labor for the Confederate military, it opened the door for all sorts of other cases and set the Lincoln administration on the rocky trail toward emancipation. And once the War Department began hiring blacks for wages, the practice initiated the breakdown of opposition to the use of blacks in other military capacities. First it was the construction of a bakery, then the erection of fortifications, and later labor as teamsters and cargo handlers. In each instance, blacks filled jobs traditionally performed by soldiers, which enabled military authorities to place more troops in combat commands as early as 1861.

As Federal armies penetrated deeper into the Confederacy, blacks flocked to Union lines for sanctuary from slavery. At first, Federal troops returned runaways who were not employed on Confederate military projects to their masters. This should not be, as Maj. Gen. George B. McClellan lectured Lincoln, a war to destroy slavery; rather, the object of the war was to save the Union. But for many northerners in and out of uniform, the situation was not that simple. Some soldiers abhorred the notion of returning anyone to slavery, while others found the practice of assisting masters in retrieval of slaves a nuisance that took away from their ability to wage war. It was also galling to civilians and soldiers alike that the Federal government was aiding individuals who had cast their lot with secessionists. By early 1862 the War Department prohibited the use of Federal troops in the retrieval of runaway slaves, and four months later, Congress went even further. In the Second Confiscation Act, it freed all escaped slaves of Rebel masters upon their entering Union lines.

Precisely how many slaves found refuge with Union forces is unknown. The best estimates range between 500,000 and 700,000 during the course of the war. While some slaves traveled great distances and undertook enormous risks to reach Union sanctuary, most had to await the arrival of Lincoln's soldiers. Personal and family hardships en route, a lack of specific information on the whereabouts of Union and Confederate forces, and the real fear of capture all acted as powerful deterrents to flight. Many slaves, therefore, had no choice but to let the Union army cut the freedom trail for them.

Such was the case for slaves on the family plantations of the crusty old fire-eater Edmund Ruffin. Situated outside Richmond, the Ruffin farms were marvels of innovation and experiment. As Federal troops pushed up the Peninsula toward Richmond in May 1862, discipline and loyalty among slaves for their masters began to erode. First a dozen fled to Union lines, while the remainder at one plantation enforced a work stoppage, despite entreaties from Ruffin's son-in-law to return to the fields. Over the next few weeks, more and more slaves slipped off to the Federals, sometimes in dribbles, other times in droves, so that by the end of June there were not enough slaves left to care for the crops and animals. Cutting losses, Ruffin's son sold much of his share of slaves and livestock and relocated his remaining bondsmen to the south near Petersburg. His father attempted to salvage what was left of his property, but the haunting question remained: Why this rash of runaways, when "no where were they better cared for, or better managed & treated, according to their condition of slavery?"[5]

With a slave population in the Confederate States of approximately three and one-half million, perhaps 15 or 20 percent reached safety with the Federals. Yet their impact was so much greater than their numbers. The war demanded a major alteration in the Confederate economy. Not only did the Confederacy have the same number of mouths to feed and bodies to clothe as before the war, but the loss of men to military service diminished the labor force significantly. In addition, the war machine consumed all sorts of material in tremendous quantities, some of which southerners had not produced before 1861. At the same time, the Federal blockade reduced the available amount of imported war necessities. The Confederacy had somehow to furnish these essentials itself and that placed even greater demands on the laboring force. White women partially offset the manpower loss, but southerners were counting on black labor to take up the slack.

Without it, workers were at a premium, commodities were scarcer, and demand significantly aided a spiraling inflation that wreaked havoc on society, driving prices up by 1865 to ninety-two times their prewar level. Thus, the Confederacy simply could not afford the loss of hundreds of thousands of black producers.

In areas such as Virginia, for example, where Federal forces campaigned frequently, the dearth of slave laborers proved critical. Soldiers on both sides, few of them well disciplined, scoured the countryside for eatables, dismantled fences for firewood, trampled fields, pilfered livestock, scattered the inhabitants, and generally wrecked agricultural output in one of the Confederacy's most productive states. Over time, Lee needed to draw more and more food and fodder for his army via railroad from the fertile Shenandoah Valley, which, remarkably, had managed to avoid the serious devastation. But the principal line, the Virginia Central Railroad, was in such serious need of repair by early 1863 that the superintendent informed Jefferson Davis its "efficiency is *most seriously impaired.*"[6] Despite a reduction of freight loads by 25 percent, the line still suffered four derailments in five days that winter due to faulty track, and this at an average rate of speed of only eight miles per hour. Repairs were impossible because laborers were unavailable. Many white workers were in the army, the superintendent complained, and black workers ran off with the Federal troops, as had nearly all the local slaves. Essentials like railroad ties, in ample supply before the war, were unobtainable, even at triple their prewar price, because there were no workers to chop down trees and make them. As a result, over the final two years of the war, Lee had to look toward the Carolinas and occasionally Georgia for more and more supplies, at greater expense to the Confederacy over railroads heavily burdened and suffering increasingly from disrepair. Nor was this problem unique to Lee's army. Over-used, inadequately maintained railroads burdened other Confederate commands as well—and the southern economy as a whole.

Runaways, moreover, undercut the sense of stability in society. The thoughts of desperate slaves, beyond the control of whites, roaming the countryside, hiding by day and traveling at night in search of Union lines, and seeking succor from fellow blacks was deeply disturbing. It also challenged perceptions of social order. Slaves whom they had known, cared for, and looked after for years, slaves in whom they had placed trust, were now abandoning them in these perilous times in search of freedom. For Edmund Ruffin and thousands of others, steeped in the delusion of the contented slave, the situation challenged their core beliefs.

Nor were runaways the only bondsmen who aided the Union war effort. Slaves who lacked opportunity to escape nonetheless found ways of contributing to Confederate defeat. At great peril to themselves, some slaves concealed, fed, and directed runaways or escaped federal prisoners of war on the journey to freedom. Others sabotaged farm and labor equipment or assumed an uncooperative attitude with owners and overseers, to slow down work and promote widespread insecurity among whites at home. In time such deeds paid great dividends, as Confederate troops deserted ranks to look after the welfare of loved ones at home.

Slave protests also fueled another potent weapon against southern whites, fear of servile insurrection. Revolts would have been self-destructive to blacks, particularly in the heightened military state of the Confederacy, and resulted only in brutal reprisals. But the fear of revolts brought deep worry to both military personnel and white civilians in the South. Confederate soldiers, always looking rearward, wondered whether the rumors of some massive slave rebellion this time came true. Their relatives and friends at home in turn lived uneasily, hearing similar tales and knowing they could some day become reality.

These acts—obstruction, unrest, and flight to sanctuary behind Union lines—alerted northerners to the changing conditions of the war and to the potential value of blacks toward Union victory. Through their behavior, slaves compelled Federal authorities to adapt their policies to match the increasing magnitude of the war. Originally, the objective of the war was simply to preserve the Union. Then, Federals as a war measure confiscated slaves employed on Confederate military projects, and later any slaves of Rebel masters. "So long as the rebels retain and employ their slaves in producing grains &c. [etc.]," explained General in Chief Henry W. Halleck to Grant, "they can employ all the whites in the field. Every slave withdrawn from the enemy is equivalent to a white man put *hors de combat* [out of action]."[7]

The next logical step was to remove slaves from Confederate hands and to direct their labor on behalf of the Union. Starting in 1862 federal officials placed women, children, and elderly and unfit males on abandoned plantations to cultivate cotton and other valuable commodities. The men served in all sorts of capacities with the army, from teamsters and cooks to stevedores and laborers, taking over the more disagreeable duties of soldiers and freeing up more bluecoats for combat. Whether northern whites wished it or not, the circumstances of war were moving the nation in the direction of black military service.

Among the small black population in the North, the desire to serve in Union blue was widespread. A group from Boston, expressing its commitment to the Union cause, vowed "there was not a man who would not leap for his knapsack and they would make it intolerable hot for old Virginia."[8] Leaders, such as Frederick Douglass, chided the Lincoln administration for failing to utilize its resources to the fullest: "this is no time to fight with one hand, when both are needed; that this is no time to fight only with your white hand, and allow your black hand to remain tied."[9] The war offered a rare opportunity to strike a mighty blow at slavery, dispel prejudice, and demonstrate to all that blacks could contribute in real and significant ways to the nation in times of crisis, and therefore merited full and equal rights. The best means of accomplishing those goals was through military service.

Blacks had already gained admission to the United States Navy. Perhaps as many as one in every ten or twelve men in the navy, or nearly 10,000, were black.[10] They manned ships in the blockade and fought on numerous occasions in river operations. Although none appear to have received commissions as officers, blacks served in every enlisted capacity, including gunners, with distinction. Four black sailors earned Medals of Honor, and Robert Smalls, who stole a vessel and piloted it out of Charleston harbor to safety, was a national hero.

But this was primarily a ground war, and it was in the army that blacks had to make their mark. "Once let the black man get upon his person the brass letters, U.S., let him get an eagle on his button, and a musket on his shoulder and bullets in his pocket," Douglass predicted, "and there is no power on earth which can deny that he has earned the right to citizenship in the United States."[11]

Unfortunately, in the eyes of many northern whites there was a giant gulf between blacks as military laborers and as soldiers in the United States Army. In the early stages of the war whites neither wanted black troops nor believed they had the capacity to withstand the rigors of soldiering. A Pennsylvanian who opposed black military service justified his opinion by saying, "God never intended a nigger to put white people Down," while a Connecticut infantryman insisted that black troops would be less valuable than hogs: "I think a drove of hogs would do better brought down here for we could eat them and the niggers we can't."[12]

Yet as the war dragged on from months to a year and more and initial enthusiasm waned, the transformation in the minds of many soldiers, politicians, and even some civilians occurred. "The character of the war has very much changed within the last year," noted Halleck in early 1863. "There is now no possible hope of reconciliation with the rebels. The Union party in the South is virtually destroyed. There can be no peace but that which is forced by the sword. We must conquer the rebels or be conquered by them."[13] The harsh realities of military life, the staggering and wholly unanticipated loss of life, and the lack of satisfactory success forced Unionists to recommit themselves to their cause and reexamine their approach to the war. A gradual escalation of the war followed. The Yankees learned to view the Confederate nation, its soldiers and civilians, as the enemy and were far less respectful of their needs and property. Northerners also concluded that the demands of the war, particularly in the area of manpower, outweighed certain traditional values and beliefs. It was in this atmosphere that Lincoln was able to garner support for emancipation and black enlistment outside abolitionist circles.

An opponent of slavery since his youth, the president had subordinated his personal views to the welfare of the country. But when hostilities reached such a scale and Union losses were so great that a peaceful reconciliation was no longer possible, he decided to issue the Emancipation Proclamation. Lincoln reasoned that slavery had been the major divisive issue between the North and South. A restored Union had to move beyond the slavery controversy, and the best way to do that was to place a peculiar institution on the road to extinction. Slavery, moreover, had enormous military value. Emancipation would strike a terrific blow at the Rebel war effort by depriving it of invaluable laborers.

At home and in military service, emancipation provided an ideological boost to the war effort. Understandably, opponents of slavery rejoiced. Lincoln had launched a powerful attack on America's great evil and resolved for all abolitionists a moral

311

problem of fighting for the Union and the Constitution that protected a reprehensible institution. Despite some initial reluctance to endorse the new policy, supporters of the Union, too, recognized its worth. Even many of those who grumbled over the proclamation, especially soldiers, acquiesced in time. They could not help but notice that Lincoln demonstrated a willingness to employ any weapon to aid them in their struggle against the Confederacy.

In the international arena, the Emancipation Proclamation pulled the rug from beneath Confederate efforts to gain recognition from Great Britain and France. For some time the British and French governments had debated whether to recognize the Confederacy as an independent nation and to offer services as mediators. Although recognition and mediation would not necessarily have led to military intervention, many benefits would have accrued to the Rebels. While the French, with dreams of an overseas empire in Mexico, urged a strong, united position for mediation, the British hesitated. The Confederacy had by no means won in the summer of 1862, and large portions of British society opposed slavery under any circumstances. As Lee drove the Federals out of Virginia and then penetrated into Maryland in August and September, the movement for recognition gained momentum in the British Parliament. But just as quickly, fortunes reversed. Lee's army fell back from Maryland after the Battle of Antietam, and Lincoln issued the Emancipation Proclamation, seizing the high moral ground for the North. By early January 1863, British antislavery forces had gained ascendancy. As Union Ambassador to Great Britain, Charles Francis Adams noted with satisfaction that "this development of sentiment is to annihilate all agitation for recognition."[14]

Still, emancipation was only part of Lincoln's policy. Its consummation was his decision to accept blacks into the army. As Douglass had explained nearly two years earlier, blacks were the largest untapped resource available to the Union. Enlistments had slowed to a trickle and Congress, hoping to avoid wholesale conscription, passed the Militia Act of July 17, 1862, that authorized the president to organize blacks and use them "for any military or naval service for which they may be found competent."[15] Lincoln, interpreting the loose phraseology to his advantage, viewed the act as congressional justification for black enlistment.

It was a bold military stroke. In one swoop he deprived the Confederacy of a great resource and converted it into one for the Federals. Not only would the Union take slaves, it would arm and train them to fight for the Confederacy's defeat.

In an unusual twist, the Federal government actually began accepting blacks into the army before Lincoln issued the Emancipation Proclamation. He decided on emancipation and black enlistment around the same time, but due to the state of military affairs, he delayed the announcement of the Emancipation Proclamation until after the next significant Union victory, which did not occur until September. Otherwise, the Proclamation would have looked like the desperate act of a nation in defeat. With the repulse of Lee's raid into Maryland, Lincoln's pronouncement came from a position of greater strength.

Because the Lincoln administration was sensitive to the controversial nature of black enlistment, it implemented the program with caution. Less than three years earlier John Brown had attempted to seize the arsenal at Harper's Ferry, Virginia, in an effort to arm slaves, to the horror of northerners as well as southerners. To be sure, the war had altered public attitudes, and the circumstances were quite different, but racism remained powerful and opposition to the black soldier was strong. Lincoln rejected one endeavor to raise black troops on the South Carolina Sea Islands in the spring of 1862, and stalled on another in Kansas, opting to await better circumstances.

He found them in distant Louisiana, where Maj. Gen. Benjamin Butler needed manpower immediately. After the Federal occupation of New Orleans, local black militiamen had tendered their services to Butler, who respectfully declined. Several months later, however, he suddenly reversed himself and swore the men into national service, spurred on no doubt by an official suggestion he had received from Secretary of the Treasury Salmon P. Chase. The New Orleans volunteers were mostly free blacks, many of them well-to-do, with a tradition of military service dating back to the war of 1812. Strangely enough, they were militiamen who in 1861 had volunteered their services to the Confederate state government of Louisiana. Now they entered the Union army with dozens of black captains and lieutenants and even a black major.

Once the Lincoln administration broke the color barrier of the army, blacks stepped forward in large numbers. Service in the army offered to blacks the opportunity to strike a decisive blow for freedom, and recognition by whites that blacks could contribute in vital ways during this national crisis. "This was the biggest thing that ever happened in my life," asserted one former slave. "I felt like a man with a uniform on and a gun in my hand." While standing there during his first roll call, another freedman proudly recalled, "I felt freedom in my bones."[16]

In order to make black military service more palatable to northern whites, and also to serve the prejudices of policy makers, nearly all officers in black units were white. The two Louisiana regimens with their seventy-five black officers comprised approximately two-thirds of all black officers in the war. With a few exceptions in 1865, the only other black officers held posts as chaplains and surgeons. Even Butler's Louisiana officers did not last. His successor squeezed them out by 1864 under the guise of their incompetence.

The basic premise for an exclusively white officer corps was that blacks lacked the qualities to become good soldiers. Many whites believed that blacks by nature were bad material, that they did not possess the requisite character, discipline, and courage to stand up to the rigors of combat. They were lazy, irresponsible, and childlike, with a strain of latent savagery—the quality that caused southerners to fear slave revolts—none of which were all suited to the development of controlled, disciplined, effective troops. The assumption was that only the best white officer could convert them into passable soldiers.

The decision for a white officer corps proved to be a mixed blessing. Unquestionably, the policy stifled opportunities for talented blacks, and even though the whites who commanded black soldiers did so voluntarily, they were men of their time and almost always held some degree of racial prejudice. But nearly all the white officers were experienced soldiers, far superior as a whole to their counterparts in white volunteer units. They had to furnish letters of testimonial vouching for their character, and had to pass an examination on a wide range of subjects, from history to general military knowledge, and from arithmetic to tactics.

Unlike officers of white volunteers, these men knew their business from study and personal experience before they took command, and black soldiers were the true beneficiaries. Early in their service, blacks performed under the microscopic eye of northern whites, many of whom keenly hoped for the failure of this great experiment. If the Lincoln administration wanted to expand the role of blacks in military service, the first units had to perform well. Worse yet, while they were new to soldiering, their Confederate adversaries were seasoned veterans. It was especially important, then, that black troops had talented, experienced officers who could prepare them for battle.

In their initial combat experiences, black soldiers demonstrated a willingness to fight. At Port Hudson, Louisiana, two black regiments, one of them with nearly all black officers, launched several gallant rushes against an almost impregnable Confederate defense. In failure, however, they earned glory and, more importantly, respect. "The men, white or black, who will not flinch from that will flinch from nothing," penned a *New York Times* correspondent on the scene. "It is no longer possible to doubt the bravery and steadiness of the colored race, when rightly led."[17] Fortunately for the black enlistment movement, neither the northern government nor public learned that the black attackers inflicted no casualties on the Confederate defenders.

Less than two weeks later, wholly untested and virtually untrained black troops repelled a vigorous Confederate assault at Milliken's Bend on the Mississippi River, when the white Union defenders fled the scene. Although their marksmanship was poor (many had only been in uniform for a week or two), these blacks fought desperately, at times hand-to-hand, against the Rebel attackers. One black regiment had almost 45 percent of its men killed or mortally wounded, and even the Confederate commander had to concede that the black troops resisted with "considerable obstinacy."[18] The performance of blacks at Milliken's Bend and elsewhere during the Vicksburg campaign convinced Grant that emancipation, in conjunction with black enlistment, "is the heavyest blow yet given the Confederacy."[19]

In mid-July 1863, black soldiers had their most important early test, the assault on Fort Wagner. The fort protected a battery that defended a portion of Charleston harbor. That alone made it an important target, but the regiment assigned to lead the charge, the 54th Massachusetts (Colored) Infantry, aroused the attention of the northern public beyond the engagement's significance. Raised with considerable fanfare throughout the North, the 54th Massachusetts had a host of sons of important abolitionists, including its commander, Colonel Robert Gould Shaw. At sunset, with northern journalists observing, the 54th Massachusetts

315

stormed the works, succeeded by several waves of white regiments. None could wrest control of Fort Wagner from the Rebel defenders.

Yet in failure, black soldiers emerged victors. Witnesses acknowledged the gallantry of the 54th Massachusetts, which suffered the greatest casualties, over 40 percent of its men. Among its dead was Shaw, who became a martyr throughout the North when Confederates attempted to insult white sensibilities by burying him "with his niggers."[20] The bravery of the men in the 54th Massachusetts, and the extensive publicity they received, ensured the continuation and expansion of what the Federal government now called the United States Colored Troops.

In spite of their fine conduct on three battlefields, considerable prejudice remained. Blacks had to fight Confederates in the front and discrimination in the rear. Riding on the combat successes, the War Department accelerated its program to create black units, and at the same time meekly accepted an opinion from its chief civilian attorney, the solicitor general, that black troops should receive inferior pay to whites. Although individual black soldiers demonstrated their leadership capacity in battle, the War Department was loathe to award any of them commissions as lieutenants or captains in combat units.

High-ranking officers, too, relegated black troops to subservient roles. Many generals refused to believe that blacks could fight as well as whites and instead employed blacks in peripheral assignments, such as fatigue labor and occupation duty, where disease, rather than Confederate bullets sapped their strength. Since some had no intention of sending their black troops into combat, they had no qualms about issuing them the worst weapons and designating very little training time. As these generals learned, however, battles occur in the most unpredictable locations, and when shooting begins, a commander wants every available soldier, black or white, on the front lines or in the designated reserve.

Of the almost 37,000 black soldiers who lost their lives, fewer than 3,000 died in combat, far below the percentage of whites killed in action.[21] That, however, represented the length of their military service and the number of major battles in which they participated and bore little relationship to their effectiveness on the battlefield. Black soldiers fought aggressively, compensating for their lack of training and experience with inspiration and dash.

316

The knowledge that this was the "War for Freedom," as one woman termed it, provided them with an added incentive.[22] "Boys, it may be slavery or Death to some of you today," announced an officer, just before an advance. A black soldier calmly replied, "Lieutenant, I am ready to die for Liberty," and just minutes later a ball pierced his heart.[23] Like white troops, they gained confidence in themselves as soldiers through extensive service and ultimately left their mark on dozens of battlefields.

With experience and achievement in combat, too, came respect from white Union volunteers. Nothing neutralized the distrust and disdain that whites held for blacks like success on the battlefield. "I never believed in niggers before," exclaimed a surprised Irish soldier, "but by Jasus, they are hell for fighting." After black troops fought gallantly to repulse an assault by Confederate cavalryman Nathan Bedford Forrest, the Union commander admitted to a similar change of heart: "I have been one of those men, who never had much confidence in colored troops fighting, but these doubts are now all removed, for they fought as bravely as any troops in the Fort." Whether it was three hearty cheers that men in the 14th U.S. Colored Infantry received from whites for their defense of Decatur, Alabama, or the cries of "Bully for you" white cavalrymen bestowed on three black regimens after a successful assault near Petersburg, whites were admitting that black soldiers were making genuine and important contributions to the war effort. Perhaps the greatest tribute white volunteers paid to black soldiers came after that same Petersburg attack, when veterans from Hancock's Corps, arguably the best in the Army of the Potomac, congratulated the men and treated them with dignity and respect. "A few more fights like that," noted an officer of black soldiers, "and our Cold [Colored] boys will have established their manhood if not their Brotherhood to the satisfaction of even the most prejudiced."[24]

In a peculiar way, Confederates helped to legitimize and enhance the reputation of blacks within the Union Army. Rebels attempted to undermine the effectiveness of black units by singling them out for especially heavy fire, declining to exchange black prisoners of war, or capturing and executing black soldiers and their white officers on the spot. Such practices, however, backfired. They not only bonded black soldiers and their white officers closer, for both faced the same fate, but elevated the standing of the United States Colored Troops in the Union army.

317

White volunteers could not help but notice that officers and men in black units incurred greater risks.

The unwillingness of Confederate officials to include black troops in prisoner exchanges also contributed in an unforeseen way. This discriminatory policy alerted Grant to the unequal nature of one-for-one exchanges. The Confederacy, with severe manpower limitations late in the war, benefited more from exchanges than the Union, and Grant halted the practice.[25]

By the end of the war, black soldiers had fought in over forty major engagements and 449 lesser firefights. Like white troops, they acquitted themselves well under good officers with satisfactory training and poorly under incompetent ones with insufficient drilling. Over all, they measured up to white troops. Lincoln himself noted in 1864: "So far as tested, it is difficult to say they are not as good soldiers as any."[26] The sixteen Medals of Honor earned by black soldiers in the war is but small testimony to their valor.

In the final year of the war, when their ranks eventually swelled above 120,000, black soldiers proved indispensable to the Union war effort. With Grant around Petersburg, thirty-three regiments were black, or approximately one in every eight soldiers. Along with the infamous Battle of the Crater,[27] the United States Colored Troops fought in many of the significant if little known battles, including Second Petersburg, First Hatcher's Run, Second Deep Bottom, Chaffin's Farm, Second Darbytown Road, Second Fair Oaks, and Third Watkins Farm.

Sherman preferred to use his black soldiers for guard and occupation duty and logistical support. Such service, while not nearly as glamorous or exciting as combat, was critical to success, especially during the Atlanta campaign, and it freed up others to serve in the front lines.

After Sherman and his army drove toward Savannah, black soldiers saw extensive action. During the Battle of Nashville in December 1864, two black brigades charged with such force that they concealed the major point of attack, the opposite flank, which resulted in a rout of Rebel forces. The next day, blacks and whites together stormed the Confederate works and contributed substantially to the decisive victory. Walking over the ground where hundreds of lifeless black and white soldiers lay mingled, an officer noticed that "the blood of the white and black man has flowed freely together for the great cause which is to give freedom, unity, manhood and peace to all men, whatever birth or complexion."[28] Several months later, blacks led the assault on Fort Blakely, near Mobile. Due to miscommunication, black troops attacked prematurely but nonetheless shattered the Confederate lines just as other Federals launched their attack.

Nearly 180,000 blacks joined the Union army, and adding the estimated 10,000 in the navy, close to 190,000 servicemen were black. They made good soldiers and sailors, on the whole no better nor worse than whites. They came in large numbers when the Union needed them most, in the final two years of the war. In addition to their military service, and their important work as laborers for the North, they helped destabilize the southern home front through their disloyalty to the Confederate cause. Thus blacks played a major role in its defeat.

Perhaps the most telling statement of black wartime contributions came from the Confederates. By early 1864, Maj. Gen. Patrick Cleburne, one of the best division commanders in the war, led a group of officers who insisted "slavery has become a military weakness." The institution turned foreign powers against the Confederacy and supplied the Union with "an army from our granaries." Its breakdown had so shaken southern whites that "the fear of their slaves is continually haunting them, and from silence and apprehension many of these soon learn to wish the war stopped on any terms." Cleburne and his subordinates called for emancipation and black enlistment in the Confederate army. They hoped that such a move would "at one blow strip the enemy of foreign sympathy and assistance," undercut the northern crusade for abolition, and expand the Rebel ranks with black troops who would earn freedom for themselves and their families in defense of their homes. While the Davis administration squashed the proposal, southerners continued to bandy about the idea, and by early 1865 Lee publicly endorsed the enlistment of blacks. He believed they could make "efficient soldiers." He added: "I think we could at least do as well with them as the enemy, and he attaches great importance to their assistance." With Lee's support, the Confederate Congress authorized the recruitment of black soldiers in March 1865. Although this was too little, too late for the Confederacy, the legislation acknowledged the vital wartime role of black people.[29]

After the war, when black leaders tried to point out the contributions of their race to Union victory, whites began to close ranks.

319

They claimed that blacks entered the war at the eleventh hour, and that blacks did not fight in appreciable numbers in the critical Virginia Theater until well after Gettysburg, which experts widely acknowledged as the turning point. But the arguments neglected two major considerations. Whites failed to recognize the devastating effect runaways and disruptive slaves had on the Confederacy. They also did not realize that the turning point thesis is predicated on Union success in 1864 and 1865. Whether one takes Gettysburg, Vicksburg, or even Antietam as the turning point, it becomes so only because of Union successes afterward. Those victories came, at least in part, because of blacks' efforts.

In 1861 few foresaw the pivotal position of blacks in the American balance of power. Through their actions as slaves and free men and women, blacks helped to force supporters of the Union to re-examine their approach to war. Unionists had to fight a war against the Rebels and adopt more vigorous methods of prosecution, such as the destruction of property and the use of blacks in the armed forces. For the Confederacy, they were a crucial workforce, providing food and essential labor for a wide range of civilian and military projects. Their steady loss to the Federals caused supply shortages, various hardships, and escalating inflation, all of which took a terrible toll on Confederate fighting men and civilians. Then, by converting blacks into soldiers, the Union not only deprived the Confederacy of a great resource, but employed it against the foe. As Lincoln explained to Grant in 1863, "I believe it is a resource which, if vigorously applied now, will soon close the contest. It works doubly, weakening the enemy and strengthening us." In time he proved right.[30]

The impact of blacks on the Civil War is comparable to the American experience in the First World War. To insist that blacks defeated the Confederacy, like assertions that the Americans defeated Germany, dismisses the efforts of all those others who had fought long and hard during the war. But like the doughboys in World War I, blacks helped to make the difference between victory and stalemate or defeat. They arrived in great numbers at the critical moment, and their contributions on and off of the battlefield, in conjunction with those of whites, were enough to force the enemy to capitulate.

Shortly after Appomattox, Major Martin Delaney told a black crowd: "Do you know that if it was not for the black men this war never would have been brought to a close with success to the

Union, and the liberty of your race if it had not been for the Negro?"[31] At the time it sounded audacious, even militant; now, it sounds plausible.

Notes

1. See Grant to Sherman, 4 Apr. 1864, for the original plan. *The War of Rebellion: A Compilation of the Official Records of the Union and Confederate Armies,* 127 vols., index, and atlas (Washington: GPO, 1880–1901), series 1, vol. 39, pt. 3, pp. 245–46. Hereafter *OR.* Later, as the plan failed to work out as Grant had hoped, he adopted more of a strategy of attrition. See After Action Report of Grant, 22 July 1865. *OR* series 1, vol. 38, pt. 1, pp. 1–3. In either case, manpower was critical.

2. Roy P. Basler et al., *The Collected Works of Abraham Lincoln,* 9 vols. (New Brunswick: Rutgers University Press, 1953–55), 8:2.

3. W. T. Boyd and J. T. Alston to Simon Cameron, 15 Nov. 1861, in Ira Berlin et al., eds., *Freedom: A Documentary History of Emancipation, 1861–1867,* series II, vol. 1 (New York: Cambridge University Press, 1982), 80–81.

4. Quoted in Robert F. Durden, *The Gray and the Black: The Confederate Debate on Emancipation* (Baton Rouge: Louisiana State University, 1972), 251.

5. Betty L. Mitchell, *Edmund Ruffin: A Biography* (Bloomington: Indiana University Press, 1981), 211.

6. E. Fontaine to Jefferson Davis, March 19, 1863, 158–F–1863. Letters Received, Secretary of War. RG 109, National Archives. Hereafter NA.

7. Halleck to Grant, March 31, 1863, *OR* series 1, vol. 24, pt. 3, pp. 156–57.

8. Morris et al., "Sentiments of the Colored People of Boston Upon the War," *Boston Journal,* April 24, 1861; "The Negro in the Military Service of the United States, 1607–1889," pp. 804–8. RG 94, NA.

9. Quoted in James M. McPherson, *The Negro's Civil War: How American Negroes Felt and Acted During the War for the Union* (New York: Pantheon Books, 1965), 162.

10. Estimates vary over the percentage of black sailors from a high of 25% by Herbert Aptheker to a low of 8% by David L. Valuska.

11. Quoted in McPherson, *The Negro's Civil War*, 161.

12. Quoted in Bell Irvin Wiley, *The Life of Billy Yank: The Common Soldier of the Union* (Indianapolis: Bobbs-Merrill, 1951), p. 120.

13. Halleck to Grant, Mar. 31, 1863, *OR* series 1, vol. 24, pt. 3, pp. 56–57.

14. Quoted in James M. McPherson, *Battle Cry of Freedom: The Civil War Era* (New York: Oxford University Press, 1988), 567.

15. The Militia Act of July 17, 1862. "The Negro," 915–16. RG 94, NA.

16. John Cimprich, *Slavery's End in Tennessee, 1861–1865* (University: University of Alabama Press, 1985), 90; Elijah P. Marrs, *Life and History of the Rev. Elijah P. Marrs* (Louisville: Bradley, 1885), 22.

17. *New York Times*, June 11, 1863.

18. Report of Brig. Gen. H. E. McCulloch, June 8, 1863, *OR* series I, vol. 24, pt. 2, p. 467.

19. Grant to Lincoln, Aug. 23, 1863, in John Y. Simon et al., eds., *The Papers of Ulysses S. Grant*, 18 vols. (Carbondale: Southern Illinois University Press, 1967–), 9:196.

20. Quoted in William Wells Brown, *The Negro in the American Rebellion: His Heroism and His Fidelity* (New York: Lee, 1867), 203.

21. Perhaps 80 percent of all black soldiers who died did so of disease in the Civil War.

22. Deposition of Sarah Reed, 26 May 1924, Pension File of Charles Cull, RG 15, NA.

23. Thomas J. Morgan, "Reminiscences of Service with Colored Troops in the Army of the Cumberland," *Personal Narratives, Rhode Island Soldiers and Sailors Historical Society*, 3, 19:29.

24. Quotation of Irishman in Dudley Taylor Cornish, *The Sable Arm: Negro Troops in the Union Army, 1861–1865* (New York: Longmans, 1956), 147; Report of Col. S. G. Hicks, April 6, 1864, *OR*, series 1, vol. 32, pt. 1, p. 549; Gus to Wife, June 15, 1864, Charles Augustus Hill Papers, in the possession of Richard S. Tracy and quoted in Glatthaar, *Forged in Battle*, 167.

25. Initially, the Davis administration announced that it would return to slavery black soldiers taken as prisoners and try white officers for inciting servile insurrection. When Lincoln threatened to retaliate man for man, Davis backed down.
26. Quoted in Cornish, *The Sable Arm*, 251.
27. At the Crater black troops suffered disproportionately heavy casualties and then fled in panic but with white troops "running back just ahead of them." Quoted in Cornish, *The Sable Arm*, 277.
28. General Orders, No. 5. HQ, 100th USCI. Feb. 2, 1865. "The Negro," 3512–13. RG 94, NA.
29. Quoted in Durden, *The Gray and the Black*, 56, 59, and 206.
30. Basler et al., eds., *Collected Works of Lincoln*, 6:374.
31. Quoted in Victor Ullman, *Martin R. Delany: The Beginnings of Black Nationalism* (Boston: Beacon Press, 1971), 328.

The Struggle for Black Rights During Reconstruction

Michael Les Benedict

INTRODUCTION

The Civil War and Reconstruction era witnessed a desperate fight for equal civil and political rights for African Americans. The legal position of black Americans had deteriorated in the first part of the nineteenth century, with racism actually growing in the North and South as slavery was rejuvenated by the development of cotton agriculture. The growth of the antislavery movement in the 1840s and 1850s, however, led some Northerners to argue that African Americans were entitled to the rights of citizenship. The Supreme Court's Dred Scott decision was a watershed that dashed black Americans' claims to citizenship. Black hopes and expectations brightened with the passage of the Thirteenth Amendment, but they were dimmed once more by the adoption of restrictive southern Black Codes. Seeing the codes as an attempt to salvage key aspects of slavery, Republicans urged the passage of the Civil Rights Act of 1866 to ensure that all Americans, regardless of color, received the basic rights of citizenship. Congress passed the bill, only to be rebuffed by President Andrew Johnson's veto. Overriding the president's veto, Republicans then passed the Fourteenth Amendment in an effort to secure African-American citizenship and rights beyond constitutional doubt.

While blacks embraced their new citizenship, they continued to demand suffrage. Among the most eloquent was Frederick Douglass, one of the greatest orators of his day. The clamor for black enfranchisement aroused apprehension among southern whites that black voters might overturn the traditional social order. The white people of Alabama were among those who voiced their fears of black dominance in a petition to Congress. Nonethe-

less, Congress imposed black suffrage on the South in the Recon-struction Act of 1867, and in 1870 the requisite number of states ratified the Fifteenth Amendment, which extended the change throughout the nation and made it permanent.

But Republicans proved unable to secure equal civil and po-litical rights for African Americans over bitter southern white resistance. A series of Supreme Court decisions narrowed the definition of federal citizenship and limited Congress's power to protect these rights. The court proclaimed that the postwar consti-tutional amendments authorized the federal government to pro-tect rights only against violations by state authorities, leaving African Americans to rely on unsympathetic state and local offi-cials to protect them against all other invasions of their rights.

REPUBLICAN RECONSTRUCTION: SCHOLARS' VIEWS

In the last few decades, Reconstruction history has undergone serious revision. Originally, historians interpreted Reconstruction as a period in which northern Republicans sought to punish rebellious southerners. Historians criticized the radicalism of the Republican effort to secure equal rights for the freedmen, suggesting that Republicans went too far in a futile cause. As Americans became committed to racial equality in the 1950s and 1960s, however, scholars came to sympathize with the Republican Reconstruction program. By the 1970s, many historians began to stress the conservatism of the Republican agenda, implying that it failed because it did not go far enough. Recently, several authors have criticized this view, asserting that Republicans did indeed intend a radical change in the social and constitutional system. In the opinion of these scholars, Reconstruction failed because the Supreme Court refused to honor the intent of the Republican program and destroyed the ability of the national government to protect the rights of American citizens in the South.

The Republican Program was Limited by Republicans' Commitment to Federalism

Historian Michael Les Benedict argues that, despite its apparent radicalism, the Republican Reconstruction program was fundamentally conservative.

Excerpted from "Preserving the Constitution: The Conservative Basis of Radical Reconstruction," Journal of American History 61 (June 1974): 66-67, 76-80, 82-84, 87-88, 90.

[An] analysis of the theoretical framework within which Republicans developed their program . . . reveals the true conservatism of Negro suffrage and may help explain why Reconstruction failed to achieve its goals and why so many Republicans appeared so quickly to abandon the struggle after 1869. For, in fact, the evidence indicates historians may be mistaken when they refer to a retreat from Reconstruction. The distaste of many Republicans for federal intervention in the South was manifest in the Reconstruction program itself. Although they insisted on guarantees for the security of loyal whites and blacks in the South and passed laws and constitutional amendments which appeared to delegate power to the national government to secure citizens' rights, most Republicans never desired a broad, permanent extension of national legislative power. Republicans framed the most limited, conservative Reconstruction possible, adhering until 1868 to the position that their legislation was merely a temporary aberration in the federal system. When continued violence in the South after 1868 forced many Republicans to endorse some permanent broadening of national power—a constitutional position which was truly radical—most Republicans tried to limit the degree of the expansion, and many others refused to make this new departure at all. Nor is it accurate to charge that the courts in interpreting Reconstruction legislation betrayed the principles and purposes of the Republicans who had framed it; rather they carried over to the judicial arena Republicans' reluctance to alter fundamentally the federal system.

. . . Republicans twice formulated conditions for the southern states to meet before Congress would recognize their restoration. Each time they conditioned restoration on the voluntary passage of state legislation, stolidly preserving the states as the primary authors of legislation, firmly refusing to force compliance through exercise of national power. . . .

From "Preserving the Constitution: The Conservative Basis of Radical Reconstruction" by Michael Les Benedict as it appeared in *The Journal of American History*, Vol. LXI, June 1974. Published by The Organization of American Historians.

The first set of conditions were the propositions embraced in the Fourteenth Amendment to the Constitution, framed in 1866. Holding that "the conquered rebels were at the mercy of the conquerors," the Joint Committee on Reconstruction offered the amendment under "a most perfect right to exact indemnity for injuries done and security against the recurrence of such outrages in the future." . . . The report emphasized the temporary nature of the exclusion of the southern states and conceded the "distracting and demoralizing" tendency of such a state of affairs. The dangerous situation would end, the committee implied, when the southern states signified their agreement to the conditions embodied in the Fourteenth Amendment by ratifying it.

. . . By the very terms of the Fourteenth Amendment, Republicans . . . demonstrated their overriding desire to preserve for the states the primary responsibility for the protection of citizens' rights. The initial section, which for the first time defined American citizenship and guaranteed citizens' rights, did not itself expand the national government's jurisdiction in areas traditionally left to the states. Its language recognized implicitly that states continued to be the primary source of the legislation which regulated citizens' rights and duties. . . . No longer could states pass laws which denied or abridged the privileges and immunities of United States' citizens, or which deprived any person of life, liberty, or property without due process of law, or which denied equality before the law. . . . So long as the states did none of these things, the national government had no more power in areas of traditional state jurisdiction than it had before the war. . . .

Republicans understood the dangers inherent in their first, conservative Reconstruction plan. Many of them feared that, without political power, blacks might be victimized by restored governments in the hands of former rebels. . . . In an effort to minimize the danger, they passed two bills which appeared to mark radical changes in the relations between the states and the national government.

The Freedmen's Bureau bill and the Civil Rights bill both seemed to place the rights of the newly freed slaves under the protection of the national government. Yet, even with the prospect of restored, white, former rebel-dominated state governments facing them, Republicans refused to offer blacks the permanent protection they realized was needed. Offered by the conservative constitutionalist Lyman Trumbull, the Freedmen's Bureau bill was avowedly a temporary measure, based primarily on Congress' war powers, a measure the authority for which would cease soon after the southern states were restored to the Union, the very time the freedmen would need its protection most. . . .

The Civil Rights bill promised to stir even more doubts. It was manifestly a peacetime measure, to be passed by virtue of Congress' power under the second section of the Thirteenth Amendment to enforce emancipation by appropriate legislation. As originally presented, the bill declared the inhabitants of every state and territory entitled to certain fundamental rights without regard to color or previous status and made it a crime for anyone to deny these rights under the cover of law. . . . Later Trumbull added a provision conferring citizenship on all persons of African descent born in the United States. . . .

Although theoretically Trumbull's bill vastly expanded the duties of the national government, in fact these new duties would not be permanent. The bill was to provide the threat of national assumption of jurisdiction over civil rights in order to force states to fulfill that role themselves. Court jurisdiction was the key to the bill's real purpose. Jurisdiction would be taken from the state courts only so long as they enforced state laws or court procedures which discriminated in the rights guaranteed to all inhabitants by the first section of the Civil Rights bill. Once the states enforced these rights equally, there could be no removal of jurisdiction from state to national courts. Thus there would be great pressure on states to change their laws in order to regain their old spheres of jurisdiction. There would be no point in resisting. Retain unequal law or procedures and blacks would simply take their cases into the federal courts.

Trumbull had found a way to force the states themselves to alter their discriminatory laws. Once they did, they would regain jurisdiction over all their citizens, and the balance of power between the state and national governments would remain unchanged . . . .

Faced with southern intransigence and growing public impatience, Republicans framed a second plan of Reconstruction in February 1867. . .

Because the Reconstruction Act required black suffrage historians have generally viewed it as a true embodiment of radical principles. By imposing Negro suffrage on recalcitrant southerners, historians have believed, Radical Republicans demonstrated their willingness to disregard traditional lines of state and national authority. But in fact by 1867 the argument for black suffrage was distinctly conservative. Republicans were unwilling to leave black Americans at the mercy of former rebels; they were equally unwilling permanently to extend the power of the national government to protect them. . . .

The enfranchisement of black men in the southern states . . . was the one measure which would provide security for the Union and its loyal southern supporters and yet allow Reconstruction to continue on a conservative constitutional basis. "Far from desiring centralization repulsive to the genius of this country . . . ," wrote [Republican leader Carl] Schurz, ". . . this is the only way in which a dangerous centralization of power in the hands of our general government can be prevented." As the *Nation* pointed out, Negro suffrage "though brought forward as a radical remedy . . . is anything but radical."

. . . Republicans continued their career of constitutional conservatism in framing that final triumph of the Reconstruction era, the Fifteenth Amendment. Here too Republicans passed the narrowest possible proposal. Framed in the negative as was the Fourteenth Amendment, the suffrage amendment was designed to preserve jurisdiction over voting requirements in the states. As the New York *Tribune* observed, "The amendment . . . confers no power whatever on Congress, but only limits the power of the States." . . .

With the passage of the Fifteenth Amendment the formative period of Reconstruction ended. The Republican policy which restored all but three of the southern states to the Union by 1869 created the context in which later efforts to protect the fruits of victory took place. Four years of apparently radical legislation had led to the restoration of a federal system virtually "as it was." To the pessimistic Henry Adams, it might seem that "The powers originally reserved by the Constitution to the States are in future to be held by them only on good behavior" and that "the first decisive, irrevocable step toward substituting a new form of government . . . ha[d] now been taken," but the more perceptive eye of James Parton discerned that although "The strict-contructionists are reduced to a feeble cohort . . . , yet Congress adheres to the tradition of their doctrines. . . ."

. . . The disastrous consequences of Republican conservatism in Reconstruction legislation are readily apparent. Congress withdrew its protection of southern citizens in 1877, unwilling any longer to exercise powers Republicans had so purposefully tried to avoid before 1868. The federal courts followed suit. Judges and justices, most of whom as Republicans remembered well the circumstances surrounding the passage and ratification of the constitutional amendments, carefully preserved the state jurisdiction upon which Republicans had been so unwilling to encroach.

The Republican Program Was Revolutionary

Law professor and historian Robert J. Kaczorowski argues that the Republican program was intended to revolutionize the federal system in order to protect the rights of the freedmen but that the Supreme Court subverted that intent.

Taken from "To Begin the Nation Anew: Congress, Citizenship, and Civil Rights after the Civil War," American Historical Review *92 (February 1987): 45, 50-51, 53-54, 68.*

In 1857, the highest court in the United States held that blacks in America possessed no rights, could never become citizens of the United States, and that Congress was powerless to abolish slavery. In the aftermath of these pronouncements, this country fought one of the bloodiest wars in its history. Fewer than ten years after the Dred Scott decision, however, Congress and the Northern states accomplished precisely what the Supreme Court declared could not be done, through constitutional amendments and a civil rights statute. . . .

Before the Civil War, . . . [t]he question of whether the national or state governments possessed ultimate authority to determine the status and enforce the rights of American inhabitants produced a national political and constitutional debate that centered on slavery and culminated in the South's secession in 1861. Seces-

From "To Begin the Nation Anew: Congress, Citizenship and Civil Rights after the Civil War" by Robert J. Kaczorowski as it appeared in *The American Historical Review*, Vol. XCII, February 1987. Copyright © 1987 by The American Historical Association.

sion, based on the constitutional theory of state sovereignty, made the legal questions of federalism and the locus of sovereignty central issues of the Civil War. The North responded with Abraham Lincoln's theory of national sovereignty, which denied the existence of any state's right to secede. The Emancipation Proclamation added the other central question, namely, which government possessed the primary constitutional authority to determine the status of American inhabitants.

. . . Northern Republicans believed that the Civil War had resolved these political and constitutional questions. They soon discovered they were mistaken. . . . White supremacists frequently met the attempts of freed blacks to assert their constitutionally guaranteed freedom with violent repression and economic intimidation. . . . In their constitutions and laws, Southern states refused to recognize that blacks were citizens possessing the natural rights of free people. . . . Southern hostility persuaded Northern Republicans and Southern Unionists that secessionist and Confederate sentiments had survived the Civil War. By the end of 1865, the constitutional and political process of restoring the Southern states to the Union had become the problem of preserving the principles for which the war had been fought.

. . . The conjunction of political ideology and political necessity resulted in congressional Republicans embracing a revolutionary theory of constitutionalism. To achieve political power in the South, to preserve their wartime objectives of Unionism and freedom for slaves, they insisted that sovereignty resided in the federal government and included primary authority to determine the status and secure the rights of all Americans, white and black. Republican supporters of the Reconstruction amendments and the civil rights statute acknowledged the revolutionary changes they had wrought in American federalism by delegating plenary authority over citizenship and civil rights to the national government. Before the Civil War, the states had exercised almost exclusive jurisdiction over fundamental rights. Under the Thirteenth and Fourteenth Amendments, as Republicans understood them, Congress could conceivably supplant the states in securing civil rights. . . . Congress exercised this authority when it determined by statute and constitutional amendment which people were citizens and what rights they were to enjoy. The states were deprived of their historical authority to make these decisions. Although congressional Republicans acknowledged the constitutional revo-

335

lution in which they were engaged, they carefully avoided carrying this revolution to its ultimate conclusion of creating a unitary political structure. Republicans did not wish to supplant the states in providing a foundation for ordinary civil and criminal justice. On the contrary, they consciously preserved federalism by avoiding unnecessary intrusions on state authority over civil rights. Intentionally recognizing concurrent authority, Congress restricted its protection of fundamental rights to situations in which states and localities failed to protect them.

The decision of congressional Republicans to preserve state authority over ordinary civil and criminal justice has led legal historians to conclude that the Thirteenth and Fourteenth Amendments and the Civil Rights Act of 1866 were modest increases in national authority. The evidence, however, supports the belief of the framers that the Thirteenth and Fourteenth Amendments and the 1866 statute would bring about revolutionary changes in federal constitutionalism. The underlying constitutional authority to enforce civil rights stemmed from the constitutional recognition of the status and rights of free people as having the status and rights of U.S. citizens. Because the civil rights inherent in citizenship were constitutionally guaranteed, the framers believed that Congress, by statute and constitutional amendment, could require the states, the traditional guardians of these rights, to secure them for all Americans. . . . By defining natural rights as constitutionally recognized rights of American citizenship, Republicans acknowledged that Americans possessed these rights independent of state law. That is, if the states were to repeal their legal recognition of these rights, citizens could still claim them as constitutionally recognized and secured rights of American citizenship. . . .

In the 1870s, the Supreme Court rejected the revolutionary congressional Republican theory of constitutionalism and read into the Thirteenth and Fourteenth Amendments the theory of states' rights promoted by congressional Conservative Democrats. The Court explicitly rejected the broader theory of a congressional civil rights enforcement authority, precisely because it was revolutionary. The Supreme Court preserved a modified theory of state sovereignty, resurrected a theory of American federalism based on states' rights, and recognized primary authority over citizenship and civil rights as residing in the states. Although American law denied the right of secession, it adopted other important elements of the antebellum theory of constitutionalism. Congressional framers of the Fourteenth Amendment and the Civil Rights Act of 1866 may have thought they were reconstructing American government and basing it on a revolutionary constitutional foundation, but the Supreme Court decided against this revolutionary constitutionalism in a reactionary resurgence of states' rights that resulted in the virtual reenslavement of Southern black Americans.

Questions

1. *Why does Michael Les Benedict say Republican efforts to secure rights to the freedmen after the Civil War were conservative? Why does he say that the Supreme Court's decisions paralleled Republican constitutional conservatism?*

2. *Can one really argue persuasively that enfranchising the freedmen after the Civil War was conservative? Could the policy have been both socially radical and constitutionally conservative?*

3. *Who do you think is more correct about the legal nature of the Republican program, Benedict or Robert Kaczorowski? How is it possible for them to look at the same evidence and arrive at such completely different conclusions? Is one right and the other wrong? Is the truth somewhere in between? Are they looking at the events from different perspectives?*

SECURING EQUAL RIGHTS: THE DOCUMENTARY RECORD

As slaves, most African Americans had been denied nearly all fundamental rights. But for much of the time before the Civil War, the civil status of free African Americans was uncertain. Many Northern states considered them citizens entitled to basic rights; most of the New England states conceded them political rights as well. Other states denied or limited the basic rights of free blacks to travel, to associate with others, and to sue and testify in court, without making clear whether they were citizens or not. It was uncertain how state citizenship related to United States citizenship. Not until the case of Dred Scott v. Sandford did the Supreme Court answer that question. In this case, the Supreme Court distinguished United States citizenship from state citizenship and held that African Americans were not citizens of the United States, whether they were citizens of individual states or not.

White southerners refused to accept the legitimacy of state governments elected by black voters, and they engaged in systematic violence to resubordinate African Americans and to paralyze the Republican state officials in the South. From 1868 to 1871 much of the violence was instigated by the Ku Klux Klan, loosely organized gangs of white terrorists that sprang up in various southern localities. From 1874 to 1876 the Democratic party organized "White Leagues," "Red Shirts," and less formal armed auxiliaries to break up the Republican party. Both white and black Republicans were victimized.

Most of the southern states passed vagrancy laws that prohibited freedpeople from buying or leasing land or homes, except in towns, and then authorized towns to make their own regulations.

The following documents will introduce you to the legislation and arguments associated with the effort to secure equal rights after the Civil War, as well as to the practical effect on the lives of ordinary people. Read them in light of the questions that follow this section, particularly considering how far Republicans intended to change the American system of government in order to protect citizens' rights.

The Thirteenth Amendment

Congress passed the Thirteenth Amendment in January 1865 and it was ratified by December of that same year. The amendment abolished slavery throughout the United States.

Section 1 - Neither slavery nor involuntary servitude, except as a punishment for crime whereof the party shall have been duly convicted, shall exist within the United States, or any place subject to their jurisdiction.

Section 2 - Congress shall have power to enforce this article by appropriate legislation.

The Black Codes

Under President Andrew Johnson's plan of reconstruction, southern state governments, elected by white men who had taken an oath pledging loyalty to the United States, passed laws specifying the rights of the freedpeople. Some were more restrictive than others. All gave freedpeople the right to make contracts and to buy, own, and sell property. Some subjected them to the same criminal laws and punishments that covered white people; others subjected them to the harsher criminal laws that had covered free black people before the war. None of the codes extended political rights or the right to serve on juries. Local communities also passed regulations that limited freedpeople's rights. The following are examples of restrictive state and local provisions that convinced Republicans to intervene.

Selections from the Mississippi Black Code conferring civil rights on freedmen and defining vagrancy are from *Laws of the State of Mississippi* . . . (1866), 82-84, 91 92.

Mississippi Black Code

An Act to confer Civil Rights on Freedmen . . .

Section 1. . . . [A]ll freedmen, free negroes and mulattoes may sue and be sued . . . in all the courts of law and equity of this State, and may acquire personal property . . . by descent or purchase, and may dispose of the same, in the same manner, and to the same extent that white persons may: Provided that the provisions of this section shall not be so construed as to allow any freedman, free negro or mulatto to rent or lease any lands or tenements, except in incorporated towns or cities in which places the corporate authorities shall control the same. . . .

Sec. 5. . . . [E]very freedman, free negro and mulatto, shall . . . have a lawful home or employment, and shall have written evidence thereof. . . .

Sec. 7. . . . [E]very civil officer shall, and every person may arrest and carry back to his or her legal employer any freedman, free negro or mulatto, who shall have quit the service of his or her employer before the expiration of his or her term of service without good cause. . . .

Mississippi Vagrancy Law

Sec. 2. . . . [A]ll freedmen, free negroes and mulattoes in this State, over the age of eighteen years, found on the second Monday in January, 1866, or thereafter, with no lawful employment or business, or found unlawfully assembling themselves together either in the day or night time, and all white persons so assembling with freedmen, free negroes or mulattoes, or usually associating with freedmen, free negroes or mulattoes on terms of equality, or living in adultery or fornication with a freedwoman, free negro, or mulatto, shall be deemed vagrants, and on conviction thereof, shall be fined in the sum of not exceeding, in the case of a freedman, free negro, or mulatto, fifty dollars, and a white man two hundred dollars, and imprisoned at the discretion of the court, the free negro not exceeding ten days, and the white man not exceeding six months. . . .

Sec. 5. . . . [I]n case any freedman, free negro or mulatto, shall fail . . . after the imposition of any fine . . . to pay the same, . . . it shall be, and is hereby made the duty of the sheriff of the proper county to hire out said freedman, free negro or mulatto, to any person who will, for the shortest period of service, pay said fine . . . .

Debate over African American Rights: The Civil Rights Act

Republicans insisted that all Americans, regardless of color, were entitled to the basic rights of citizenship. In response to the black codes and other deprivations of rights in many states, North and South, they proposed a civil rights act.

Congress passed the Civil Rights bill on 15 March 1866, with southern congressmen still not permitted to take their seats. The bill made it a crime for anyone acting "under the color of law" or "custom" to deny the rights specified in Section 1. It also allowed those denied their rights in the states to transfer civil and criminal cases to the federal courts.

President Johnson vetoed the Civil Rights bill, giving his reasons in the message excerpted below from *The Congressional Globe*, 39th Congress, 1st Session, 1679-81 (27 March 1866).

To the Senate of the United States:

I regret that the bill which has passed both Houses of Congress . . . contains provisions which I cannot approve, consistently with my sense of duty to the whole people and my obligations to the Constitution of the United States. . . .

By the first section of the bill, all persons born in the United States, and not subject to any foreign Power, excluding Indians not taxed, are declared to be citizens of the United States. This provision comprends the Chinese of the Pacific States, Indians subject to taxation, the people called Gypsies, as well as the entire race designated as blacks, people of color, negroes, mulattoes, and persons of African blood. . . .

The right of Federal citizenship thus to be conferred on the several excepted races before mentioned, is now, for the first time, proposed to be given by law. If, as is claimed by many, all persons who are native-born already are, by virtue of the Constitution, citizens of the United States, the passage of the pending bill cannot be necessary to make them such. If, on the other hand, such persons are not citizens, as may be assumed from the proposed legislation to make them such, the grave question presents itself, whether when eleven of the thirty-six States are unrepresented in Congress, at this time it is sound policy to make our entire colored population and all other excepted classes citizens of the United States? Four millions of them have just emerged from slavery into freedom. Can it be reasonably supposed that they possess the requisite qualifications to entitle them to all the privileges and immunities of citizens of the United States? . . .

Thus a perfect equality of the white and black races is attempted to be fixed by Federal law in every State of the Union, over the vast field of State jurisdiction covered by these enumerated rights. . . . In the exercise of State policy over matters exclusively affecting the people of each State, it has frequently been thought expedient to discriminate between the two races. By the statutes of some of the States, northern as well as southern, it is enacted, for instance, that no white person shall intermarry with a negro or mulatto. . . .

Hitherto every subject embraced in the enumeration of rights contained in this bill has been considered as exclusively belonging to the States. They all relate to the internal policy and economy of the respective States. . . .

In all our history, in all our experience as a people living under Federal and State law, no such system as that contemplated by the details of this bill has ever before been proposed or adopted. They establish, for the security of the colored race, safeguards which go infinitely beyond any that the General Government has ever provided for the white race. In fact, the distinction of race and color is, by the bill, made to operate in favor of the colored and against the white race. They interfere with the municipal legislation of the States, with the relations existing exclusively between a State and its citizens, or between inhabitants of the same State_an absorption and assumption of power by the General Government which, if acquiesced in, must sap and destroy our federative system of limited powers, and break down the barriers which preserve the rights of the States. It is another step, or rather stride, towards centralization and the concentration of all legislative powers in the national Government. The tendency of the bill must be to resuscitate the spirit of rebellion, and to arrest the progress of those influences which are more closely drawing around the States the bonds of union and peace.

Senator Trumbull's Response

Republican senator from Illinois Lyman Trumbull managing the bill in the Senate, successfully argued for passage of the Civil Rights Act of 1866 over the president's veto. Taken from The Congressional Globe, *39th Congress, 1st Session (4 April 1866), 1756-58, 1760-61.*

What is the bill? It declares that there shall be no distinction in civil rights between any other race or color and the white race. It declares that there shall be no different punishment inflicted on a colored man in consequence of his color than that which is inflicted on a white man for the same offense. Is that a discrimination in favor of the negro and against the foreigner—a bill the only effect of which is to preserve equality of rights?

. . . Why, sir, the very object . . . is to prevent discrimination, and language, it seems to me, could not more plainly express that object and effect. It may be said that it is for the benefit of the black man because he is now in some instances discriminated against by State laws; but that is the case with all remedial statutes. They are for the relief of the persons who need the relief, not for the relief of those who have the right already; and when those needing the relief obtain it, they stand upon the precise footing of those who do not need the benefit of the law.

. . . The bill neither confers nor abridges the rights of any one, but simply declares that in civil rights there shall be an equality among all classes of citizens. . . . Each State, so that it does not abridge the great fundamental rights belonging, under the Constitution, to all citizens, may grant or withhold such civil rights as it pleases; all that is required is that, in this respect, its laws shall be impartial.

. . . This bill in no manner interferes with the municipal regulations of any State which protects all alike in their rights of person and property. . . . How preposterous, then, to charge that unless some State can have and exercise the right to punish somebody, or to deny somebody a civil right on account of his color, its rights as a State will be destroyed.

The Fourteenth Amendment

To secure African-American citizenship and rights beyond constitutional doubt, Congress passed the Fourteenth Amendment later in 1866.

Section 1. All persons born or naturalized in the United States, and subject to the jurisdiction thereof, are citizens of the United States and of the State wherein they reside. No State shall make or enforce any law which shall abridge the privileges or immunities of citizens of the United States; nor shall any State deprive any person of life, liberty, or property, without due process of law; nor deny to any person within its jurisdiction the equal protection of the laws. . . .

Section 5. The Congress shall have power to enforce, by appropriate legislation, the provisions of this article.

Frederick Douglass Argues in Favor of Black Suffrage

Even before the Civil War ended, African-American leaders and radical Republicans were insisting that the national government secure the freedmen the right to vote. By 1867 most Republicans agreed, and by 1869 they were considering a constitutional amendment to bar racial tests for voting. Frederick Douglass, the great African-American orator and newspaper editor, explained "What the Black Man Wants" to a Boston audience in 1865. Note Douglass's allusion to the fact that women did not have the right to vote at this time. Note also his brief appeal to the anti-Irish prejudices of his Republican audience.

Excerpted from The Frederick Douglass Papers—Series One: Speeches, Debates, and Interviews, Volume 4: 1864-80, *ed. John W. Blassingame and John R. McKivigan (New Haven, 1991), 62-63, 66-68.*

I have had but one idea for the last three years to present to the American people. . . . I am for the "immediate, unconditional and universal" enfranchisement of the black man, in every State of the Union. (Loud applause.) Without this, his liberty is a mockery; without this, you might as well almost retain the old name of slavery for his condition; for, in fact, if he is not the slave of the individual master, he is the slave of society, and holds his liberty as a privilege, not as a right. . . .

It may be asked, "Why do you want it? Some men have got along very well without it. Women have not this right." Shall we

345

justify one wrong by another? That is a sufficient answer. Shall we at this moment justify the deprivation of the negro of the right to vote because some one else is deprived of that privilege? I hold that women as well as men have the right to vote (applause), and my heart and my voice go with the movement to extend suffrage to woman. But that question rests upon another basis than that on which our right rests. We may be asked, I say, why we want it. I will tell you why we want it. We want it because it is our right, first of all. (Applause.) No class of men can, without insulting their own nature, be content with any deprivation of their rights. We want it, again, as a means for educating our race. Men are so constituted that they derive their conviction of their own possibilities largely from the estimate formed of them by others. If nothing is expected of a people, that people will find it difficult to contradict that expectation. By depriving us of suffrage, you affirm our incapacity to form an intelligent judgment respecting public men and public measures; you declare before the world that we are unfit to exercise the elective franchise, and by this means lead us to undervalue ourselves, to put a low estimate upon ourselves, and to feel that we have no possibilities like other men. . . . [H]ere, where universal suffrage is the rule, where that is the fundamental idea of the government, to rule us out is to make us an exception, to brand us with the stigma of inferiority, and to invite to our heads the missiles of those about us. Therefore I want the franchise for the black man.

. . . It is said that we are ignorant; I admit it. But if we know enough to be hung, we know enough to vote. If the negro knows enough to pay taxes to support the Government, he knows enough to vote—taxation and representation should go together. If he knows enough to shoulder a musket and fight for the flag, fight for the Government, he knows enough to vote. If he knows as much when he is sober as an Irishman knows when drunk, he knows enough to vote, on good American principles. (Laughter and applause.)

. . . What have you asked the black men of the South, the black men of the whole country to do? Why, you have asked them to incur the deadly enmity of their masters, in order to befriend you and to befriend this government. You have asked us to call down, not only upon ourselves, but upon our children's children, the deadly hate of the entire Southern people. You have called upon us to turn our backs upon our masters, to abandon their cause and espouse yours; to turn against the South and in favor of the North; to shoot down the Confederacy and uphold the flag—the American flag. . . . And now, what do you propose to do when you come to make peace? To reward your enemies, and trample in the dust your friends? . . . Do you mean to give your enemies the right to vote, and take it away from your friends? . . . In time of trouble we are citizens. Shall we be citizens in war, and aliens in peace? Would that be just?

. . . What I ask for the negro is not benevolence, not pity, not sympathy, but simply justice.

The Nation Supports Black Suffrage

The weekly journal The Nation *was founded in 1865 to support radical solutions to the problem of restoring the Union. The journal endorsed black suffrage.*

Excerpted from "Universal Suffrage And Universal Amnesty," The Nation *(29 November 1866), 430.*

[T]he Federal Government is bound by every consideration of justice, honor, and decency either to see that the freedmen enjoy complete security or to furnish them with the means of protecting themselves. In other words, we are bound either to give the freedmen a police—to see that every man of whom we claim allegiance can eat or sleep in peace—or we are bound to see that he enjoys a fair share in the making of the laws and the selection of the officers who are to execute them. . . . The former of these courses is not strictly in accordance with the spirit of our institutions; the latter is. . . .

[T]he ballot will do for the negro what it does for the poor ignorant Irishman, or German, or Englishman, but no more. It will secure him against flagrant class legislation, or cruel or unusual punishments, and against all oppression which is on its face oppressive. It will do more than this; it will cause politicians and public men—sheriffs, policemen, and the whole race of functionaries, actual and expectant—to treat him with civility, even with deference. It will put a stop to outrages and assaults of various kinds on negroes, and to all open expressions of contempt for them or dislike of them. . . .

But more than this the ballot will not do for the negro. It will not make him a good judge of the value or importance of measures not bearing directly and patently on his personal comfort or convenience; it will not enable him to tell the difference between statesmen and demagogues; between honest public men and knavish public men; between his own real friends and his real enemies; to distinguish laws contrived by scoundrels for his spoliation, under a show of immediate benefit, and schemes contrived by statesmen for his permanent advantage.

Opposition to Black Suffrage

The Reconstruction Act of 1867 enfranchised both black and white southerners, with the exception of those whites who as officeholders had sworn to uphold the Constitution of the United States and then joined the rebellion. It put the southern states back under military control temporarily. In exchange for restoration to normal relations in the Union, the Reconstruction Act required each southern state to frame a new constitution that would secure equal civil and political rights regardless of race. In the following document, a number of white Alabamans protested against the process.

Excerpted from the Petition and Memorial File, Records of the House of Representatives, 40th Cong., Record Group 233, National Archives, Washington, D.C.

The White people of Alabama send this their humble petition.

We beseech your Honorable Bodies to withdraw yourselves from the influence of the passions and contests of the hour, and contemplate for a brief period, our miserable condition . . . .

. . . [I]t is well known by all who have knowledge on the subject,—that while the negroes of the South may be more intelligent and of better morals than those of the same race in any other part of the world . . . —yet they are in the main, ignorant generally, wholly unacquainted with the principles of free Governments, improvident, disinclined to work, credulous yet suspicious, dishonest, untruthful, incapable of self-restraint, and easily impelled by want or incited by false and specious counsels, into folly and crime. . . .

Are these the people in whom should be vested the high governmental functions of establishing institutions and enacting and enforcing laws, to prevent crime, protect property, preserve peace and order in society, and promote industry, enterprise and civilization in Alabama, and the power and honor of the United States? Without property, without industry, without any regard for reputation, without controul over their own caprices and strong passions, and without fear of punishment under laws, by courts and through juries which are . . . created by and composed of . . . themselves, or of those whom they elect,—how can it be otherwise than that they will bring, to the great injury of themselves as well as of us and our children,—blight, crime, ruin and barbarism on this fair land? . . .

Will you, nearly three years after the war has ended, . . . suffer a whole State full of your kindred civilized white inhabitants, not only those who had opposed the Government, but women, children, and loyal men who had adhered to it,—to be thus consigned over to the horrid rule of barbarian negroes! . . .

. . . [D]o not, we implore you, abdicate your own rule over us, by transferring us to the blighting, brutalizing and unnatural dominion of an alien and inferior race: A race which has never shown sufficient administrative capacity for the good government of even the tribes, into which it has always been broken up in its native seats; and which in all ages, has itself furnished slaves for all the other races of the earth.

The Fifteenth Amendment

To make black enfranchisement permanent and to extend it to the north, Congress passed the Fifteenth Amendment in 1869 and sent it to the states for ratification. The required number of states ratified it in 1870.

Section 1. The right of citizens of the United States to vote shall not be denied or abridged by the United States or by any State on account of race, color, or previous condition of servitude.

Section 2. The Congress shall have power to enforce this article by appropriate legislation.

Violent Resistance to Equal Rights in the South

The following documents describe Klan activities from several perspectives. Amzi Rainey, a black South Carolina sharecropper, described how the Klan terrorized his family in testimony excerpted from Proceedings in the Ku Klux Trials, at Columbia, S. C. in the United States Circuit Court, November Term, 1871 *(Columbia, S.C., 1872) 279-80.*

Former Senator James Chesnut of South Carolina testified before a congressional committee investigating the Klan. Simpson Bobo, a white lawyer and jack-of-all-trades, testified before the same committee. Their testimony is excerpted from Testimony Taken by the Joint Select Committee to Inquire into the Condition of Affairs in the Late Insurrectionary States, *vol. 1 and 2,* South Carolina *(Washington, D.C., 1872) 1:446, 449, 2:796-97.*

[Amzi Rainey's Testimony]

I looked out of the window, and I see some four or five disguised men coming up, and I ran up in the loft, and they came on; come to the door; and when they come to the door, they commenced beating and knocking. "God damn you, open the door! open the door! open the door!" . . . and my wife run to one of the doors and they knocked the top hinges off of the first, and she run across the house to the other, and agin that time they got the two hinges knocked off the other door, and the bolt held the door from falling, and she got it open . . . and when they come in, they struck her four or five licks before they said a word . . . .

They asked her who lived here. She said, "Rainey—Amzi Rainey." "What Amzi Rainey? What Amzi Rainey?" And she said, "Amzi Rainey," and he struck her another lick, and says: "Where is he? God damn him, where is he?" And she says: "I don't know." And one said: "O, I smell him, God damn him; he has gone up in the loft." He says: "We'll kill him, too," and they come up then. . . .

I was in a box, and they said: "Oh, he is in this box, God damn him, I smell him; we'll kill him!" and the other says: "Don't kill him yet;" and they took me down. This man that struck my wife first, ran back to her and says: "God damn her, I will kill her now; I will kill her out;" and the one that went after me, he says: "Don't kill her;" and he commenced beating her then; struck her some four or five more licks, and then run back and struck me; he run back to her then, and drawed his pistol, and says: "Now, I am going to blow your damn brains out;" and the one by me threw the pistol up, and says: "Don't kill her." He aimed to strike me over the head, and struck me over the back and sunk me right down. Then, after he had done that, my little daughter—she was back in the room with the other little children—he says: "I am going to kill him;" and she runs out of the room, and says: "Don't kill my pappy; please don't kill my pappy!" He shoved her back, and says; "You go back in the room, you God damned little bitch; I will blow your brains out!" and fired and shot her . . . .

. . . [A]nd then they took me . . . [o]ff up the road, about a hundred and fifty yards; and they wanted to kill me up there, and one said, "No, don't kill him, let's talk a little to him first." Then, he asked me which way did I vote. I told him I voted the Radical [Republican] ticket. "Well," he says, "now you raise your hand and swear that you will never vote another Radical ticket, and I will not let them kill you." And he made me stand and raise my hand before him and my God, that I never would vote another Radical ticket . . . .

[Ex-Senator Chesnut's Testimony]

There is a deep dissatisfaction . . . in the hearts of the people of this State. . . . Three hundred thousand white people here around us, who had been accustomed to self-government, who had had an orderly government and had participated in that government, whose property had been taxed only by those who paid the taxes, beheld the whole thing suddenly subverted and themselves placed at the mercy of ignorance and of corruption . . . . These people are under an absolute despotism, and you will find that the countries where governments are most despotic are precisely those in which secret associations appear; small associations of parties ardent and seeking redress for real or fancied wrongs which they think cannot be avenged through the government. That is the true secret of this thing.

[Simpson Bobo's Testimony]

We have gone through one of the most remarkable changes in our relations to each other that has been known, perhaps, in the history of the world. The negro that was our slave has become our master suddenly . . . ; the bottom rail has got on top . . .—any one living here and knowing all about it, will be surprised that there has been as little disturbance as there has been. If the Government had give us a good government; if it had let us remain under a military government, none of these troubles would have been in this country. . . . There have been a great many . . . cases of the whipping of negroes in this county and some of the adjoining counties, some for one purpose and some for another. I think some of them have been political, and some of them have been with a view of answering special ends. . . . [T]he lower class of white people have a great prejudice against the negro, because he is a competitor for common labor, and wherever they come into collision, these fellows form themselves into a Klan, and take up negroes that come in their way, and punish them. . . . [F]or instance, a white man rents a tract of land to a negro. Some white man wants to get the land. The owner prefers giving it to the negro. For the purpose of punishing the negro, he will then get up a parcel of neighbors, and in disguise they will go and whip the negro half to death.

The Supreme Court Limits the Ability of the Federal Government to Protect Rights

In a series of cases interpreting the Fourteenth Amendment, the justices of the Supreme Court made it difficult for the federal government to protect the rights of American citizens in the south. In the Slaughter-House Cases, the Court distinguished between the rights people held as citizens of the United States and those they held as citizens of their states. The rights Americans thought of as basic to citizenship were those they held as state citizens, not as citizens of the United States. The Fourteenth Amendment, the justices said, only authorized the federal government to protect the latter.

Abridged from the Slaughter-House Cases, *83 U.S. 36, at 72-78 (1873).*

The Slaughter-House Cases

The first section of the fourteenth article . . . opens with a definition of citizenship—not only citizenship of the United States, but citizenship of the States. . . .

It declares that persons may be citizens of the United States without regard to their citizenship of a particular State, and it overturns the Dred Scott decision by making all persons born within the United States and subject to its jurisdiction citizens of the United States. . . .

It is quite clear, then, that there is a citizenship of the United States, and a citizenship of a State, which are distinct from each other, and which depend upon different characteristics or circumstances in the individual.

We think this distinction and its explicit recognition in this amendment of great weight in this argument, because the next paragraph of this same section . . . speaks only of privileges and immunities of citizens of the United States, and does not speak of those of citizens of the several States. . . .

The language is, "No State shall make or enforce any law which shall abridge the privileges or immunities of citizens of the United States." It is a little remarkable, if this clause was intended as a protection to the citizen of a State against the legislative power of his own State, that the word citizen of the State should be left out when it is so carefully used, and used in contradistinction to citizens of the United States, in the very sentence which precedes it. It is too clear for argument that the change in phraseology was adopted understandingly and with a purpose.

Of the privileges and immunities of the citizen of the United States, and of the privileges and immunities of the citizen of the State, . . . it is only the former which are placed by this clause under the protection of the Federal Constitution . . . .

The latter must rest for their security and protection where they have heretofore rested . . . .

[The Court then quoted an earlier lower court decision that defined the privileges and immunities of state citizenship:]

"What are the privileges and immunities of citizens of the several states? We feel no hesitation in confining these expressions to those privileges and immunities which are fundamental; which belong of right to the citizens of all free governments, and which have at all times been enjoyed by citizens of the several states which compose this Union. . . . They may all . . . be comprehended under the following general heads: protection by the government, with the right to acquire and possess property of every kind, and to pursue and obtain happiness and safety, subject, nevertheless, to such restraints as the government may prescribe for the general good of the whole."

. . . Was it the purpose of the 14th Amendment, by the simple declaration that no state should make or enforce any law which shall abridge the privileges and immunities of citizens of the United States, to transfer the security and protection of all the civil rights which we have mentioned, from the states to the Federal government? And where it is declared that Congress shall have the power to enforce that article, was it intended to bring within the power of Congress the entire domain of civil rights heretofore belonging exclusively to the states?

. . . We are convinced that no such results were intended by the Congress which proposed these amendments, nor by the legislatures of the states, which ratified them.

Civil Rights Cases

In the Civil Rights Cases, the Court ruled that the Fourteenth Amendment only authorized the federal government to protect people against deprivations of their rights by state officials or people acting under color of state authority.

Abridged from the *Civil Rights Cases*, 109 U.S. 3, at 10-11 (1883).

The first section of the Fourteenth Amendment . . . is prohibitory in its character, and prohibitory upon the States. It declares that:

"No State shall make or enforce any law which shall abridge the privileges or immunities of citizens of the United States; nor shall any State deprive any person of life, liberty, or property without due process of law; nor deny to any person within its jurisdiction the equal protection of the laws."

It is State action of a particular character that is prohibited. Individual invasion of individual rights is not the subject-matter of the amendment. . . . [T]he last section of the amendment invests Congress with power to enforce it by appropriate legislation. To enforce what? To enforce the prohibition. . . . This is the legislative power conferred upon Congress, and this is the whole of it. It does not invest Congress with power to legislate upon subjects which are within the domain of State legislation; but to provide modes of relief against State legislation, or State action, of the kind referred to. It does not authorize Congress to create a code of municipal law for the regulation of private rights. . . .

The Effect of "Redemption" on Black Southerners

The Supreme Court's narrow interpretation of the Fourteenth Amendment made it difficult to prosecute southern violence. Between 1873 and 1875, the resolve of the federal government to protect the rights of citizens in the south waned. By 1877, southern white Democrats regained control of southern state governments. Southern whites referred to their success as "redemption," and they used fraud in many states to prevent Republicans from regaining power. The following plea from Wilson H. Williams for help from the national government suggests how the change affected African Americans in the South. It had been illegal to teach slaves to read or write, so Williams's literacy, with all its spelling errors, was quite an accomplishment.

From Wilson H. Williams to Senator John Sherman, care of Rev. John D. Haynes, 15 January 1879, John Sherman papers, Manuscript Division, Library of Congress, Washington, D.C.

We poor coul[ored] men have got no more show then a good Dog. The White people is tareing all over the land picking up the poor coul men acreing [forcing] them back to thar old Homes giving them no triel but butchering them up for things that [got] don in 20 and 30 years a go. God hoe [who] made the wourld knows that it is not rite and we know you all ought to do sum thing for ous for we are healpletts cant do eney thing nor say eney thing [P]lease you all stop that thing for it has been going on long anuffe. . . .

Questions

1. *Describe the issues of social justice that affected the lives of free African Americans at the time the Civil War broke out.*
2. *Why did President Andrew Johnson oppose the Civil Rights Act? Did it discriminate in favor of African Americans, as he charged?*
3. *What reasons did proponents of African-American suffrage give for supporting it? Aside from the racism of the petition, did the petitioners have a point about enfranchising former slaves so soon after emancipation? How would Frederick Douglass have answered? Given the hostility of white southerners toward equal civil rights for African Americans, what would you have done to secure their rights?*
4. *To what degree were the Supreme Court decisions interpreting the Fourteenth Amendment consistent with the spirit in which they were passed?*
5. *Over all, to what degree did the civil status of African Americans change during the era of Reconstruction? How much did their status improve? What were the limitations of the change?*

FURTHER READING

The standard, prize-winning work on Reconstruction in general, providing a wealth of information about the effort to restore the Union on the basis of equality of rights, is Eric Foner's *Reconstruction: America's Unfinished Revolution, 1863-1877* (New York, 1988). A briefer and more focused work is Foner's "Rights and the Constitution in Black Life during the Civil War and Reconstruction," *Journal of American History* 74 (December 1987): 863-83. Herman Belz addresses constitutional questions more directly than Foner in *Emancipation and Equal Rights: Politics and Constitutionalism in the Civil War Era* (New York, 1978). Peyton McCrary offers another argument for the radicalism of Republican Reconstruction policy in "Republican Ideas about Politics and Social Change," *Civil War History* 30 (December 1984): 330-50. Robert J. Kaczorowski criticizes the Supreme Court for retreating from the Republican commitment to rights in *The Politics of Judicial Interpretation: The Federal Courts, Department of Justice, and Civil Rights, 1866-1876* (New York, 1985).